D1514782

Library of
Woodbrooke College,
Selly Oak,
Birmingham.

EVANGELICALS IN ACTION

1. The Revival Meeting

361.9

Evangelicals in Action

AN APPRAISAL
OF THEIR SOCIAL WORK
IN THE VICTORIAN ERA

by

KATHLEEN HEASMAN

a content.

GEOFFREY BLES · LONDON

© KATHLEEN HEASMAN, 1962

Printed in Great Britain
by The Garden City Press Ltd., Letchworth
and published by
GEOFFREY BLES LTD.
52 Doughty Street London W C 1
Australia:
33 York Street Sydney
531 Little Collins Street Melbourne
47-53 Castlemaine Street Brisbane
CML Building King William Street Adelaide
New Zealand:
Wyndham Street Auckland
Canada:
10 Dyas Road Don Mills Ontario
South Africa:
PO Box 8879 Pallstate House
51 Commissioner Street Johannesburg

First published 1962

W2989

Acknowledgments

IT IS difficult to decide which was more exciting, the writing of this book with the discovery of conclusions which in some instances I was most surprised to find, or the visiting of numerous societies and missions which I hardly knew existed and often in places where I had never been before. I might receive the heartiest of welcomes and be almost deluged with facts, or I might be regarded with a certain amount of suspicion until I had fully explained my purpose, but I always received all possible help. In every case I must thank the many voluntary societies who so kindly supplied me with information, often regaled me with lunch or tea, so eagerly helped me to write this book, and in a very real way have made it their own. In particular, I should like to mention those societies which lent me photographs or prints for the illustrations; Miss Daniell's Soldiers' Home, the London Haven for Women and Girls, Quarrier's Homes, the Regent Street Polytechnic, the Seamen's Christian Friend, and Mrs. Smyly's Homes.

The information which this book contains formed part of my Ph.D. thesis on "The Influence of the Evangelicals upon the Origins and Development of Voluntary Charitable Institutions in the second half of the Nineteenth Century" which was accepted by the University of London in 1960; and for this reason I have supplied few references or notes in the text of my book. Those who would like to verify my facts, or to have fuller details, should turn to the thesis itself, copies of which are housed in the University Library and the library of Bedford College. Thus, perhaps, my greatest thanks should be given to Dr. Ivy Pinchbeck, who was my supervisor and who took unlimited pains to guide me, to read through my several drafts, and to encourage me at every stage.

Nor should my indebtedness to the Rev. Ian Douglas-Jones, the rector of Rushden, be overlooked, for it was he who urged me to make this study in the first place, and who has taken a personal and continuing interest in it. Miss C. E. Curryer, who taught me when I was at school at Walthamstow Hall, has given me invaluable help, both in reading the manuscript and making suggestions as to improvements in style; and Miss Blanchard has cheerfully undertaken the onerous task of typing my manuscripts, often at unprecedented speed.

I owe a debt of gratitude to the various libraries which allowed me to borrow and consult their books, and to their untiring librarians who helped me in my searches; among them the London Library with its amazing stock of nineteenth century material, the British Museum which unearthed many forgotten reports of societies, the Evangelical Library with its store of Evangelical biographies and accounts of different missions, Dr. Williams' library, the Women's Service Library, the Family Welfare Association Library, and, for much of my American material, the Library of Congress. I am grateful to the editor of *Moral Welfare* for permission to publish some facts on the Midnight Meeting Movement, first printed in the issue of January 1960.

Last, but by no means least, I should thank my husband, who forbore with the constant demands of "getting on with the book", who read and re-read my manuscripts, who urged me on when my interest flagged, and without whose co-operation I doubt if this would ever have been written.

K. J. H.

London, 1962

Contents

Contents

Illustrations

* *by courtesy of the Radio Times Hulton Picture Library*
† *The Illustrated London News*

CHAPTER I

Social Work in the Nineteenth Century

NINETEENTH-CENTURY England marks the change
from a rural to an urban society. Family after family, driven by
the prospect of better wages, moved from the countryside to the
towns. Few had any concept of what life in the towns would be
like, though most were agreed that it would be better than life in
the villages. Like all first-generation emigrants they took with
them their familiar conceptions of social relationships, only to be
baffled by the unfamiliar conditions which they found. During the
second half of the century they, their children and sometimes their
grandchildren passed through a painful process of adjustment
which in the end adapted them to town dwelling. The chief concern of the numerous voluntary charitable organisations of the
period was to help them in this process.

Not only was there this movement of people to areas of denser
population, but the population itself was growing at an unprecedented rate. The census reports show a figure which doubled
itself in the first fifty years of the century and almost repeated the
process in the next half-century. The younger element in the
population was therefore coming to the fore and so was in particular need of help to fit itself into the urban environment.

It was also a period of *laissez-faire*. The growing material progress and prosperity blinded the wealthier people to the problems
which this social adjustment caused:

If there was poverty, private philanthropy and charity would alle-
viate it; if there were sweated labour in mine or mill, mild legislative
restrictions would remedy that; if agricultural and industrial interests
seemed at cross-purposes, free discussions coupled with the removal
of old and burdensome restrictions would smooth out these conflicts;

I

if there were harsh penal laws, they would be gradually and carefully removed.[1]

Though few of these social problems were new, it was in the towns that they were accentuated, and it was in the towns that the greater part of the social work was done.

The size of the manufacturing towns, and of some of the sea-ports as well, was growing, as it were, overnight. Every available piece of land was built upon, and until late in the century there was no authorised control. London, in particular, spread in this way. Different districts tended to be occupied by different social classes, and the poorer the people the more densely were they packed together. Thomas Beames, writing in 1850, gives a vivid description of one of the "rookeries", as the slums were called at that time:

> Stories piled on stories in the older parts of our towns, not each floor, but each room tenanted by a family, in some cases the dormitory of several occupants thrown together in the chance scramble for a night's lodging, each swelling the gains of some middleman, whose heart is seared by the recollection of his own poverty, and who learns to grind as he once was ground by others.[2]

Areas of this type were to be found in St. Giles, Drury Lane, and Saffron Hill in the centre of London; Whitechapel, Bethnal Green and Hoxton in the East End; Notting Hill in the West; and the so-called "dusthole" of Woolwich in the South.

Most of such property was converted from the houses of the rich. As the poorer people moved in, so those of higher income moved out. Gardens were built upon, houses divided up, and a veritable rabbit warren of courts and alleys would emerge. The majority of the new dwellings were built as commercial under-takings with capital which had to compete with more remunera-tive investment. Thus resources were restricted to essentials, little more was provided than was absolutely necessary, and rents were governed entirely by demand. Working people had little choice but to live in such quarters for they needed to be near their jobs

[1] David Thomson, *England in the Nineteenth Century*, Pelican 1951, p. 232.
[2] Thomas Beames, *The Rookeries of London*, 1850, pp. 5–6.

and such areas usually offered subsidiary employment to other members of the family.

Taine, the French critic and historian, in his *Notes on England*, compiled during the late sixties and seventies, describes a visit which he paid to such an area in Shadwell, where

> low houses, poor streets of brick under red-tiled roofs cross each other in every direction, and lead down with a dismal look to the river. Beggars, thieves, harlots, the latter especially, crowd Shadwell Street. One hears a grating music in the spirit cellars; sometimes it is a negro who handles a violin; through the open windows one perceives unmade beds, women dancing. Thrice in ten minutes I saw crowds collected at the doors; fights were going on, chiefly between women; one of them, her face bleeding, tears in her eyes, drunk, shouted with a sharp and harsh voice, and wished to fling herself upon a man. The bystanders laughed; the noise caused adjacent lanes to be emptied of their occupants; ragged, poor children, harlots—it was like a human sewer suddenly discharging its contents. Some of them have a relic of neatness, a new garment, but the greater number are in filthy and unseemly tatters.[1]

Public houses or gin palaces stood at the major street intersections, most of them flashy and brightly lighted, attracting by their comparative comfort and warmth men and women of all ages. For the teenagers there was the "penny gaff", usually a shop converted into a music hall, where both drink and dancing were offered. Henry Mayhew the well-known journalist, who was not easily shocked by things he saw, was disgusted by the obscenity which he found in one of these:

> If there had been any feat of agility, any grimacing, or in fact, anything with which the laughter of the uneducated classes is usually associated, the applause would have been accounted for; but there were two ruffians degrading themselves each time they stirred a limb, and forcing into the brains of the childish audience before them thoughts that must embitter for a lifetime, and descend from father to child like some bodily infirmity.[2]

Living conditions such as these presented many and various

---

[1] H. Taine, trans. F. Rae, *Notes on England*, 1872, pp. 33–4.
[2] Peter Quennell, ed., *Mayhew's London*, 1952, p. 85.

problems to the social worker, the fundamental one of which was poverty. "Nowhere", says Taine, "in his experience was the division between the rich and the poor more horrifying and more dramatic than in London."[1] Mayhew's colourful descriptions of the environment and occupations of those who gained their living in the streets tended to obscure this, but William Booth, the founder of the Salvation Army, was nearer reality when he described the very poor as "the submerged tenth" of the population. Many had nowhere to live but the cheap lodging house; some slept on the streets. Though wages were slightly higher in the second half of the century than earlier, employment was erratic, many of the jobs were casual and a trade depression threw most of such workers completely out of employment. Few could afford anything but second-hand clothes and possessions were in and out of the pawnshop as wages were paid and spent.

It was probably the children who suffered most. The long hours which their parents worked left them little time to care for the home, and the degrading conditions of living supplied little incentive to them to show much concern for their parental duties and responsibilities. Some of the children were homeless, others were neglected, and cruelty was by no means uncommon. Mayhew found such children

> fluttering in rags and in the most motley attire. Some are orphans and have no one to care for them; others have left their homes and live in lodging houses in the most improvident manner, never thinking of to-morrow; others are sent by their unprincipled parents to beg and steal for a livelihood; others are the children of poor but honest and industrious people, who have been led to steal through the bad companionship of juvenile thieves.[2]

It is not surprising that drunkenness, prostitution, and crime were prevalent. The ease with which alcoholic liquor could be obtained was a continual temptation to the susceptible, and the lack of regulation of its sale made it available for all age groups. Many used it to deaden their troubles, and a disproportionate part of the family income was often spent in this way. The irregularity of employment made it necessary to find some casual activity and

[1] Taine, *op. cit.*, p. 33.   [2] Peter Quennell, ed., *London's Underworld*, 1952, p. 133.

2. The London Samaritan Society clothes the Poor

people too often fell back upon petty pilfering and prostitution. It was taken for granted that there would be a congested quarter given up to such pursuits in every growing town.

If society had little place for the healthy poor it could find even less for the sick. Government reports of the mid-century leave little doubt that the insanitary conditions of the towns were an important cause of the prevalent ill-health. Many of the lodging houses were sources of contagion, and in the dark and dismal cellars fever was rarely absent. Robust health was enjoyed by few of those dwelling in the very overcrowded areas, and it was usual for the expectation of life to be appreciably shorter in such places than in the rest of Britain. Except for the really ill, who usually could gain admission to a hospital, the sick were left to the care of their family or a neighbour. No attention whatsoever was paid to the early stages of sickness and very little to convalescence.

The same lack of concern was shown to the handicapped. They stood little chance of gaining employment in the overcrowded state of the labour market, and frequently had to resort to the streets to earn a precarious livelihood. The crippled bird-seller tells Mayhew:

I was born a cripple, sir. . . . When I was very young he (my father) took me to almost every hospital in London, but it was of no use. . . . When I was thirteen my father put me in the bird trade. . . . I've been bird-selling in the streets for six-and-twenty years or more. . . . Before father died, the parish allowed us 1s. 6d. and a quartern loaf a week; but after he was buried, they'd allow me nothing; they'd only admit me to the house. I hadn't a penny allowed to me when I discharged myself and came out. I hardly know how ever I *did* manage to get a start again with the birds. I knew a good many catchers, and they trusted me. Yet, they was all poor men. I did pretty tidy by bits, but only when it was fine weather, until these five years or so, when things got terrible hard. Particularly just the last two years with me. Do you think times are likely to mend, sir, with poor people?[1]

As for the aged, the meagre provisions of the existing almshouses reached only a few, and when they were ill the old were unacceptable at the hospitals. Their choice lay between entering the workhouse, where they were cut off from their friends and

---

[1] Peter Quennell, ed., *Mayhew's Characters*, 1952, pp. 156–8.

families, or remaining at home. Here they were usually unwanted, not so much because their families discarded them, as because the size of the family income left little margin for dependants, and overcrowding little room where they could live.

For all these groups of poor people the State, in theory, made some provision through the Poor Law. There had been, in England, since the reign of Elizabeth I, a certain degree of State intervention which recognised the right of the indigent, the infirm and the unemployed to State assistance. But by the end of the eighteenth century the conditions under which such assistance was granted had become increasingly easier and the cost to the State proportionately increased. Thus the nineteenth century attitude to State intervention had been toughened. The poor were only helped if they were destitute; in most cases they had to enter the workhouse for relief, and the conditions there were made such that they should compare unfavourably with those outside.

This deterrent approach can be explained by the Victorian attitude that it was the duty of everyone to help themselves, and only in the last resort to appeal for outside assistance. Samuel Smiles, in his popular books, *Self-Help* (1859), *Character* (1871), and *Thrift* (1875), had emphasised the principle that a man should, by his own efforts, provide for himself and his family, and that he could do so by the careful and thrifty use of all his endowments. This was the attitude which had produced the self-made industrialist of the early decades of the century, and it was the view that dominated the outlook of the middle classes and the higher paid workers throughout the century.

When working men found that personal independence was difficult to achieve on their own they formed themselves into friendly societies and affiliated orders which provided help in periods of sickness, unemployment and old age. Most of the trade unions, co-operative societies, building societies and working men's clubs started benefit schemes which in return for small weekly contributions would provide food, clothing and other essentials at times of necessity. Similarly many of the trades and professions organised benevolent institutions for their members to which they could appeal in time of need. Many of the poor, however, did not qualify for admission to these societies, nor was their employment sufficiently regular for them to pay weekly contributions. They could not be classed as destitute, and so eligible for poor relief, and yet their standard of living was extremely low and the slightest misfortune would make them poverty-stricken. Sometimes this was their own fault, but more usually it was the result of circumstances entirely beyond their control. Trade depressions, in particular those of the mid-sixties and early eighties, accounted for very large numbers of such people, seasonal and casual employment were permanent causal factors, and "sweated" labour, especially in trades employing women, produced much distress. It was for people such as these that most of the voluntary charitable institutions of the second half of the nineteenth century were formed.

From very early times the poor had benefited from charity and almsgiving. After the dissolution of the monasteries in England, which had been the fountain head of help to the poor, the number of secular charities greatly increased. Most of them were endowed, which meant that their income was derived from legacies or bequests, and many were very small in amount and assigned by the donor to some particular purpose. These were not often suitable to meet the needs of the nineteenth century. Circumstances had greatly changed since most of them were founded, and few of them were assigned to the newer urban areas. Hence the setting up of a permanent board of Charity Commissioners in 1853 to reallocate the funds of out-dated charities to more pressing needs. On the other hand voluntary charity was becoming increasingly popular. It took the form of donations or annual subscriptions which were offered in the lifetime of the donor. These became the income of the charity to which they were allocated; they could be altered at will, increased when circumstances demanded and withheld if for any reason the donor was unsatisfied with the methods of the society. No external control was exercised over their allocation and the beneficiaries could be dealt with in any manner considered suitable at the time.

Samuel Gurney, speaking at the International Philanthropic Conference in 1862, describes the organisation of such voluntary charities:

London is the headquarters of agencies which are at work throughout the country. Here the central bodies deal with the funds remitted
from charitable residents in all parts of the United Kingdom. These
are raised by bringing the objects of each society under the notice of
the benevolent by personal canvass, by circular, or by public advertisement; occasionally by public dinners and fancy fairs; or in the
case of missionary societies by a comprehensive system of local
associations. The central executive consists usually of unpaid and
paid officers, the unpaid being a president, treasurer, committee, and
perhaps an honorary secretary, the paid being secretary, collectors
and other subordinate officers.   Generally the president is a noble-
man or gentleman of influence in the philanthropic world, the
treasurer a member of the firm which are bankers to the society. The
committee meets from time to time to pass accounts, draw cheques
and direct the management of affairs; and issues to subscribers
annually a report of the year's proceedings, with a statement of
receipts and expenditure.[1]

By the mid-nineteenth century this voluntary method had become as important as the endowed. Figures in this respect can only
be approximate, but by the 1870's the Charity Commissioners reported an annual income of around £2·2 million for endowed
charities in England, and Sampson Low, the compiler of the hand-
books of London's voluntary charities, estimated in 1861 an income of £2·4 million for voluntary purposes in the metropolitan
area alone. There is no doubt that there was a remarkable increase
in these voluntary charities between 1850 and 1900. The number
of such charities in London increased by a quarter in the decade
from 1850 to 1860 and their income by 35 per cent. Though this
rate of increase was not maintained in the following decades it did
not fall far short, and by the end of the nineteenth century the
trend of donations and subscriptions was still on the upward move.
Voluntary societies had become, in the second half of the nineteenth century, the main means by which those in need received
private as distinct from State and mutual assistance.

The attitude of the State towards voluntary charity gradually
became more favourable. Whereas the Royal Commission on the
Poor Laws of 1834 had condemned it as competing with State

[1] Samuel Gurney, *Charitable Societies of London*, a paper read to the International
Philanthropic Conference of June 1862.

relief and causing the poor to concentrate in areas where such charity was available, the Goschen Minute of 1869 suggested a division of the poor between the destitute who should be left to the care of the authorities, and the rest who were suitable recipients for such charity. By 1909 the Royal Commission on the Poor Laws went so far as to state that voluntary charity filled a definite need which was not "out of proportion to the obvious needs of those who may be in want of relief from such charities".[1]

These voluntary societies were to be found in an ever-increasing variety of fields. During the eighteenth century their work was largely confined to the education of the children of the poor, at first in charity schools and then in the Sunday Schools, and also to the opening of general hospitals and dispensaries for the care of the sick. In the middle of this century a small group of philanthropists came to the fore, among them John Fielding, the Bow Street magistrate, Robert Dingley and his younger brother Charles, both London merchants, Jonas Hanway, for a time a partner in their firm, and John Thornton of the Clapham Sect. One or other of these was connected with the opening of the Foundling Hospital (1739) for illegitimate children, the Magdalen Hospital (1758) for prostitutes, the Female Orphan Asylum (1758) for parentless children, the Marine Society (1756) to train homeless boys, and the Philanthropic Society (1788) for children on the verge of crime. They are an important group, for they were the forerunners of the specialised societies of the nineteenth century.

The early years of the nineteenth century were noteworthy for the numerous visiting societies and general or domestic missions which appeared in the big towns. They used large numbers of voluntary workers who would visit from house to house to assess the needs of the inhabitants and do what they could to help them. In the later years of the century, the Christian missions superseded the general missions and large numbers of specialised societies were formed to meet practically every possible contingency. There were infant nurseries for babies, homes for older children, evening institutes for teenagers, reformatories for children convicted in the courts, organisations to try to reduce drunkenness, crime and

---

[1] *Royal Commission on the Poor Laws*, report, Cd. 4499, part vii, par. 215.

prostitution, asylums for the insane, care for the families of service-men and for those whose jobs took them away from home, and canteens for workers in some of the outdoor occupations. In fact, most of the social services of today can trace their origins to these voluntary societies of the later nineteenth century.

There were various reasons for this increase in voluntary charity which developed during the nineteenth century. In the first place there was a growing awareness of the existence of social problems. The liberal humanitarian motives of the eighteenth century formed the nucleus for the study of wider problems in the nineteenth. Such things as prison abuses, juvenile delinquency, alcoholism and prostitution were subjects for governmental investigation and private discussion. The National Association for the Pro-motion of Social Science, founded in 1857, held annual con-ferences and gave many controversial subjects a hearing. All shades of opinion were represented and matters on which little was known were brought to the general notice, and the public were made aware of these through the annual publication of the trans-actions of the Association.

There was also a deepening sense of guilt at the inequality of wealth and the appalling conditions of living of an appreciable proportion of the population. Even if the ordinary citizen never visited the slums, he was brought into constant contact with people from them. He would meet such characters as the street sweeper, the costermonger and the flower girl almost daily and be approached whenever he went out by some beggar or street seller. The growing recognition of their needs in comparison with his own affluence often prompted him to support some form of voluntary charity.

A less worthy motive, though typical of the materialism of the Victorian era, was the desire for publicity and power. Many of the voluntary societies were what was known as "voting charities". It was the large subscriber who was elected to honorary office and whose name was published in the annual report. Beneficiaries were chosen by the vote of donors, the number of votes which each donor could exercise being determined by the size of his subscrip-tion. Each beneficiary had to approach the donor to plead his case before he could even be considered by the committee. Such voting charities offered ideal conditions for those who desired to be widely known for their benevolence.

Such a vast number of voluntary charities could never have come into existence had there not been the money available to invest in them. Much of this money was derived from the profits of industry and trade, and in this way social work received a share of the surplus income available for investment at that time. As in the business world, free competition tended to sort out the good from the bad, those organisations which showed reasonable results in relation to the amount subscribed being likely to gain further support, and those performing relatively little tending to disappear. The height of Victorian prosperity, from the fifties to the mid-seventies, corresponded with the greatest increase in the annual income of these organisations. After this voluntary charity began to depend more and more upon the benefactions of millionaires like George Peabody, and upon the growing availability of charitable trusts.

The women's movement of the second half of the nineteenth century played an important part in recruiting workers for such societies. The primary purpose of this movement was to improve the status of women and to open paid occupations and professions to them. It encouraged educated women to stand for election as Poor Law guardians and school board officers and to accept paid positions of authority in voluntary and State institutions. Indirectly the movement inspired many middle-class women with the desire for emancipation, and so helped to swell the numbers of voluntary part-time social workers. The unequal proportion of men to women at that time left many women unmarried and large numbers of these found some compensation for the lack of a home of their own in living and working among the poor. Male social workers were not nearly so numerous. They were usually persons of considerable wealth and almost always held positions of control.

As the century progressed, social work became much more closely connected with religious beliefs. Humanitarian motives were translated into religious terms, and people began to feel that the existing conditions of poverty and need were not in keeping with the teaching of the churches. Voluntary charitable organisations tended increasingly to have some religious connections.

From the early days of the Tractarian movement, Dr. Pusey had encouraged the sisterhoods to take up "moral welfare" work, and such groups as the Community of St. Mary at Wantage, and that of St. John at Clewer, made this an important part of their duties. Similarly, several of the High Church slum parishes were outstanding for their social work. It would be impossible to underestimate the social activities of Father Lowder, who for twenty-one years carried on his mission at St. George's-in-the-East, or of Father Dolling at St. Saviour's, Poplar, and of the many sisterhoods, such as Kilburn and All Saints, Margaret Street, which made social work one of their main functions.

The so-called Broad Church expressed its views mainly through Christian Socialism. Their desire to improve the status of the under-privileged is usually thought to have been confined to the somewhat abortive experiment of producers' co-operation. But it also found an outlet in progressive social work. The provision of better housing and of open spaces in the big cities owes its origin almost entirely to the lifework of Octavia Hill, whose principles of dealing with the poor formed the basis for the approach of the Charity Organisation Society. In the same way, another Christian Socialist, Canon Barnett, vicar of Whitechapel and founder of Toynbee Hall, set the pattern for the settlement movement which is still a means of helping the underprivileged and of training social workers.

These two streams came together in the later decades of the century through their emphasis upon social justice. The Christian Social Union, formed in 1889, was supported by both the High and the Broad Church in its endeavours to interpret the signs of the times and to formulate some *modus vivendi* by which Christian principles could be expressed in terms of a more equalitarian outlook.

The Unitarians also had some part to play in the development of social work. Their inspiration came from Boston, where in the twenties the domestic missions of Dr. Joseph Tuckerman gave a practical slant to the preaching of Dr. William Ellery Channing. Their close connection with Unitarians in Liverpool and London led to the establishment of domestic missions in these cities and their methods were frequently followed by the great Christian missions of the second half of the century. This emphasis on social work among the Unitarians produced some of the great social pioneers of the century. Among them were William Rathbone, responsible for the early organisation of district and workhouse nursing, Mary Carpenter who fought to keep children out of the prisons, and whose reformatories and industrial schools were the forerunners of our approved schools; and James Stansfeld whose unselfish support at a critical stage helped to win the campaign for the repeal of the Contagious Diseases Acts. Less well known was the work of Henry Solly in instituting working men's clubs; Mary Dendy in dealing with the feeble-minded; Frances Power Cobbe in caring for the needs of domestic servants; and Mary Shipman Beard's furtherance of nursery schools. Much of this work still awaits full documentation, and the important place that the Unitarians hold in the development is rarely realised.

Both the Roman Catholics and the Jewish community were influenced by this spate of social work, though they were principally concerned with their own people. Roman Catholic social work developed after England became an ecclesiastical province of the Roman Church in 1850, and then it was almost entirely educational. Jewish social work was centred in the Jewish Board of Guardians set up in 1859 to help the poorer members of their community, particularly those who had recently come to this country.

In spite of the importance of the fore-mentioned social work, it was small in comparison with that of the Evangelicals. It is difficult to say just what proportion of the voluntary charitable organisations were Evangelical in character, since no appropriate statistics exist. The only way of discovering which societies were Evangelical is to examine the lists of charities supplied by Sampson Low for London, and after 1881, by the *Charities Register and Digest* of the Charity Organisation Society, and see whether any well-known Evangelicals appear among their office-holders or supporters. This can be checked to some extent from the societies mentioned in the weekly periodical, *The Christian*, which reported only those which had some Evangelical allegiance. But these sources give little indication of the number of societies outside London, and in one or two cases omit an important London society. Therefore only a rough generalisation can be given, but it does appear that as many as three-quarters of the total number of voluntary charitable organisations in the second half of the nineteenth century can be regarded as Evangelical in character and control. The greater proportion of these were formed in the decades immediately after the mid-century, many of them as a result of the revival of that time.

Of these societies, a very large number were Christian missions for the general benefit of the poor. Many were for children, and for the first time the needs of the teenager began to be considered. Attention was paid to the misfits in society, the drunkard, the criminal, and the prostitute, usually with the purpose of helping them to conform, and it was gradually realised that after-care was as crucial a part of social work as the giving of immediate help. Finally, among the organisations for the benefit of small groups of people with some particular need, the Evangelicals tended to concentrate upon the soldier and sailor, the railwayman and the navvy, the needlewoman and business girl, and the domestic servant.

In the last decade of the century there was a gradual increase in the desire for more State intervention. It was beginning to be realised that social distress was not necessarily the fault of the character of the individual but quite often was caused by economic factors entirely outside his control. Various suggestions were put forward for sharing this responsibility between the individual concerned, the State, and sometimes the employer, which finally resulted in the National Insurance Act of 1911. Meanwhile, State social workers were becoming more common. School board visitors were added to the ranks of relieving officers, and, with the opening of employment exchanges in 1905 and the provision of old age pensions in 1908, the employees of their offices were introduced into the realm of social work.

Thus the partnership between voluntary and State social service began to develop. In many instances the voluntary services set the pattern for those taken over by the State, and in some cases voluntary societies still continue to hold the field. In the process the Evangelicals played an important part, both in beginning and developing many of these voluntary services, and in suggesting lines of action which were later followed by the State.

CHAPTER II

The Evangelicals and Their Part in Such Work

THE EVANGELICALS are remembered for what they did rather than for their theology. As Dr. Cornish, the author of *The English Church in the Nineteenth Century* says:

> they are known to the world, not by their writings, which are forgotten, but by their lives, which never can be forgotten.[1]

The journeys of the Wesleys through the countryside of England are familiar to most people and today many of the chapels which they founded are still in use. Few have not heard of the part played by Wilberforce in the fight for the freedom of the slave, nor of Lord Shaftesbury's demands for factory legislation. But the widespread social work of the Evangelicals in the nineteenth century is as yet uncharted, and many people are unaware of the numerous societies which they formed to help the distressed, and of the many different types of need which they met.

The term "evangelical" is usually used to describe those Protestants who believe that the essential part of the Gospel consists in salvation by faith through the atoning death of Christ. From the time of St. Paul there have been those who have emphasised this truth, but this was particularly the case after the reformation. The Pietists of the German Lutheran Church in the seventeenth and early eighteenth centuries and the Moravians, led by Count von Zinzendorf in Saxony in the 1720's, were examples of this, and both had their influence upon English Evangelicalism. It was the Moravians who first introduced John Wesley to Evangelical beliefs, and the Pietists who inspired some aspects of Evangelical social work.

In England, Evangelicalism was revived in the eighteenth

[1] F. W. Cornish, *History of the English Church in the Nineteenth Century*, 1910, vol. i, p. 15.

15

century by the Wesleys and other preachers both within and outside the Established Church. It restored to the religion of the day the force and energy which had been lost by the rationalism of the preceding decades. In fact, Lecky, the historian of the eighteenth century, considers that these eighteenth century Evangelicals

> gradually changed the whole spirit of the English Church. They infused into it a new fire and a passion of devotion, kindled a spirit of fervent philanthropy, raised the standard of clerical duty, and completely altered the whole tone and tendency of the ministers.[1]

Some writers have confined this term "evangelical" to those members of the Church of England who, like John Newton and Charles Simeon, introduced a spirit of enthusiasm into the worship of the Established Church. But there is little difference between what they believed and the outlook of the different Nonconformist denominations. Their theology might differ on points such as baptism, and their forms of service vary, but they were all agreed upon salvation by faith and the infallibility and over-riding importance of the Scriptures. They all feared the growing influence of Roman Catholicism and the rapid spread of Tractarianism. They were united in their stand against rationalism and the theories of evolution which seemed to undermine the literal truth of the Bible. Even the works of a staunch Evangelical, such as Henry Drummond who tried to reconcile these new views with Evangelical theology, were regarded as suspect by many.

Their unity was demonstrated in the exchange of pulpits and in joint open-air preaching, in the revivals in which they all joined, and the religious conventions which they all attended. The great Evangelical societies at the turn of the eighteenth century, the Religious Tract Society (1799), the British and Foreign Bible Society (1804), and the Sunday School Union (1803) were interdenominational, and so was the Evangelical Alliance which was formed in 1846 to bring together Evangelicals of different countries. It is small wonder, therefore, that the majority of the voluntary societies formed by the Evangelicals

[1] W. E. H. Lecky, *History of England in the Eighteenth Century*, 1899, vol. ii, p. 527.

for social work were also interdenominational. Thus, in this context, the Evangelicals include those who were members of the so-called "Low" Church of England as well as of the Non-conformist denominations. Only the Unitarians have been excluded, not because of their views on the Trinity, but because few Evangelicals associated with them or joined with them in their particular forms of social work.

In a very general way the different Evangelical denominations tended to appeal to certain social classes. The Evangelical Church of England, and probably also the Plymouth Brethren, though their numbers were very small in comparison, consisted mostly of middle-class people. Both the Congregationalists and the Presbyterians, with their intellectual approach, attracted people who had been successful in trade or industry and the lower ranks of the professions. Many of the Quakers who were from old established families, such as the Cadburys, Frys, Rowntrees and Gurneys, were leading industrialists, and though they too were relatively small in numbers, the amount of welfare work which they did was remarkable. Only the Baptists, whose "tabernacles" were to be found in the leading thoroughfares of the poorer districts, and the Methodists who appealed largely to newcomers to the industrial areas, attracted large numbers of the working class.

To some extent the middle-class Evangelicals tended to congregate in certain towns. Clapham was a centre of this type at the end of the eighteenth century, and Cheltenham, Bath and Tunbridge Wells in the nineteenth. Here well-to-do Evangelicals would settle, get to know one another and meet for prayer and the study of the Bible. They would join together for most social activities and formed a source from which many of the social workers of the second half of the century were drawn.

A very general idea of the numbers of practising Evangelicals in relation to the rest of the population can be gained from the religious censuses of 1851, 1886, and 1902–3. The first of these formed part of the official census of that year; the second was conducted by the *British Weekly* and counted worshippers in London as they entered church or chapel on a particular Sunday; and the third, that of the *Daily News*, estimated church attendance

in the different London boroughs during the winter of 1902-3.
The figures do not show a close degree of accuracy, for such
things as weather and the fact that people might attend more than
once on a Sunday have to be taken into account. But the general
conclusion which can be reached is that just under half the total
population of London attended a place of worship, of which
probably as many as three-quarters were Evangelicals in the
terms of our definition. The extent to which this estimate can be
applied to the country as a whole is questionable, particularly in
view of the fact that in areas where Nonconformity was strong
the number of Evangelicals were likely to be much larger.

But church and chapel attendance did not include all who
followed the Evangelical way of life. There were many with less
definite religious convictions who adopted the same manner of
living. The Evangelical Revival of the eighteenth century had
left its imprint upon English society. Victorian middle-class
families, with their large households of children and servants, all
followed a very similar pattern of living. Each member, whether
master or servant, had his own particular position with its
appropriate duties and responsibilities, but together they presented
a united front to the world. Such things as family prayers and
family anniversaries held them together. They clung strictly to a
system of rigid class distinction which had few dealings with a
class below themselves, except in a spirit of benevolence and
sometimes, unfortunately, of condescension. This was true not
only of the middle-class itself, but also of the shopkeepers, the
artisans and the skilled workers. Only the lowest income ranges
did not conform to this pattern, and then largely because circumstances made such conformity impossible. This helps to explain
the emphasis which Evangelical social work placed upon the
family, and why attempts were constantly made to try to teach
the poor the middle-class manner of life.

Philanthropy came to form an essential part of this way of life.
This may seem strange, since Evangelical beliefs are based on a
personal experience called "conversion", which is essentially
introspective and encourages faith rather than good works as a
means to salvation. The religious philosopher, William James,
defines this experience as

the process gradual or sudden, by which a self, hitherto divided and consciously wrong, inferior and unhappy, becomes unified and consciously right, superior and happy in consequence of its firmer hold upon religious realities.[1]

but he also points out that one important result of conversion is charity or brotherly love, which has always involved the care of the needy members of the Christian faith and which has quite often been extended to include others who happened to be in trouble. It was this which led the German Pietists to start their charitable institutions at Halle at the end of the seventeenth century, and Wesley and his followers to open orphanages, first for the children of their members and then for others in need.

The widespread poverty and distress of the nineteenth century caused the Evangelicals of that period to adopt the same attitude to those in trouble. As Harold Begbie points out in *Broken Earthenware:*

> Those who know life deeply and intimately, who are profoundly acquainted with all the suffering, sorrow, misery, and sin of cities and villages, those whose studies are not limited to books read in a library, or to discussions accidentally started in a drawing room, know as the first axiom of their knowledge that religion alone among all the forces at work for the improvement of humanity has power to alter the character and regenerate the soul of evil people. Legislation may better house the poor, may educate their children, limit the opportunities for drink and crime, and punish evil-doers with a saner and more determined effort at their moral reformation, but without religion they will never give spiritual joy and invigorating strength to the posterity on which evolution depends.[2]

They began to feel that it was part of their duty to make some attempt to relieve the suffering which they saw around them and to help those who were so obviously in need. Yet there was a conflict in this new approach, since Evangelicalism had always regarded the winning of others to their beliefs as of first importance. Their social work was therefore bound up with evangelism. Some thought that evangelism should precede material help, since a change in heart would make the person more responsive

---

[1] William James, *Varieties of Religious Experience*, 1903, p. 189.
[2] Harold Begbie, *Broken Earthenware*, 1909, p. 285.

to such help. Others felt that as the poor were so deeply sunk in misery, spiritual help would be of little effect without some improvement in their physical conditions. But in every case evangelism was the outstanding motive for such work.

This burning concern of the Evangelicals for the state of the soul had a further effect upon the nature of their social work. Each particular person was of infinite worth. Thus they tended to adopt an individualistic attitude to the work which they did, to show little interest in what non-Evangelicals might be doing in the same field, or stop to consider whether there were any basic principles underlying the conditions which they found. Their concern was centred upon the individual and his family, and it was to help them that these numerous charitable organisations were formed.

This individualistic outlook is also to be seen in the importance of personalities in the guidance of Evangelical social work. Some gave their patronage and money to organisations which, with their support, were sure of success. Others were leaders in the field, either blazing a new trail or opening up extensive areas of operation. A few awakened the social conscience in the religious groups to which they belonged. Little is generally known about most of them; hence their introduction in the following paragraphs.

The "Clapham Sect" was the driving force in the first decade of the century. Here, in a house on Clapham Common, Evangelicals such as William Wilberforce, Thomas Fowell Buxton, Admiral Lord Gampier, William Smith and Hannah More had gathered to discuss the outstanding social problems of the period. With some of the leading Quakers, they formed a vigorous reforming minority, using many of the more recent methods of publicity such as the lecture, the pamphlet, the newspaper and the billboard. Furthermore, as Dr. Howse points out in his recent book, *Saints in Politics*, they were by no means indifferent to the sufferings of the poor in England, but were to be found on the committees of many voluntary societies of the period which sought to ameliorate such conditions. It is interesting to notice how many of the social leaders of the later decades can trace their parentage to a member of this "sect". Among such are Josephine Butler, Florence Nightingale, Charles Booth, Lucy Smith who was prominent in work for the aged, and Catharine Tait, the wife of the archbishop.

Lord Shaftesbury was the immediate successor of the Clapham Sect. He used their methods both within and without parliament to further different social causes of the mid and later decades of the century and lent his support to a very large number of charities, so that his influence is to be found in almost every field of social work from the forties until his death in 1885. Closely associated with him were Samuel Morley, a director in the well-known firm of stocking-knitters, and Lord Mount-Temple, Lord Shaftesbury's brother-in-law, whose conferences for the discussion of religion at Broadlands, Hampshire, attracted a curious mixture of Evangelicals and High Churchmen, all bent upon helping the needy.

Then there were the Aberdeens, the Kinnairds, and the Waldegraves, all upper-class families whose young people took a prominent part in the mid-century revival meetings and who helped the well-known American revivalist, D. L. Moody, in his campaigns in this country. They directed much of the social work which sprang from these revivals and this brought them into touch with others, such as Quintin Hogg, the Hon. T. H. Pelham and Henry Drummond, and with several well-to-do middle-class families, the Bevans, the Trittons, the Barclays and the Dennys, some of whose members were partners in the banking house of Barclay, Bevan, Tritton, Ransome, Bouverie and Company which managed the affairs of many Evangelical charities.

Among the wealthy traders who subsidised Evangelical charity were the Corys, a firm of Cardiff shipbuilders and colliery owners, the Crossley brothers of Manchester, William Palmer the biscuit manufacturer, and Francis Peek, a London city business magnate. Professional men who helped to organise such charity included Sir Arthur Blackwood, the chief of the Post Office in the 1880's, Sir Robert Anderson of the C.I.D. department of Scotland Yard, and General Gordon of Khartoum. In the different denominations support was given by bishops such as Thorold, Tait and Walsham How, Hugh Price Hughes of the Methodists,

F. B. Meyer and Dr. Clifford of the Baptists, and members of the
Quaker families of Fry, Cadbury, and Rowntree.

But the beginnings and co-ordination of much of the Evangelical social work can be traced to the Rev. and Mrs. Pennefather,
who in 1856 started their annual conferences for Christians of
all denominations, at first at Barnet, where the Rev. William
Pennefather was vicar of Christ Church, and then at St. Jude's,
Mildmay, in North London. Though the conferences were
primarily religious, a day was always set aside for the discussion
of contemporary social problems and accounts of work performed
by leading Evangelical voluntary organisations. Mrs. Pennefather
was herself associated with several of these organisations and at
the time when she started her well-known deaconess institution
at Mildmay was in constant touch with Evangelical social workers
of all types. It is not generally realised that here, in 1862, seven
years before the Charity Organisation Society was formed, Mrs.
Pennefather had started her Association of Female Workers,
which included the leaders of most of the Evangelical voluntary
organisations and which acted as a focal point from which new
ventures were started and old ones expanded. This Association
anticipated much of what was to be done in later years by the
Charity Organisation Society.

Smaller groups of the same type were organised by Annie
Macpherson at her Home of Industry in the Ratcliffe Highway,
and by Mrs. Meredith at the Conference Hall, Nine Elms,
Clapham. The purpose of both of these was to deal with local
problems and to co-ordinate the work of their areas. They held
monthly meetings for the social workers in the district, and the
serious problems which they came up against were dealt with
by the Association of Female Workers. Similarly there were
co-ordinating organisations for specialised types of work, the
Ragged School Union for those working among the children of
the poor, and the Reformatory and Refuge Union for workers
dealing with deprived children, those convicted at the courts,
young prisoners and prostitutes. Thus although Evangelical social
work was essentially individualistic, it did recognise the need for
mutual discussion and co-ordination.

We therefore find that there was a fairly close-knit group of

Evangelicals responsible for a very large part of the social work which was performed in the second half of the nineteenth century. They came from the upper and middle classes and from the various denominations. There were certain functions at which they all tended to meet. One of these was the religious conference, held first at Perth in 1868, at Dublin in 1873, and then annually at Keswick from 1875 onwards. Secondly there were the "May Meetings" which were the annual meetings of the different societies, usually held in May at the Essex Hall in the Strand. These were not only business affairs but also social occasions, and it was quite the usual thing for wealthier Evangelical families from different parts of Britain to spend that month in London so that they might attend as many meetings as possible.

Most of the social work done by these Evangelical societies was performed by a vast number of "ladies", who would give a day or so to such activities. They were largely middle-class people, either married women who were relieved of their domestic chores by the numerous servants available at that time, or single women with little else to do. Social work was regarded as a "suitable" occupation for them, though in view of the way in which they were protected on other occasions it is difficult to understand why, in the course of their social work, they were allowed to see sights and meet people who were unmentionable in polite society. They had very little training other than that of the experience of managing a large Victorian household, and the methods which they used were those which they followed in their own homes. Much of the work they did themselves, but where paid help was engaged, as happened with biblewomen and district nurses, they supervised. The result was a surprising degree of success, though there was always a tendency for them to be critical of interference by those in control, and to be slow in making friends with other social workers in the district.

There were various ways in which the need for such workers was made known. Perhaps the most important was through the popular literature which circulated in the homes of the middle class. In the early part of the century the purpose of Evangelical fiction had been largely moral. Most children of the middle class were brought up on Mrs. Sherwood's *The Fairchild Family* or on

Mrs. Sewell's *Mother's Last Words*, both of which had, as their background, life in a middle-class household. But by the middle of the century a change was taking place. The setting of such writings became the homes of the poor, and their teaching the duty of those in better circumstances to help those who were not so well off.

There were unforgettable books such as *Jessica's First Prayer* (1866) by Hesba Stretton, which is the simple story of a girl waif awakening to the meaning of religion, and which shows an extraordinarily accurate knowledge of the life of destitute children in a large city. Its popularity led to the sale of over one and a half million copies, and it was translated into every European language, as well as some Asiatic and African ones. Mrs. O. F. Walton fascinated the children of the time by *Christie's Old Organ*, the story of the hard life of poor old Treffy the organ-grinder, *A Peep behind the Scenes* which describes the adventures of a family in a travelling circus, and *Saved at Sea*, the tale of a lighthouse keeper. Amy le Feuvre captivated them by *Teddy's Button*, a story of village life, and *Probable Sons*, an account of the difficulties of an adopted child.

These stories were written in a highly emotional style, with dramatic conversion and death scenes. But the children loved them, read them again and again, and began to take an interest in similar people in real life. To foster this, societies for children of the middle-class to help those in the slum areas were formed, among them the League of Ministering Children (1885) to befriend poor children in general, the Sunbeam Mission (1891), to help the paralysed and sick, and the Children's League of Pity in connection with the work of the N.S.P.C.C. Each middle-class child was placed in touch with a poor child of similar age and was expected to write and send presents of toys and clothes. Thus the youth of the middle class were introduced at an early stage to social work.

Similarly, grown-ups of the middle class were attracted by writers such as Catharine Marsh, Mrs. Ranyard, Mrs. Wightman, and Mrs. Bayly, whose accounts of the forms of social work which they did were widely popular. Catharine Marsh's first book, *English Hearts and English Hands*, which described her work among the navvies who were erecting the Crystal Palace at Sydenham in the 1850's, reached a sale of 74,000 copies in the first year. Mrs. Ranyard's *Missing Link* (1860), an account of the work of her biblewomen, the "link" with the poor in the slums of St. Giles, had almost as large a sale, as did Mrs. Wightman's *Haste to the Rescue* (1859) which pointed out the need for dealing with drunkenness. Mrs. Bayly, in her *Ragged Homes and How to Mend Them*, and *Mended Homes and What Repaired Them*, both written in 1859, suggests how lady visitors might help the poor to make the best of the conditions in which they were forced to live.

These books shared the same dramatic style, with long descriptions of the circumstances of actual people whom the author had met and how she had helped them. Except for the lack of modern scientific jargon, they might well have been modern case histories. As Mrs. Wightman points out in her preface, they were intended chiefly for the educated classes "to stir up every heart to more earnest and prayerful effort to rescue those who are placed by God in a less favourable position".[1] Mrs. Ranyard's books, in particular, are full of interesting details. The district and task of each of her biblewomen is described. Thus Martha works among the dust heaps of Paddington where the women were employed as sorters and sifters, and here change of clothing is the greatest need. Priscilla's district is Limehouse, which is densely populated with coal whippers, costermongers and dockers whose womenfolk are chiefly employed in needlework. She is therefore chosen because she is a good needlewoman and so can both help and understand the difficulties of such people. Barbara works among the sailors in the gin palaces of Shadwell and her chief job is to protect the women and children.

Not only did these writings attract many voluntary workers and give them some ideas as to how to deal with their children; they also were the means of inspiring some of the pioneers in social work. Thus Agnes Weston attributes to Catharine Marsh's books her interest in the welfare of sailors, Miss Sandes her work for soldiers, and Mary Sumner her concern for the well-being of the family. Mrs. Wightman consulted Catharine Marsh before

---

[1] Mrs. Charles Wightman, *Haste to the Rescue*, 1859, preface p. xi.

starting her temperance work in Shrewsbury, and Mrs. Bayly, in her turn, asked the advice of Mrs. Wightman with regard to her mothers' meetings in Notting Hill. Suggestions and advice circulated freely between these early pioneers.

The magazines of the larger societies, such as the *London City Mission Magazine* and *The Missing Link Magazine* of Mrs. Ranyard's Mission, were also useful in rousing interest in social work, and they too were full of case histories and how the workers dealt with particular people. A wider range of the community was reached by periodicals like *Leisure Hour* and *Good Words*, which, though not essentially Evangelical magazines, frequently contained articles describing the work of Evangelical societies and short biographies of outstanding Evangelical social workers. Similarly *The Sunday at Home*, *The Sunday Magazine* and the children's papers such as *The Boys' Own*, *The Girls' Own* and *Little Dots* all contained accounts of work for the poor.

A particularly useful form of publicity was the Evangelical weekly, *The Christian*, which was read by most Evangelicals. It had been published first from 1859–70 as *The Revival* to record the spiritual and charitable results of that episode, and it was continued as a religious paper of general Evangelical interest. Its editor, R. C. Morgan, was always willing to publish accounts of any reputable Evangelical charity, and through its columns many forms of social work were started or extended. An organisation recommended by this paper could be sure of widespread support.

A certain number of workers were gained through the periodic religious revivals which took place in the latter part of the nineteenth century. These revivals, like those of today, were primarily to win converts and to deepen the religious life of Christians, but in the second half of the nineteenth century revivalists began to encourage their converts to engage in some form of social work. This connection between revivalism and social service seems first to have been made by Charles G. Finney in America, where he preached that "conversion" meant not only a fitness of the individual for a future life, but some attempt to make the world a more suitable place to which Christ should return. His visits to England in 1849–51 and 1858–9 probably had some influence upon the mid-century revivalists, since for the first time in this century revivalists urged their converts to take up social work, with the result that many societies for this purpose were formed.

D. L. Moody gave a more precise expression to this attitude during his visits in 1867, 1873–5, 1881–4 and 1891. He suggested that a personal faith might be a means of helping to solve such problems as destitution, immorality, drunkenness and crime. His converts were instructed to seek out such people and to offer them both spiritual and material help. His campaign methods made this possible, since for the first time in the history of revivalism a plan of action was decided in advance. Funds were raised, halls booked, meetings announced and workers trained. Their centres were usually the big industrial towns where poverty and degradation were apparent, so that the workers, in their pre-campaign visiting, would become familiar with the conditions in the slums and would be able to suggest what forms of social work might be undertaken by the converts. Many organisations, in particular those for young people, can trace their origin or development to one of Moody's campaigns.

Similar in approach were the requirements which were laid upon the members of the various Christian Unions. Modelled on the class meetings of the Wesleys, these unions consisted of an inner circle of adherents whose function was to support one another in prayer and to devote what available time they had to some form of Christian service. This had been the original intention of the Y.M.C.A. and the Y.W.C.A., though other unions were usually formed in connection with some occupational group, such as soldiers and sailors, commercial travellers, navvies, the police, postal and telegraph workers, employees in the banks and the stock exchange and students. Their members were responsible for welfare work in their own particular occupations and for starting any social work which might be needed in the district where they lived.

In these ways it gradually became an accepted fact that social work, in one way or another, was the duty of every earnest Christian. The attitude of Evangelicals towards philanthropy passed through a subtle change. From having looked upon

charity as a duty to less fortunate members of the Church, and
perhaps to those who were obviously in urgent need, it was
extended to include all who were in any way underprivileged.
The social distress of the late nineteenth century partly accounted
for this, but it was also due to a mellowing of the Evangelical
outlook. Evangelicalism passed away from the somewhat intro-
verted and introspective attitude of personal salvation which it
had tended to assume in the eighteenth century to an active
benevolence which attempted to demonstrate the spirit of Christ
by helping other people who were in need.

Evangelical influence in this respect was far wider than its own
religious group. It included those who might no longer count
themselves among the Evangelicals, but who could point to an
Evangelical home and background. Many of the social pioneers
and reformers at the turn of the nineteenth century can be placed
in this category. This spirit of philanthropy and the methods
which it followed was also caught by others outside the confines
of Evangelicalism. Numerous people of no particular religious
allegiance were persuaded to undertake social work by the
pattern of life around them. Such work became regarded as one
of the common virtues and was followed by most of those who
looked upon themselves as responsible members of the community.

CHAPTER III

The Great Christian Missions

UNTIL CHARLES BOOTH published his famous survey of
Life and Labour in London at the end of the nineteenth century, no precise account of poverty existed. Sir F. M. Eden's
State of the Poor, written in 1797, gives some idea of poverty at the
end of the eighteenth century, the Manchester and London Statistical Societies produced some local surveys in the middle of the
century, and journalists, like Henry Mayhew, James Greenwood
and George Sims, wrote somewhat lurid accounts of the slums of
London in the later decades. But just how many poor there were,
and what their state was, has to be left to conjecture. There is no
doubt that there were numerous families living at a very low standard of existence. When their income was regular and circumstances normal, they could just manage to keep going, but unemployment, sickness or some other adversity would cause untold
distress. This was particularly so in periods of slack trade such as
the sixties and the eighties and early nineties when destitution was
widespread.

The attitude of the authorities to these people was that if they
were in real need they could apply to the relieving officer who
would arrange for their admittance at the workhouse or in special
circumstances grant them out-relief. Otherwise they should be
encouraged to take care of themselves. It was people such as these
whom the Christian missions tried to help. Their workers visited
them in their homes, encouraged them to join clothing and fuel
clubs, provided them with free or cheap meals, offered them recreational facilities, and at times of great need were ready to do
what they could.

Charles Booth noted in the nineties that London was

dotted over with buildings devoted to this work. In the poorer parts especially, in almost every street, there is a mission; they are more numerous than schools or churches, and only less numerous than the public-houses.[1]

The majority of them were Evangelical missions, started in the middle of the century, and they usually owed their origin to a group of individuals, or sometimes to a single person. Booth found that

> in some cases, and these are perhaps the most interesting, a poor man, a man of the people, a born missionary, himself filled with Christian zeal, has tried to bring conviction to others and has gathered round him a band of co-workers. After a prolonged struggle and many disappointments, he at length encounters and touches the heart of someone with wealth. Then the work gradually becomes professional. In other instances, the reverse happens, and a person with means, having thrown his or herself into mission work, seeks paid assistance in order to carry it on more regularly. The undertaking may begin with a class of boys or girls and slowly develops into a club or school or mission centre; or visiting in poor streets, followed by the employment of a woman of the people to assist, may lead to the holding of mothers' meetings, to the systematic giving of charitable relief, and perhaps to a soup kitchen. Others again begin with medical relief, preaching the Gospel to all who come for treatment. And finally, there are some whose initial motive is hostility to the action of those who hold divergent religious views.[2]

The size of these missions varied from the minor mission, housed in a converted stable or outhouse, to the large scale mission with a central hall and outlying stations. The smaller ones would come and go, some succeeding, others failing, and those which were shut one week would often open again the next week under new leaders. Most of the large missions had at one time been small, and their expansion was usually due to good management and to their methods of appeal to the public.

The large general missions included the Field Lane Institution (1841) at Clerkenwell, the George Yard Mission (1854) in Whitechapel, the South London Mission (1861) in Bermondsey, the

---

[1] Charles Booth, *Life and Labour in London*, 3rd series, vol. vii, p. 270.
[2] *Ibid.*, pp. 282–3.

Golden Lane Mission (1862) in the City, and the Tower Hamlets Mission (1870), all of which had immense Sunday schools, large provident clubs and huge mothers' meetings, were elaborately organised with up-to-date equipment and had numerous paid and voluntary workers.

The Field Lane Institution and the South London Mission, both of which concentrated upon helping the "down-and-outs", illustrate two extremes in the methods of doing this. The Field Lane Institution, which had been started as a ragged school, opened refuges in 1850 for the destitute in the area. By the later decades it had large dormitories for homeless men and women, who had been carefully selected and who were housed and fed until work was eventually found for them. The South London Mission, on the other hand, which had been started by William Carter, a chimney sweep converted in the mid-century revival, provided free meals and shelter for much greater numbers of destitute people, but with seemingly little selection or attempt to rehabilitate them.

The George Yard and Golden Lane Missions were characteristic of missions run by the middle-class. Both George Holland, the superintendent of George Yard, and W. J. Orsman, the superintendent of Golden Lane, were men of some means and close friends of Lord Shaftesbury. These missions were very well known, highly organised, and there was keen competition whenever a vacancy for voluntary workers occurred. Both men were on the committees of many of the more specialised societies and so could pass on appropriate cases to them where necessary.

The Tower Hamlets Mission is interesting in that its superintendent was Fred Charrington, a member of the well-known firm of brewers. He introduced his titled friends to the work, many of them coming down daily to help. In fact one wag is said to have remarked that most of St. James's was now in Tower Hamlets, since Fred had gone there. As might be expected, the chief concern of the mission was the closing of the public houses and gin palaces in the area, and constant warfare was waged against the publicans.

At the other extreme were such missions as the East Plumstead Mission (1895), which occupied the skittle saloon at the back of the Prince of Orange, and the Hammersmith Mission (1871) in a small

cottage in the area. Both did little more than hold evangelistic services and organise meetings for mothers and children, though the
Hammersmith Mission did employ a biblewoman part-time to
do some visiting.

But whether the mission was large or small, the primary purpose
was to preach the Gospel. Thus they all had their Sunday services,
their prayer meetings, their Sunday schools and their Bible
classes. A few, like the Open Air Mission (1853), which visited
race courses, fairs, holiday resorts, factories, shipyards and markets, and the Evangelisation Society (1864), which provided
speakers for meetings in churches, school rooms and missions,
confined their activities to preaching. But the majority set out to
train the children, to guide the mothers in the care of their families,
to provide centres for relaxation and enjoyment, and to offer help
in sickness and comfort in distress.

Work among children was frequently the first activity undertaken by a new mission, since the children were the easiest to
attract, and once interested, would encourage their parents to
come. A ragged school would be started for the children who were
too dirty and poor to attend the local school. Evening classes
would then be commenced for those who were at work, with
games for the less studious. A few missions, such as the Children's
Mission, Camberwell (1896), and the Juvenile Christian Mission
(1875) concentrated entirely upon the young.

For women, the mothers' meeting was the main attraction. In
many missions it consisted of little more than a cup of tea and a
reading from the Bible. But if managed on the lines adopted by
Mrs. Bayly at the Latymer Road Mission, Notting Hill (1858), it
could be used to help them in their daily living. Mrs. Bayly's
popular book, *Ragged Homes and How to Mend Them*, describes her
first meeting for the mothers of the children who attended the
ragged school at the Mission:

About seven or eight women assembled who looked at her with
curiosity. She read to them a few verses of scripture and then explained that the purpose of the meeting was to help them to manage
their homes better. She started by teaching them needlework, providing material for them to buy at a reduction of 2d. in the 1/- to be

paid for a few pence at a time, with a pattern thrown in. During the winter they made several garments for themselves and their children. The following year the meetings took a more definite form. Experiments in simple cookery were introduced, and ways of looking after children were discussed. Clothing and saving clubs were formed, and whitewash brushes and saucepans hired out. They were taught how to whitewash the walls of their dwellings and given instructions in the cheapest way of making nourishing soup. Thus she hoped to improve the homes of poor women living in the potteries and piggeries of Notting Hill.[1]

Most missions had a maternity society which lent out sheets and other things needed by the expectant mother for the birth of her child, and some had infant nurseries to look after the babies of widows and other mothers, forced by circumstances to go out to work. Many organised sewing meetings which both taught mothers to make clothes for their families and employed the elderly in making garments which were sold at a nominal price to those who needed them.

The men invariably proved more difficult to attract. Social evenings were tried, clubs started, working men's associations formed, but they hardly ever lasted long. This was partly due to the excessive hours of employment and the shift system which made leisure time variable. But it was also the result of the influence of secular thought which had a far greater hold on the men than on the women. Halls of Science were a powerful attraction to the man who liked to think for himself and who regarded the mission as a resort for women. The few missions run by men of the working class for their own social group, therefore, had a special appeal. The New Cut Mission, Lambeth (1877), was of this type. It was started by T. C. Young, a convert of William Carter and for a time a worker in his South London Mission. As a lad of nineteen he had taught himself to read and write, and had gradually built up a large mission for the people among whom he lived. It had an annual income of £1,000, more than £100 being collected locally in small coppers, four branches, a thriving Sunday school of some 500 children, clubs for men and women, a soup kitchen and a brass band. At the same time he had managed to

[1] Mrs. Bayly, *Ragged Homes and How to Mend Them*, 1859, p. 116.

get himself elected to the board of guardians and the Southwark borough council in order to draw the attention of the authorities to the many problems of the poorer people in the district.

Most missions made some provision for the underfed and the starving. Some had kitchens which distributed free meals in winter to the hungry, but only the Homerton Mission, sometimes known as the London Samaritan Society, did so on a large scale. It financed the distribution of food at the different ragged schools and missions throughout London, but left the actual organisation to the local social workers. Usually those who received such meals were carefully selected, but this was not the case with the free meals which were offered to try to attract people to attend the mission. The "sabbath breakfasts" provided by Moody's followers during his Scottish campaigns were of this type, and so were the "thieves'" and "tramps'" suppers organised by some of the more reputable missions. Thus there arose a conflict of principle between those who held that the Gospel should be furthered at any cost, and those who felt that feeding tramps and thieves on "meats of various kinds, plum pudding, tea and coffee"[1] only encouraged them to continue in this way of life.

Nearly all the missions had a nurse to attend cases of sickness reported by the district visitors. In the larger missions she had some training, though in the smaller she was usually some kindly person willing to help in this way. A few missions, like the White-cross Street Mission (1876) opened a dispensary for the provision of free medical attention and drugs, and many of the larger missions had seaside or country homes for convalescents and those in need of a rest.

An activity common to all was the social evening. All connected in any way with the mission were invited and supper was usually provided, to be followed by music or games. Sometimes it took the form of the rather prim "parlour meeting" to which formal invitations were issued and the guests expected to behave in the manner of the middle class. One wonders how much they enjoyed themselves, and how far they were successful in this metamorphosis. More riotous occasions were the Christmas parties

[1] *Evangelical Christendom*, 1878, vol. xix, p. 366.

when they were fed on roast beef and Christmas pudding and allowed to amuse themselves in their own way.

It quite often happened that missions which began with general social work found that their activities were channelled in some specialised direction. It is rarely realised that Dr. Barnardo's Homes were merely started as an offshoot of his East End Juvenile Mission (1867), nor that the social work of the Salvation Army was an after-thought of the East London Christian Mission, started by the Methodist pastor and his wife, William and Catharine Booth, in the sixties. Similarly the St. Giles Christian Mission (1860) began in 1877 to concentrate on ex-prisoners and their families, and the Hoxton Hall Mission became the centre for the "Gospel temperance" movement. Street traders were the special concern of the Costermongers' Cottage Mission (1871) and the Golden Lane Mission donkey parades were held to encourage costers to care for their animals. It is said that on one occasion Lord Shaftesbury was presented with a costers' donkey and cart.

Outstanding among the large missions was the London City Mission, first formed in 1835 by David Nasmith. A strange and somewhat unstable character, he had taught at an early age in a Glasgow Sunday school. Then, as clerk to a group of religious and benevolent societies, he noticed the extent to which the funds were maldistributed and the work overlapped. He, therefore, started the Glasgow City Mission in 1826 on a comprehensive basis, dividing the city into districts each under its own missionary. The rest of his life was spent in forming similar missions in other large towns. Before his death in 1839 he had started forty-five city missions in the British Isles and thirty-six in the United States and Canada. Very few of them survived because he rarely remained long enough in one place to gain staunch supporters who could carry on when he left. But in those cities where they did survive, they frequently became the central organisation for social work.

The London City Mission was different from the rest in that, after its early years when it did a certain amount of moral welfare work, it confined its activities exclusively to evangelism. London was divided into districts, each under a superintendent who was responsible for the missionaries in his area. These missionaries were working-class men, usually in charge of a particular number of dwellings, though a few were assigned to certain groups of people. There was a missionary to soldiers, to cabmen, to postmen, to policemen, and to gipsies. The city missionary became a well-known figure in the poorer districts. He would visit regularly from room to room, inviting the people to services in the Mission Hall. Social gatherings, mothers' meetings and other communal functions would be arranged, and more often than not a ragged school started for the children. But in spite of the fact that the missionaries were not allowed to engage actively in social work, they would direct those in need to a suitable agency, and their reports, published in the monthly London City Mission Magazine, acquainted a wide range of people with conditions in the slums.

To help the women with their problems, Mrs. Ranyard had, in 1857, started the London Bible and Domestic Mission which was at first run on similar lines to the City Mission. As a child she had visited with the local representative of the Bible Society, and when she married and came to live in Bloomsbury continued to do so. But here the people of the "rookeries" of St. Giles were particularly uncouth and often slammed the door in her face. She came to realise that only a woman of their own social standing was likely to penetrate successfully into their homes. Marian Bowers, who had offered her services to the Bloomsbury Baptist Mission, was chosen, and for several hours a day would go from room to room, talking to the women and reading the Scriptures to them.

Mrs. Ranyard had not intended that her "biblewomen" should do any social work. But the biblewoman usually found that "she would set out in the morning to visit her district and before she returned home she had probably been welfare worker, instructor in cookery and hygiene, minor-ailment nurse and above all best friend to many a weary woman."[1] She therefore arranged for them to set aside certain times for evangelistic work, and at others to give material help.

Each biblewoman was under the control of a lady superintendent, who would supply her with such things as bedding, clothing, and food for the needy, who would visit with her on occa-

[1] Elsbeth Platt, *The Story of the Ranyard Mission*, 1937, p. 78.

sions, and to whom she had to make weekly reports on the cases visited. The central activity was the mothers' meeting, conducted by the superintendent, at which sewing and cookery classes were held and demonstrations on hygiene and the care of children given. For a time dormitories were opened for poorly paid girls, mainly shirtmakers and tailoresses, at Dudley Street, St. Giles and Parker Street, Holborn. But the most useful form of social work which they did was to nurse the sick poor in their homes, and it was on this that the Mission concentrated increasingly after 1868, until in 1917, when the Mission was renamed the Ranyard Mission, this became its exclusive function.

Mrs. Ranyard, through her friendliness with leading Evangelicals such as Lord Shaftesbury, Bishop Thorold, the Kinnairds, and the Pennefathers, and her writings, did all she could to encourage others to follow her methods. Biblewomen were soon to be found in most provincial towns and in some cities abroad. But she made no attempt to link up their work with hers, and similar organisations, such as the Church of England Parochial Mission Women's Association (1860) were entirely independent. The city missionaries and the biblewomen usually worked together in a district. Between them they would visit the inhabitants and each deal with appropriate cases, and the Mission hall would often be the centre for the biblewoman's meetings. Thus they provided a network of social services which, because they were undenominational, were often more acceptable to the people concerned.

The importance of Mrs. Ranyard in the history of social work is that for the first time the paid social worker appears. She was expected to be "a clean, tidy, humble, cheerful, pleasant-spoken matron with a good character, a character of real piety without cant—with a quiet, energetic missionary spirit about her",[1] and she received a few pence a day, was engaged in the first instance on a month's probation, and given a small amount of practical training.

We have to turn to the undenominational deaconesses if we are to discover the first instances of careful training. The deaconess institutions at Tottenham and Mildmay were the chief examples of this. The inspiration for their work came from Germany, where

[1] Platt, *op. cit.*, p. 47.

at Kaiserswerth in 1836 a Lutheran, Pastor Fliedner, had begun to train women for nursing and social work on the lines which were thought to resemble those of the deaconesses of the fourth century in the Christian Church. The Tottenham deaconesses, started by Dr. Laseron, an immigrant German Jew, in 1857, closely resembled Kaiserswerth in concentrating almost entirely upon nursing, but the Mildmay Institution developed a widespread and elaborate network of social services.

The Rev. and Mrs. Pennefather had moved from Barnet to St. Jude's, Mildmay, in North London in 1864. They had already opened a home for orphans of the Crimean War and a coffee house for workers, but at Mildmay they developed a far wider range of social services. Though the Rev. Pennefather died in 1873, Mrs. Pennefather continued to organise the social work of the Institution, and in particular to superintend the training of the deaconesses. She describes the beginnings of the deaconess work in the following way:

> It was on the 17th of August, 1860, a sweet, quiet, summer morning that a few friends assembled in a cottage home in the little town of Barnet, with the desire of consecrating its walls and its inmates to a new and sacred purpose. . . . We started with Kaiserswerth and its hallowed associations fresh in our minds, but the work was not intended, for many reasons, to be a copy of that valuable institution. In the first place, while we felt sure that the great principles of Christian work are the same in all countries, the domestic rules and practical details essentially belonging to the habits of another land must not be followed out on English grounds; we may learn but not transplant. Secondly, the hospital and infirmary nursing, though included in our scheme, would not, at least in the early stages of our present undertaking, occupy so prominent a place in our training as it does in the work of the German deaconess. Thirdly, the name and dress (though our sympathies might go with both) would enlist a host of opponents, whose only idea of such distinctions were associated with nuns and sisterhoods of Romish reputation. We began, then, simply as a Training Home for female missionaries . . . the only qualifications were consistent Christian character, earnest love for souls, and a fair amount of intelligence and education.[1]

[1] H. J. Cooke, *The Story of the First Deaconess Institution*, 1893, pp. 43–4.

By the time that the Institution was well established, the period of training of the deaconess was two years. After a month's probation, she was accepted by the central training home at Mildmay where lectures were given by Mrs. Pennefather and other senior deaconesses, and where the trainee could help in the men's night school, the dorcas society which taught simple needlework to poor women, the Bible Flower Mission which distributed flowers to the local hospitals, and the orphanage. She would then be allocated to one of the outlying missions to learn more general social work. There were eleven of these missions in North London and six south of the Thames. She would live either at the central home at Mildmay, or the home in South London in Effra Road, Brixton, and from there would travel daily to her mission. Here she would learn to help with mothers' meetings, to organise boys' and girls' clubs, to undertake elementary dispensing at the medical mission and to supervise the distribution of food to children and invalids. When qualified she might take further training in nursing at one of the two hospitals of the Institution, or in moral welfare work at the rescue home in South London, she might continue to work at one of the Mildmay missions in London or one of their five affiliated institutions, be sent to help in the social work of a parish or, after some experience, be invited by an outside agency to supervise or re-organise their work. She took no vows, nor any promise that she would remain unmarried or work for a definite period, but she was expected to make her work her principal aim in life and to pursue it as long as she could.

Though in numbers the Mildmay deaconesses were few, only some 200 working at any one time in comparison with the large numbers of biblewomen and other social workers, their work was outstanding and their example of training was followed by others. Dr. Barnardo began to train his workers in a similar manner at Bow in 1875, the Y.M.C.A. in 1891, and the Star Mission at Manchester in 1894. Thus this remarkable institution played an important part in the development of nineteenth century social work. Though Thomas Chalmers, in his experiment in a Glasgow suburb in 1819, had laid down certain principles and methods to be followed by his deacons in their dealings with the poor, he by no means gave them the careful training which was instituted at

Mildmay. Here it was intended to equip the worker to enter social work on a full-time rather than a voluntary basis and to make social work her permanent career. Both the theoretical and practical aspects were dealt with, the former in lectures given to trainees by persons experienced in social work, and the latter through working in the different departments of the Institution. The two years' general training for the younger workers and the shorter more specialised course for the more mature, set the pattern for the social science courses which were introduced at some of the universities in the twentieth century. The Evangelicals, therefore, made their contribution to the more scientific approach which was developing towards social work at the end of the century.

Large Christian Missions such as these, however, were rarely to be found outside London. Among the exceptions were the Star Mission at Manchester (1889), started in a music hall by Frank Crossley, the owner of a large engineering firm, and eventually including among its various activities the management of a small working class housing estate; the Carrubbers' Close Mission in Edinburgh (1858) which was encouraged by D. L. Moody to become the centre for social work in the district; and the Irish Church Missions (1849) which organised much of the Protestant social work in Southern Ireland. Most urban centres possessed town or city missions, and these, unlike the London City Mission, either organised the social work of the area themselves or acted as centres for those who did.

It was far more expensive to organise similar missions for the country folk, and they did not suffer to the same extent from the effects of poverty as did the inhabitants of the towns, since they mostly had means of adding to their income in kind. Thus country missions, such as the Country Towns Mission (1837) and Mrs. Daniell's Village Missions (1857), were almost entirely evangelistic and educational. Similarly the Island and Coast Mission (1833) which covered much of the coastline of Scotland, and the Highway and Hedgerow Mission (1885) which worked among gipsies, coastguards, sailors, soldiers and navvies, had itinerant missionaries who started Sunday schools in the different villages and visited them from time to time.

The sphere of action of these Christian missions was mostly confined to the very poor who had some home of their own. Only a few of these missions, as for example the Field Lane Institution and the South London Mission, made any provision for the homeless and destitute. They could go to the common lodging houses, where for 4d. to 6d. per night a bed and cooking facilities could be obtained. But, as Lord Shaftesbury told the House of Lords in 1853:

> It is scarcely possible to describe the filthy conditions of the houses—the loathsome beds filled with vermin, the overcrowding which caused fever to be rarely absent, the abandoned inmates, comprising the lowest classes of vagrants, thieves and prostitutes.[1]

The State was really supposed to provide for the homeless in the casual wards of the workhouse, and these casual wards were not too bad, as the following rhyme scribbled on the wall of one of them maintains:

> Dry bread in the morning, ditto at night,
> Keep up your pecker and make it all right,
> Certainly the meals are paltry and mean,
> But the beds are nice and clean.
> Men don't tear their bedsheets or rugs,
> For there are neither lice, fleas or bugs
> At the little, clean union of Trysicle.[2]

But the genuinely destitute had to be desperately in need to seek admission to such wards. They disliked the lack of freedom, the repulsive companionship, and particularly the fact that they could not leave the next morning before the prescribed task of work had been done, when it was usually too late to find employment that day. Furthermore large towns offered insufficient accommodation, and in times of maximum unemployment could not begin to cope with the large numbers needing help.

Therefore, charitable shelters, of which there were several in London, were opened. The first of these, the Nightly Shelter for the Homeless Poor, had been started by Elizabeth Fry in 1819, and by the thirties the Society had three shelters with room for

---

[1] *Parliamentary Debates*, House of Lords, 3rd series, vol. cxxvii, May 13, 1853.
[2] *Vagrancy and Mendicity*, C.O.S. pamphlet No. 7.

2,000 inmates. It was careful with regard to those whom it admitted, not permitting applicants with a legal claim for poor relief to stay for more than three nights.

By the sixties the numbers of the homeless had greatly increased, and other shelters began to be opened, most of them by Evangelicals. The Metropolitan Free Dormitory Association, organised by Lord Shaftesbury and the Rev. Pennefather in 1857 to cover the poorer parts of London, was the largest of these. It had shelters at Paddington, Whitechapel, Holloway, Greenwich, Woolwich, Lambeth, and Chelsea, where meals and sleeping accommodation were offered to "respectable and homeless men and women".[1]

Ellen Barlee, in her book *Our Homeless Poor*, describes one of these shelters:

> Rooms, which are as large and airy as can conveniently be procured are divided on either side by wooden partitions that serve as beds, a pathway being left down the centre of the room. These beds resemble troughs more than anything else, raised so that its occupant rests on an inclined plane, affording relief to the posture and raising the head and shoulders. At one end of the room are the implements and apparatus for washing, each applicant for admission being very properly required to perform her ablutions before retiring to bed. A rude mattress and mat covering is placed in each crib. In winter the rooms are well warmed and cheerful fires are kept. On entering, and before leaving the asylum in the morning, a penny roll is given to each person, with sometimes the addition of a cup of coffee. The gas is kept burning all night.[2]

The unemployment of the 1880's and the 1890's once again raised the need for such shelters, and this time they were provided on a much larger scale by denominational agencies. The London Congregational Union opened free shelters at the Medland Hall in the Ratcliffe Highway and Colliers' Rents in the Borough where the homeless were allowed to sleep on forms and given a free breakfast before they left in the morning. Similarly the Salvation Army, which until this time had been an evangelistic mission, began its social work for the "submerged tenth". Their first shel-

---

[1] *The Revival*, August 6, 1868.
[2] Ellen Barlee, *Our Homeless Poor*, 1860, pp. 13–14.

ters, opened in 1888, were providing accommodation for as many as 4,000 nightly in 1892, half of whom paid a few pence for their lodging and food. These shelters were much criticised at the time on the grounds that they competed with the workhouse and merely encouraged the poor to depend on others. This was probably true where the accommodation was entirely free and where all and sundry were admitted. But the Salvation Army did institute what they picturesquely called "elevators" where those willing to work were employed until a job could be found for them. Similarly the Church Army cared for the homeless, though on a far smaller scale, and rarely sheltered people whom they were not intending to employ in their own "labour" homes.

Most of these shelters provided food for the destitute. But there were also food charities which gave free or very cheap meals to the hungry. Peter Bedford, the Quaker philanthropist, had set the example in 1797, when to feed the hungry in war-time he had opened the Spitalfields Soup Kitchen. Some thousands were served every day with a quart of soup for 1d., the additional cost being met by the city companies, banks and offices. By the 1850's and 1860's free soup kitchens in some of the poorer areas had become so numerous that it was possible for the astute to collect several free meals per day, and quite common for families to depend upon the soup kitchen at the end of the week when wages were spent. There were even instances of bogus advertisements in the newspapers describing cases of slow starvation and asking for contributions for their relief.

This was not, however, true of all food charities. Many of the Christian Missions gave food to the needy only after careful scrutiny by their visitors, and some had invalid kitchens from which food was taken to the sick or provided for children. It was organisations such as these which Charles Booth commends when he writes:

> Soup kitchens again are characteristic of the ordinary parish view of poverty and its needs. They provide, at the lowest possible cost, necessary nourishment, which all who will can buy, and which is offered freely to prevent starvation. The kitchen is not always open, but it is always in readiness in case of need occurring, and such need is calmly looked forward to as an inevitable incident of life connected

with bad trade or a cold winter. . . . Because of their need the starving family, the victim of sickness, and the hungry child, require and receive relief.[1]

A rather interesting and significant experiment was tried by a group of Evangelicals in the East End of London in the winter of 1860. At the suggestion of two of the mid-century revivalists, Reginald Radcliffe and Richard Weaver, the East End Mission and Relief Committee was formed to help the families of those out of work. The wives of the unemployed were engaged at 6d. per hour in sewing garments which they were later allowed to buy at a nominal price. The experiment was repeated in Lancashire at the time of the cotton famine, and was revived in London by Lady Hobart and the Hon. Elizabeth Waldegrave whenever unemployment was severe. It is an example of the way in which the Evangelicals recognised the needs of the family as a whole.

Emigration was a further possibility for the very poor. In the early decades of the century it had been tried as a means of relieving unemployment, but although the authorities had the powers to assist prospective emigrants, they rarely made use of them, and what little emigration did take place was almost entirely in private hands. Most of the societies for this purpose were formed in periods of trade depression, particularly in the late sixties and eighties, they concentrated almost entirely upon men and single women, and few were run by Evangelicals.

The Evangelicals, however, as so often happened, made good the deficiencies in the existing organisation by making arrangements for emigrating families rather than individuals and taking steps to improve the comfort of those who were travelling. Their largest society was the East End Family Emigration Society (1868) which was an adjunct of the East London Mission and Relief Society. Others included the British and Colonial Emigration Society organised by Admiral Fishbourne, the Cow Cross Emigration Society connected with the Cow Cross Mission, and the Clerkenwell Emigration Society run by the vicar of St. Paul's, Clerkenwell. The larger missions, such as George Yard, Tower Hamlets, Golden Lane and the London Samaritan Society also

---

[1] Booth, *op. cit.*, p. 285.

assisted family emigration. It is not likely that very large numbers were sent in this way, but at least families were not broken up and in most cases some arrangements were made for their reception on arrival.

Lady Kinnaird and Lord Radstock were both concerned with making the transit easier and more comfortable. Conditions on the emigration ships were usually very poor. Men and women were huddled together, with few sanitary arrangements, insufficient food, and very little to do on a voyage which might last several weeks. Some of them had waited for days at the port of embarkation before leaving, and few had friends to meet them on arrival or a definite job to which to go. Mary Jane Kinnaird helped to found the British Ladies' Female Emigration Society (1849), which provided matrons for ships taking single women. The task of these matrons was to care for those who were sick, to organise needlework and other classes to while away the time and to arrange contacts in the colonies for the women on arrival. Lord Radstock opened the Emigrants' Home at Blackwall, near the London Docks, in 1883 to accommodate both families and single persons while they were waiting for departure. It could take some six to seven hundred people who would otherwise have found it difficult to get lodging for the night, and was widely used by the shipping companies until the end of the century, when the emigration societies began to make their own arrangements for the accommodation of travellers.

Thus the Evangelicals met most of the general needs of the poor. They visited them in their homes to see what material help and advice they could give; they offered them some recreation and amusement outside their homes; they made arrangements for the feeding and shelter of the homeless and destitute; and they encouraged family emigration. The widespread work of the larger organisations, such as the London City Mission, the Mildmay Institution, the Ranyard Mission and the other great Christian Missions reached a very large number of those in need who would otherwise have received no help of any sort at that time. It was they who introduced payment and training into the field of social work. Though pay was at first given only to members of the lower class, and though training was in some cases meagre and inadequate, the principle began to be recognised that this was a field of work in which the paid employee held an increasingly important place and in which his job was one of skill which required some prior teaching and experience.

In particular they looked upon the family as the unit for care. Unlike the Poor Law authorities, they tried to keep the family together and when they helped individual members it was usually with the purpose of benefiting the family as a whole. This is an approach which was lost when a more scientific attitude was adopted towards social work and when greater specialisation was introduced. It is only now beginning to be re-emphasised.

Yet they received much criticism. In the first place it was said that they usurped the duties of the Poor Law authorities whose purpose it was to relieve the destitute. No doubt they did in some instances, but it has to be borne in mind that in many unions the guardians were very loth to grant out-relief and in times of heavy unemployment workhouse accommodation was restricted. Furthermore, Charles Booth pointed out in the nineties that these Christian Missions did not on the whole help the destitute, who were the people for whom the Poor Law was intended, but the slightly more respectable who only occasionally fell in need.

A second category of charges brought against them was indiscriminate relief, inefficient management of their organisations, and waste of the public's money. There were undoubtedly cases of indiscriminate help, particularly in the societies which offered food and shelter. But in such cases help was needed immediately, and it was more difficult to make enquiries. It was usually the smaller organisations which were less efficiently managed, though some of the larger ones appeared from time to time on the Charity Organisation Society's "black list". As to wasting the money of the public, there was certainly much money spent in vain, but until adequate statistics were available it was difficult to estimate exactly what was wanted, and again as Charles Booth says "in spite of many failures, much beneficial work was done".[1]

Where the Evangelicals can be justly criticised is in their failure to consider the causes of the poverty and distress which they tried to relieve. They paid little attention to the low level of wages in

[1] Booth, *op. cit.*, pp. 273-4.

certain trades, to the reasons for unemployment or to the environment in which the poor lived. It is frequently said that they turned their faces resolutely against any alteration in the structure of society, or the introduction of some form of State social security. This was not so; and the next chapter will show the contribution that the Evangelicals made to the general change in attitude to these matters which took place in the last decades of the century.

CHAPTER IV

The Social Work of the Churches and Chapels

THOUGH MOST of the Evangelicals preferred to carry out their social activities through the Christian Missions and other societies, a certain amount of this work was undertaken by the churches and chapels. Until the 1880's this was comparatively small, but during that decade the "social conscience" of the churches was aroused, and expressed itself both in an immediate extension of social activities and, in certain instances, in the development of a social policy.

The immediate reason for this change in attitude was the publication of a penny pamphlet, *The Bitter Cry of Outcast London*, in October 1883. No author's name appears on the cover, but it is said to have been written by the Rev. W. C. Preston, a Congregational minister, from facts supplied to him by the secretary of the London Congregational Union, the Baptist minister and members of the East London Tabernacle, and some of the London City Mission workers. It attracted attention at once in both the secular and religious Press, and in many of the reports of charitable societies. The headmaster of Harrow is said to have waved a copy in his hand as he preached from the pulpit of the University Church at Oxford, and Canon Barnett, who shunned most sensationalism, agreed that the *Bitter Cry* played an important part in gaining support for the foundation of Toynbee Hall.

It opens with the challenging words:

Whilst we have been building our churches and solacing ourselves with our religion and dreaming that the millenium was coming, the poor have been growing poorer, and the wretched more miserable, and the immoral more corrupt. The gulf has been daily widening which separates the lowest classes of the community from our churches and chapels, and from all decency and civilisation. It is easy to bring an array of facts which seem to point to the opposite conclusion—to speak of the noble army of men and women who penetrate the vilest haunts, carrying with them the blessings of the Gospel; of the encouraging reports published by Missions, Reformatories, Refuges, Temperance Societies; of theatre services, midnight meetings and special missions. But what does it all amount to? We are simply living in a fool's paradise if we suppose that all these agencies combined are doing a thousandth part of what needs to be done, or a hundredth part of what *could* be done by the Church of Christ. We must face the facts, and these compel the conviction that *this terrible flood of sin and misery is gaining upon us*. It is rising every day. This statement is made as the result of a long, patient and sober enquiry undertaken for the purpose of discovering the actual state of the case and the remedial action most likely to be effective. Convinced that it is high time some combined and organised effort was made by all denominations of Christians, though not for denominational purposes, the London Congregational Union have determined to open in several of the lowest and most needy districts of the Metropolis, suitable Mission Halls, as a base for operations for evangelistic work.[1]

The publication of the *Bitter Cry* would probably have caused less concern had it not appeared at a time when the unemployment and under-employment of the 1870's and early 1880's was beginning to gain the attention of the public. Widespread discussion of social conditions was taking place both among the workers and the intellectuals, and socialist ideas were being revived. The *Bitter Cry* was the response of those Evangelicals who appreciated the situation and who wished to apply similar remedies with an Evangelical emphasis. This method of approach was quickly seized upon. William Stead made it the basis of an article in the *Pall Mall Gazette*, and it inspired the *Liverpool Daily Press* to publish some vivid accounts of "Squalid Liverpool". It also suggested the lines which were followed in 1890 by William Booth's *In Darkest England*—a book which was widely read in the last decade of the century, and roused not only the

[1] *The Bitter Cry of Outcast London, an Enquiry into the Conditions of the Abject Poor,* October 1883, by the London Congregational Union, p. 1.

Salvation Army, but other groups of Evangelicals to recognise their social duties.

Until this time the social work of the churches had been comparatively sparse and meagre. In the early nineteenth century most of the denominations had tried to extend their work among the industrial groups of the larger towns, both in the slums and the growing suburbs. Inspired by the foreign missionary movement, "home missionary" societies had been formed at the turn of the eighteenth century, the Baptist Home Missionary Society in 1797 and the General Home Missionary Society, which was largely Congregational, in 1819. But their purpose was as much to increase their own membership as to help the needy, and they can hardly be regarded as carrying out social work. The Church of England followed the same policy in the thirties with the formation of two Evangelical societies, the Church Pastoral Aid Society (1836) and the Additional Curates Society (1837), to supply more clergy for the heavily populated areas. This enabled some of the problems of the slum parish to be tackled. William Champneys at St. Mary's, Whitechapel, in 1837 began to open Church day and Sunday schools, to organise mothers' meetings, to institute provident clubs and to start a young men's institute; and William Cadman did the same, some ten years later, at St. George's, Southwark. The Church Home Mission, with William Cadman as its secretary, extended such work to other parishes. Further strides were made when deaconess orders were introduced into the Church of England, Elizabeth Ferard of the North London Deaconess Institution being the first to be ordained in 1861. Such orders were the Low Church counterpart of the High Church sisterhoods which had been formed in the 1840's, but instead of concentrating upon devotional occupations, they were intended to help the clergy in the general work of the parish. The social work of the Rochester and Southwark deaconess order, started by Deaconess Gilmore and Bishop Thorold, was typical of these institutions. As well as superintending the Sunday school and teaching scripture in the day school, the deaconess would visit from house to house, distribute the endowed parochial charities, organise benefit societies, hold meetings and clubs for different age groups, and would usually be trained in first aid, so that, at a time when district nurses were few, she could help the doctor and nurse the sick.

The Baptists were the only other denomination to develop social work on any scale, and they did so through the formation of domestic missions, in the charge of a layworker, in connection with their large city chapels. Both the Bloomsbury Chapel and the Regent's Park Chapel supported domestic missions of this type, the one at St. Giles and the other at Camden Town. George McCree provides a good example of the efficient and versatile layworker of this period. He was not only in charge of the Bloomsbury Domestic Mission, but also took part in the midnight meeting movement and in temperance work, and when moved to the Borough Road Chapel was conspicuous for the donkey and barrow clubs which he organised to help costermongers to purchase their own equipment.

The Quakers, as a religious group, would have little to do with organised social work at this time. The Meeting for Sufferings was mainly concerned with Quakers in need, and the Yearly Meeting feared to sanction any home missionary work lest by placing a particular individual in control the "guidance of the spirit" should be lost. Yet individually they undertook a great deal, probably more than any of the other denominations, and much of this work was associated with the name of Peter Bedford. He was an older member of a group of Quakers which included Elizabeth Fry, William Allen and Thomas Buxton, all of whom had been stirred to action by the evangelistic preaching of Stephen Grellet in the early years of the nineteenth century. They cared for the poor, helped to draw attention to the problems of juvenile delinquency and visited in the London prisons. Their general work for the underprivileged was conspicuous for its careful organisation and for its personal enquiry and observation of each case before relief was given. The various activities which they started in London were consolidated in 1865 when the Bedford Institute was opened, and this is still a centre of Quaker social work.

There were, however, isolated instances of very useful work, usually connected with one of the larger London congregations, the Metropolitan Tabernacle in South London, to which C. H.

Spurgeon had come in 1853, being a good example. Here, he organised a wide variety of social services, manned by members of his congregation. In the Tabernacle were twenty rooms for classes and clubs, and the adjoining almshouses provided quarters for seventeen poor women. The ladies of the congregation organised the benevolent society, managed provident societies, and ran a maternity society for expectant mothers; and an evangelistic association visited in the public houses and lodging houses. Several specialised societies sprang from the efforts of members of the congregation, among them Orsman's Golden Lane Mission, Mr. Hampton's Mission to the Blind and the Stockwell Orphanage. But all this was exceptional and due to Spurgeon's popularity which placed at his disposal not only a much wider choice of leaders but also much larger funds than were usually available to the ordinary church. The *Bitter Cry* was therefore not far wrong when it deprecated the lack of real interest in the welfare of the poor by the majority of the churches, called for more concentrated action from them, and drew attention to the ways in which social distress was increasing and undermining the social stability of the community.

The immediate result of the *Bitter Cry* was the calling, by the London Congregational Union, of a conference with the other Free Churches to discuss the relationship of their work to the needs of the poor. No general plan appears to have been formed, but each denomination seems to have taken stock of its welfare activities and formulated some plan for improving these in the future. This awakening of the social conscience of the churches became known as the "forward movement". All denominations were affected by it though in different ways. They all realised that there were large numbers of very poor people whose conditions of life were appalling and who had not the faintest idea of the meaning of Christianity. They agreed that these people would never come to the churches nor would they be acceptable if they did, and so must be sought out and helped both materially and spiritually. But they differed as to how such help should be given. Some followed the traditional method of the mission; others adapted it to meet these special circumstances, and a few, such as the Christian Socialists, felt that group action was necessary.

In fact the *Bitter Cry* made it quite clear that without some change of environment and some interference by the State little could be done. As the pamphlet states:

> We shall be pointed to the fact that without State interference nothing effectual can be accomplished upon any large scale. . . . The State must make short work of this iniquitous traffic (this refers to the rebuilding of the slums and the consequent necessity for the poor to move to other quarters) and secure for the poorest the rights of citizenship; the right to live in something better than fever dens; the right to live as something better than the uncleanest of brute beasts. This must be done before the Christian Missionary can have much chance with them.[1]

The Congregationalists were the first to take action and their method was to open "halls" for the homeless where all who came could find shelter and some food. With the help of Samuel Morley three disused Congregational chapels, at Colliers' Rents in Bermondsey, the Wheatsheaf Hall, South Lambeth, and Caine Hall, Vauxhall, were opened for this purpose, and when the Rev. Wilson Gates was appointed superintendent of the social work of the London Congregational Union in 1891 the Medland Hall in the Ratcliffe Highway, the Hope Mission in Banner Street, St. Luke's, and a hall in the Old Gravel Lane, Wapping, were added. They hoped to attract the very poor by offering them free accommodation of the simplest type and by allowing them to do much as they liked in the way of smoking, cooking their own food and washing. In practice, this led to overcrowding, disorder and abuse and to much widespread and indiscriminate relief. Thus, after experimenting for some years, the "halls" were closed and the more usual form of Christian Mission substituted.

The Methodists modified these methods by using the "hall" as the centre of activities, and by organising around it a carefully selected and controlled pattern of social services. The Primitive Methodists and the Bible Christians, on account of their flexible organisation and close contacts with the poor, were the first groups to introduce such systematic social work, but it was the Wesleyans who took the lead in the "forward" movement. At a

[1] *The Bitter Cry of Outcast London, op. cit.,* p. 2.

meeting of their London ministers in 1884 it was decided that central missions should be opened in the needy districts where the preaching of the Gospel should be closely linked with social work.

In a very poor neighbourhood it was usual for them to choose as their central mission some place with which the people were familiar, frequently a disused public house or dance hall. Thus, the Rev. Peter Thompson, who was appointed to take charge of such work in the East End in 1885, acquired first Paddy's Goose in the Ratcliffe Highway, which consisted of two small music halls and a public house, and used it for a coffee house with rooms for meetings and various social functions, and later the Old Mahogany Bar as a centre for work among young people. Not only did he conduct all the usual social activities of that time, but through his membership of St. George's vestry and the local board of guardians, he took an active part in local politics, where he maintained a firm stand against drunkenness and indecency in the area, and caused a general clearing up of some of the more disreputable places. He encouraged the people themselves to take a part in municipal affairs and provided classes in citizenship for them and a free library which became the nucleus of the Passmore Edward's Library for St. George's-in-the-East. This method of combining social work with a demand for a more enlightened social policy on the part of the local government authorities was typical of the Methodist "forward" movement.

Central missions on these lines were started in other parts of London; in St. John's Square in Central London (1886), at St. James' Hall, Piccadilly, in West London (1887), at the Old Lockfield's Chapel in South London (1889), and at Poplar and Bow in the East End. The first to be formed in the provinces was the Manchester and Salford Mission (1886), and this was followed by others in the larger cities.

The most prominent of these was the West London Mission, under the superintendency of the Rev. Hugh Price Hughes, who was president of the Wesleyan Conference in 1898. He had taken part in the first interdenominational meeting which had resulted from the *Bitter Cry*, and his mission was supported by many non-

3. A Soup Kitchen in the Ratcliffe Highway

4. The Blind Basket-makers

Wesleyans. Two of his halls, Wardour and Craven, were disused Congregational chapels, many of his workers were from other Evangelical groups, and the famous Baptist minister, C. H. Spurgeon, gave the opening address of his Mission on October 21, 1887.

More than half the theatres and music halls of the Metropolis were in this area, with hotels, restaurants, and questionable "massage" establishments in the mean streets off the main thoroughfares. There was as well a respectable element, consisting of men and women employed in the business houses, some factory girls, and soldiers and nurses from the neighbouring barracks. The work was, therefore, divided between that at the main "hall", St. James', later to be replaced by the present Kingsway Hall, which was used as a centre for meetings and classes for business people and the more respectable groups, and the branch mission "halls" in the back streets for the people in those areas. The activities were similar to those of the East End Mission, but in addition there was an employment bureau, an enquiry office for those in need of advice or help (possibly the first instance of a modern citizens' advice bureau), a "Poor Man's Lawyer", and a guild for crippled and deformed children. Moral welfare work was available for middle-class girls, a group which was much neglected at that time, and incurables discharged from the local hospitals were cared for. Attempts were made to improve the standard of "turns" in the music halls, not by suggesting that such halls should be closed nor coarse fun excluded, but by trying to stop indecency. The workers were not only encouraged to become members of the local vestries, the boards of guardians, and the school boards, but to work in close co-operation with the Charity Organisation Society, the Metropolitan Association for Befriending Young Servants, and other voluntary societies. Thus the innovations introduced to the Methodist "forward movement" by Hugh Price Hughes were an endeavour to suit his agencies to the requirements of the neighbourhood, and an attempt to fit in with all the other social agencies in the district.

His wife, Catharine, with her band of "sisters of the people", took an active part in the work, several being attached to each of the "halls" and others undertaking more specialised duties, such as nursing in the homes of the poor, caring for the children in the day nursery, or looking after the "cripples' parlour". They were drawn from all Evangelical groups, took no vows, were under no specified rules or regulations and were allowed to choose the type of work which most interested them. These "sisters of the people" were not the first "sisters" in the Methodist denomination, since T. B. Stephenson of the National Children's Home had employed "sisters" specially trained to look after his children, and the Rev. Peter Thompson had "lady workers" to help him in the East End, but they were the type which was copied by the other central missions, both in London and the provinces, and they set the example for the use of deaconesses in the social work of the Primitive Methodists, the Congregationalists and the Baptists. By the last decades of the century much of the social work of the denominations was carried out by these devoted women, frequently for little or no remuneration.

The Wesleyan forward movement quickly spread to the provinces and became an essential part of their work in any heavily populated urban area. Here their social work depended very much upon what was already being done in the area, and they made it their purpose to fill in the gaps so that none might be left without some kind of help. Thus, the first of these provincial centres, the Manchester and Salford Mission (1886), under the superintendence of the Rev. S. F. Collier, was particularly concerned with the prisoners discharged from the Strangeways Gaol, many of whom were not brought into contact with the existing Discharged Prisoners' Aid Society. Mission workers at first met them at the gaol gate, and later were permitted to interview them before their release. They found employment for some and personally conducted others to their home or family. Many of these Methodist central missions are still to be found in the poorer parts of our cities.

The effects of the "forward movement" upon the Baptists were neither so sudden nor so spectacular as they were among the Congregationalists and the Methodists, since many of their chapels were already engaged in some forms of social work. The "movement" was not officially recognised by the London Baptist Association until 1889 and then its purpose was to extend the social work of the Baptist chapels in the poorer areas rather than to create new centres for such work. The only instance of a central hall was the West Ham Central Mission (1898), opened by Robert Rowntree Clifford in connection with his work as pastor of the Barking Tabernacle.

The result was that the social work of the different Baptist chapels developed in entirely different ways. Some men, like the Rev. Archibald Brown, at the East London Tabernacle in Stepney, and the Rev. William Cuff at the Shoreditch Tabernacle, clung to the old method of social agencies attached to a particular congregation; and others, like John Wilson of the Woolwich Tabernacle and J. C. Carlile in Bermondsey, were chiefly concerned with the community approach. As Charles Booth remarked:

> Except in their financial boldness, in the buoyant faith shown in the construction of such a building (the Woolwich Tabernacle), and in the common name "tabernacle", although both are Baptists, there is little resemblance between this congregation and that which maintains the Spurgeon tradition at Newington.[1]

These divergent attitudes were skilfully brought together by the Rev. F. B. Meyer, who, as honorary director of the Baptist Forward Movement, formed the link between the more conservative and the newer approaches. Brought up under the influence of Dr. Brock at the Bloomsbury Chapel, he had imbibed the more orthodox methods at an early age, only to have them shaken by D. L. Moody in 1873. Thereafter he began to use more spectacular methods during his ministry at Leicester from 1874–88. Opening Melbourne Hall as an interdenominational chapel and centre for such work, he started a prison-gate mission, a home for friendless boys, a wood-chopping yard and a window-cleaning brigade for the unemployed. It was a common sight in Leicester at that time to see carts carrying wood with F. B. Meyer, "firewood merchant", inscribed on the side, or to meet men engaged in window cleaning with "F. B. Meyer" on their hats. Thus, when he came to London as minister of the Regent's Park Chapel in 1888, and took over the direction of the "forward

[1] Booth, *op. cit.*, 3rd series, vol. v, pp. 105–6.

movement", he was well experienced in such work. Though never fully sharing the views of the more progressive, such as Dr. Clifford, he had the confidence of most shades of opinion in the Baptist denomination.

The Presbyterians and the Quakers both made only very small contributions to the "forward movement", though for very different reasons. The Presbyterian Church of England was relatively new and had few working class congregations. Its appeal was to the middle income groups and its chief concern the gathering together of lapsed Presbyterians. A Church Aid and Evangelisation Committee was, however, formed in 1893 with the novel purpose of linking the work of existing churches in the poorer areas with that of some wealthy congregation. Thus, Kentish Town was linked with Frognal and Hampstead, and Victoria Docks with Enfield and Palmers Green. But this was not very successful, and it was only when the Presbyterian Settlement was founded in 1901 with a band of women workers to help the ministers in the social work of the East End congregations that much progress was made.

The Quakers, on the other hand, had formed their Home Mission Committee a year before the *Bitter Cry* was published. This operated with the Bedford Institute to meet the increasing distress in the East End. Sunday Morning Breakfasts for the homeless were tried, a labour agency was opened to help find work for the unemployed and a medical mission and sick fund started. But the younger generation of Quakers, led by John Wilhelm Rowntree, felt that this was not the complete answer to the problems of poverty and unemployment. They thought that a far deeper study should be made of current social problems before any further action was taken, and a special conference was held to consider the matter, which was followed by two summer schools at Scarborough and Birmingham. John Wilhelm had always dreamed of a Quaker college where such problems could be thoroughly discussed, and George Cadbury brought this into being with the gift of "Woodbrooke", near Birmingham, in 1904.

A distinctive response to the *Bitter Cry* was the social work of the Salvation and Church Armies. The intention of both was to reach those who were "down-and-out"—the submerged tenth as William Booth picturesquely called them—and for this purpose both started as evangelistic organisations and used spectacular methods which could be understood by the most ignorant. Both employed a disciplined body of workers, men and women, many of them from the lower income groups, and both found it difficult to make progress unless some social work was added. Thus they both began, in 1886, three years after the publication of the *Bitter Cry*, to employ "slum" sisters who visited, nursed and generally helped the very poor.

The Salvation Army had been started as the East London Christian Mission in 1865 by a Methodist minister and his wife, William and Catharine Booth. For a time they followed the usual methods of a Christian mission, but found these inadequate for dealing with the vast amount of misery which they encountered. They therefore began to place their workers under sterner discipline, to train them for their jobs and to provide them with uniforms, ranks and the band accompaniments with which we are familiar.

There is no doubt that Wilson Carlile, the founder of the Church Army, copied these methods to some extent, though it was indirectly due to Moody that he did so. As musical director in Moody's London campaign in 1875, he learned the appeal that singing could make, and when he decided to continue evangelistic work, Moody advised him to use similar methods for attracting the poor. He tried this out in his first parish, St. Mary Abbots, Kensington, and though many Anglicans were profoundly shocked, others realised that this was a successful means of bringing the Church of England to the very poor. Here lay the chief distinction between the two "armies". Whereas the Church Army became, in 1885, an integral part of the Church of England, entering the parishes only on the invitation of the incumbent, the Salvation Army has continued as a religious group without any affiliation to a denomination.

The year 1890 was a decisive one for both of them, since in that year they both published their schemes for relieving social distress. The Church Army claimed a slight priority in time, since *Our Tramps* was published seven months before William Booth's *In Darkest England and the Way Out*, but whereas *Our Tramps* was little more than a pamphlet, *In Darkest England* could boast of being a full-grown book. They both put forward similar schemes. They envisaged food, shelter and work for the unemployed of the cities, farm training colonies in the countryside and organised emigration for suitably trained persons. These schemes, however, were by no means original. They had already been tried in a modified manner by the Christian missions and were to be found on a more elaborate scale on the continent. But they were far better organised than anything that had been proposed before in England, and in the case of the Salvation Army, the arresting style of *In Darkest England* quickly gained supporters and funds.

The social services which were eventually established were also similar. Both had temporary shelters where the destitute could spend the night, though the Church Army made a careful selection of those they helped, while the Salvation Army took all who came and supplied them with cheap or free food. Most of those who were sheltered by the Church Army were trained in their "labour homes", but only the selected few found their way to the Salvation Army training homes, or "elevators" as they were called. Both established farm colonies to train men for agricultural labour, the Salvation Army at Hadleigh in Essex, and the Church Army at Newdigate in Surrey; but neither was very successful with its emigration schemes. The Salvation Army failed to persuade any of the colonies to accept their plan of large-scale emigration, and all that the Church Army could do was to use the Church Emigration Society to send abroad a few of those they trained.

Yet both did much to relieve the distress of the late nineteenth century. In 1896 the Salvation Army reported that in the previous year they had provided shelter for a million persons, had sold $3\frac{1}{4}$ million meals and employed four to five thousand persons in their "elevators". The Church Army, for the same year, claims to have dealt with 9,000 people in various ways. A certain amount of criticism was raised at the time with regard to their methods, in particular with regard to the huge expenditure of the Darkest England Trust Fund. But the committee which investigated this found few significant faults and Charles Booth, who was usually very critical of "mis-directed charity and cadging hypocrisy" regarded only the cheap food and shelters of the Salvation Army as helping "to perpetuate the way of life of the classes for which such provision is made"; the rest of the work of both Armies, he thought, compared favourably with that of most other missions.

In assessing the value of the work of these two "armies" it must be remembered that the Church Army, as part of the Church of England, was able to use the services of the other Church agencies, such as the Church of England Temperance Society and the Police Court Mission, to supplement its work. This meant that in actual fact the scope of its social work was far more widespread than it appears. Its connection with the Church of England also tended to make its work more acceptable to the community as a whole. On the other hand, if the contemporary Salvation Army statistics are to be trusted, their work covered a far greater proportion of the underprivileged than any of the other denominational schemes and reached many who would otherwise have received no help. The Salvation and the Church Armies both continue to play an important part in the social work of the community by providing services for its least privileged members.

Thus the *Bitter Cry* had some success in rousing the social conscience of the churches. Much more social work was done by the different denominations than ever before, and congregations began to regard the care of the poor in their district as an important responsibility. But except in the case of the "armies", it is doubtful if they really reached the poorest classes for whom they were intended. Charles Booth found that it was more often those who already had some slight connection with religious denominations who benefited. The *Bitter Cry* also made some contribution to the development of social work training. Each of the denominations had its deaconesses or "sisters" and the Salvation Army its "lassies", who received some instruction and plenty of practical experience in dealing with different types of people and their needs. Most of the denominations had their own training homes, and all placed their less experienced workers under supervision, with the result that social workers with some training were more plentiful than previously.

The main success of the *Bitter Cry* lay, however, in the work of the progressives who combined suggestions for social reform with schemes for improved social work. These progressives were in the Free Churches rather than the Church of England. At one of the meetings of the London Congregational Union, immediately after the publication of the *Bitter Cry*, two ministers, G. S. Reaney and C. Fleming Williams, had tried to make suggestions on the lines of the Christian Socialists, but had been talked down by those in favour of the ordinary mission activities. Hugh Price Hughes and John Scott Lidgett of the Wesleyans, J. B. Paton of the Congregationalists, and F. B. Meyer, John Clifford and J. C. Carlile of the Baptists led this progressive party, and their general attitude to the "forward movement" can well be summed up in the following words of John Scott Lidgett:

> I am not willing that it should be merely an ambulance to gather up the casualties of our industrial system, without being equally anxious to lessen the causes of these casualties.[1]

Christian Socialism had drawn attention to the sufferings of the underprivileged in the fifties, and the Rev. F. D. Maurice, in particular, had shown that there was much in common between Christian theology and socialistic ideals. The influence of these Christian Socialists, especially of Maurice and Kingsley, can be found in the social outlook and methods of work of the progressives. It appeared in the preaching of Hugh Price Hughes and the writings of John Scott Lidgett, it helped to frame the socialist views of J. C. Carlile, and it moved John Clifford to use politics as an instrument of Christian social reform. These men attempted to combine evangelical doctrines with a strong opposition to the *laissez-faire* individualism of the time. Hugh Price Hughes made this plain in a series of sermons preached in St. James' Hall, Piccadilly, in 1887 and 1888, in which he pointed out that Evangelicals had dealt too long with the individual aspects of Christianity, seeking to help the underprivileged by reforming their personal lives—Christ had come to save society as well as the individual, and it was time to apply this principle to the group and to make it possible for all to share in the good things of life.

Like the Christian Socialism of the Broad Church of England,

[1] R. E. Davies, ed., *John Scott Lidgett*, 1957, p. 161.

it found an expression in the opening of settlements, but in a somewhat modified form. The Evangelical settlement tried to combine evangelisation with the "settlement idea" of living among the people and reaching them by personal influence. The Wesleyans, urged by Dr. W. F. Moulton, the headmaster of Leys School, Cambridge, were probably the most successful in this, starting the Leysian Mission in the City in 1886 and the Bermondsey Settlement in 1891. Though resembling the Christian mission in many ways, the Leysian Mission did provide a residential hostel for its workers where Old Leysians and other Wesleyan business men were encouraged to come and live and spend their free time in working with the Mission.

John Scott Lidgett, at the Bermondsey Settlement, went somewhat further in trying to conduct extensive evangelism and at the same time provide the broadest possible educational and social services. Like the Browning Settlement, its Congregational counterpart, it tended to break away from strict Evangelicalism, but unlike the Congregational settlement, it did not link itself closely with the Labour movement. The purpose of the Browning Settlement, under the guidance of its warden, F. Herbert Stead, the brother of W. T. Stead, was to show through an active participation in local politics the desire to practise Evangelical Christianity. The comment of Charles Booth was:

> the success attained is considerable, but somewhat spasmodic and strained. It seems to lack the full flow of Wesleyan enthusiasm, and not to possess the solid character of Baptist work.[1]

A second way in which the more progressive Evangelicals tried to overcome the individualism of their voluntary organisations was by forming the Christian Union for Social Service. It was suggested by J. B. Paton, the leading Congregational minister in Nottingham, at a conference of Evangelical social workers in 1873, and had been tried out in a modified way in that town for several years. The inspiration had come from the German Inner Mission, which had arisen in the 1840's when poverty was widespread and charity inadequate. Under the leadership of Dr. J. H. Wichern of the Rauhe Haus, Hamburg, congresses of Lutheran

---

[1] Booth, *op. cit.*, 3rd series, vol. iv, p. 87.

clergy and laity met yearly from 1848 to 1871 to discuss the current social problems and to find and put into practice Christian solutions. They worked through the different voluntary organisations of the district, which were linked together and closely co-ordinated with any government services. Groups of deacons and deaconesses were trained for both voluntary and government institutions; and financial aid was provided by the authorities.

J. B. Paton, with the help of Hugh Price Hughes, F. B. Meyer, Scott Lidgett, John Clifford and a few Anglican clergy, tried to form a similar organisation in England in 1896. The Christian Union for Social Service opened two colonies for the unemployed at Lingfield in Surrey and Starnthwaite in Cumberland, and a band of Christian "brothers" from the different denominations was trained and placed in control. But the authorities could not be persuaded to co-operate, and there was little opportunity for future employment on the land in this country for men from these colonies. The Christian Union thus failed to achieve the widespread collective action for which J. B. Paton and his supporters had hoped, and it had to concentrate upon certain specialised forms of social service which were not being performed by other organisations.

It was in the Christian Labour Movement that the progressive Evangelicals achieved their success. Its purpose was to offer to the working man a form of Christianity which would appeal to him and which fitted in with his awakening belief in social equality. Charles Booth was of the opinion that the average working man would have little to do with church or chapel, not because he really believed in free thought, but because he despised the professionalism of the clergy, the class consciousness of the conventional church or chapel-goer, and the benevolence of the social worker. Herbert Stead, the founder of the Browning Settlement, agreed that "for parsons and for churches they have scant respect; but they have reverence for religion; they have reverence for Christ".[1] Thus an interpretation of Christianity which had no set doctrines and no authoritative clerics, but

---

[1] F. Herbert Stead, *The Labour Movement in Religion*, an address delivered at the Browning Settlement, January 6, 1895.

emphasised the social side of the Gospel was likely to make an appeal.

The origins of this movement can be traced to two sources, the Chartist churches, which had been formed in the 1840's, and the Pleasant Sunday Afternoons, known familiarly as P.S.A.'s, which had resulted from the Moody campaigns of the 1870's. The Chartist churches had catered for those who had felt unable to remain within any denomination but did not want to give up religion entirely. They were succeeded in the later decades of the century by Labour churches, under the leadership of the Rev. John Trevor, the minister of the Upper Brook Street Free Church in Manchester. There were about thirty of these churches at the end of the century, most of them in the North of England, and they had thriving Sunday schools, largely because many working men preferred to send their children to schools where capitalism was not taken for granted.

The first P.S.A. had been started by John Blackham in connection with his Bible class at the Ebenezer Congregational Church, West Bromwich, in 1874. Enquiring why so few men attended his class, he was given the answer, "Well, Guvnor, we'en got nothin' agin' the Bible . . . but you 'ave all yer things so blessed dull. Couldn't yer liven 'em up a bit?" Taking the hint he introduced some of the tactics which he had seen Moody use at his men's meetings—a short snappy talk with plenty of music and opportunities for the men to make their own comments. Such meetings proved highly successful in the Midlands, won the approval of F. B. Meyer, John Clifford and Hugh Price Hughes, and became the usual way of conducting men's meetings in the Free Churches which took part in the "forward movement". In time they dropped much of their Bible Study and concentrated increasingly upon a Christian interpretation of social problems. Similarly many of them changed their name to "brotherhood" meetings, thereby stressing the importance of social equality. They based their teaching upon the Gospels, maintaining that the social ideal of Christ was to bring about the kingdom of God on earth, and this necessitated a belief in social equality. As Arthur Henderson, a strong supporter of the movement stated:

Any attempt to separate the spiritual being from the social unit, or to isolate individual salvation from the social idea of original Christianity and the teaching of the Brotherhood is likely to fail. The day is past when we could treat man as a brother when concerned with the salvation of his soul, and be content to leave him as a bond-slave or machine when social and economic interests are concerned. We can only re-kindle the perception as to the supreme worth of Christianity to the mass of the people, by accepting all the obligations of the Brotherhood. We must make it clear that Christianity teaches the worth of every human life that God has made and redeemed in Jesus Christ.[1]

Though this teaching closely resembled that of the Christian Socialists, it did not necessarily require membership of any particular church or denomination. As Keir Hardie put it:

The Brotherhood Movement is, as its name implies, an association for the promotion of fellowship among those who love Jesus. It does not recognise any particular group nor is it attached to any particular church; taking the teaching of Jesus as set forth in the Gospels, it seeks to interpret and apply the spirit of these to the problems of modern life.[2]

It therefore proved attractive to working men both within and outside the recognised Christian churches, and many future leaders in the Labour party belonged to it.

The Browning Settlement in the Walworth Road, South London, became the centre for the Christian Labour movement, and its nucleus was the Fellowship of Followers which consisted of those members, both men and women, who were pledged to put its principles into action. They had a thriving brotherhood meeting which attracted several of the leaders in the Labour movement, among them Philip Snowden, George Lansbury, Arthur Henderson and Will Crooks, and it was here that the most progressive of the Evangelicals gathered to consider the social reforms which they felt should be supported. They would discuss these problems at their P.S.A. meeting, decide what action could be taken, and then proceed to put it into effect, giving to the whole process a spiritual fervour as well as a social significance.

---

[1] J. W. Tuffley, *Grain from Galilee, a history of the Brotherhood Movement*, 1935, p. 71.
[2] *Ibid.*, p. 62.

Old age pensions were the first major problem with which they dealt, and in this they won the adherence of Charles Booth, who spoke for them on several occasions and supported the methods which they adopted. The National Committee of Organised Labour for Promoting Old Age Pensions was set up at the Settlement, and nine years later—in 1908—their proposals were put into effect with only slight modifications. Similarly, when the overcrowding of central London was under discussion, three conferences on housing and locomotion were held under their auspices in 1902, Charles Booth speaking at both of them. The result was the setting up of a Royal Commission on London Traffic which suggested better arrangements to enable working people to live in the suburbs and travel daily to work. Sir John Gorst was invited to speak on the subject of the unemployed at one of their Brotherhood meetings, which resulted in their taking a leading part in the campaign for the passage of the Unemployed Workmen Act of 1905.

Thus the Christian Labour Movement not only had some marked success in dealing with the social problems which it tackled, but it also provided a meeting ground for progressive Evangelicals and the leading socialists. It offered membership of the Brotherhood to those who had been brought up in the Christian faith but found it difficult to reconcile the teaching of the churches with their socialist principles, and the discussions on social reform which the brotherhoods held throughout the country gained the adherence of large numbers of working men and coloured the attitude which they took upon social matters. This Evangelical infiltration into the labour movement helped to give it its Christian character which is said to distinguish the movement in England from similar movements on the continent.

And so *The Bitter Cry of Outcast London*, in spite of its emotional character and tract-like form, and its lack of detailed statistical information, served a very important purpose. It roused the social conscience of the churches to an extent and in a way not previously followed, with the result that much more social work was performed by the churches and chapels. In some denominations the response was greater than in others, and the quality of the work more discerning. But all were affected. Furthermore

certain groups within the denominations became aware of the
need for social reform, and a few of them went so far as to
attempt it.

A highly important by-product of this social work was that it
involved co-operation between the denominations and so brought
them much closer together. This had been the aim of the
Christian Union for Social Service, and both the central missions
and the settlements accepted workers from all the Evangelical
churches. Thus the "forward movement" paved the way for the
formation of such bodies as C.O.P.E.C. (the Christian Order in
Politics, Economics and Citizenship), and was a step on the road
towards the closer bond of the Protestant churches.

Contrary to what is frequently thought today, the more progressive of the Evangelicals did realise their social responsibilities.
They were prepared to take a part in the changes in social policy
which characterised the turn of the nineteenth century and urged
their church members to do the same. They were to be found on
most local government committees in the poorer districts which
dealt with social problems and they did their utmost to check
abuses and to improve the social services. They thus exercised a
considerable influence in helping to bring about the social reforms
of the present century and in laying the foundations of the
welfare state.

CHAPTER V

The Ragged School Movement

WORKING CLASS children of the nineteenth century had few of the benefits available to such children today. Those whose parents were described at that time as the "independent" poor—who had a reasonably regular wage—were usually fairly well fed and clad and received some small amount of education. But little attention was paid to their needs as children; they hardly ever left their squalid surroundings and they started work at a very early age. But such children were far more fortunate than those whose parents either could not, or would not afford to feed, clothe, or care for them properly. Most of these went around barefoot, clad in rags, and picked up a meal when and where they could. Such "street arabs", as they were called, might make a precarious living by sweeping crossings, by selling matches, flowers or watercress, but often they were forced to beg or steal. Many were cruelly treated, others were deformed or handicapped, and all lacked the security of a happy home. Numbers of them had no home at all, either because their parents were dead or missing, or because they had been abandoned. Occasionally a neighbour took pity on them when they were very young, but as they grew up they were usually forced to take to the streets, having to eat, feed and sleep there. Dr. Barnardo estimated in 1876 that there were about 30,000 of such neglected children under the age of sixteen living on the streets of London.

The general attitude towards these children was that their care was the duty of the parents. The State could take such children "into care" only if the parents were dead or proved missing, were inmates of the workhouse, or a widow on out-relief. Relatively few of the children of the poor fell into this category, and the rest had to depend upon private charity for their needs. Some were looked after in the numerous orphanages and children's homes which sprang up in the middle of the century, but most were given some sort of help in their existing circumstances, much of which was associated with the ragged school movement.

During the eighteenth century the chief concern for the poorer child had been with its education. Charity schools were set up for this purpose in the parishes, and Sunday schools in the later decades for children who were employed during the week. The growth of the urban areas made more schools necessary, and the British and Foreign Schools Society and the National Schools Society were formed to provide them in 1808 and 1811. But none of these schools had a place for the dirty, shabby, undisciplined child of the streets. As the Select Committee on the Education of Destitute Children stated in 1861:

> It appears to be established by the evidence before us, that there exists in many of our great cities and towns a class of children whom the system of national education supported by Parliament, and administered by the Committee of Privy Council for Education, does not reach, and who are excluded, in consequence either of the faults or of the misfortunes of their parents, from any participation in its benefits. This class consists partly of the children of very poor persons, many of them actually paupers in receipt of parochial relief, others in a condition scarcely superior to that of paupers, who are unable to spare the fees charged in the National and British schools, or to provide their children with the dress suitable to those schools, partly of the children of dissolute parents, of whom some are actually engaged in criminal pursuits, and others are abandoned to careless and self-indulgent habits; all of them being unwilling, though not absolutely unable, to put themselves to the expense and trouble of sending their children to school; and partly of children who have lost their parents and are deprived of proper guardianship and control. We have collected no precise statistics as to the extent of this class of children, but we have before us sufficient evidence to show that it is very considerable.[1]

These children were described by William Locke, the honorary secretary of the Ragged School Union in London, as

the children of the coster-mongers, who sell in the streets and at the

[1] *Select Committee on the Education of Destitute Children*, report, 460 of 1861, p. viii.

5. A Tea-Meeting for Mothers at the One Tun Ragged School

6. The Ragged School Union Prize-Giving

stalls fruit, vegetables and so on, or of those who go with barrows about the streets; they are the children of brick-makers, a large class about Notting Hill and elsewhere; of pig-feeders, persons earning a deal of money, but altogether careless about the education of their children; the children of rag-dealers and Spitalfield weavers out of employment, and many others of uncertain occupations, who are in a dreadful state during the winter months. Sometimes the children of labourers, who are out of work in frost or bad weather, or who are thrown out of work at the docks frequently by ships not arriving; the children of knackers and cats' meat men; of slop-tailors, who form a large number, who earn a bare subsistence, and who yet will not condescend to accept parochial relief; the children of washer women who go out to work in the daytime, neglecting their children; the children of crossing-sweepers and street-musicians, and the lowest mendicants and tramps, and persons who get their living by theft, who altogether neglect their children; the children of hawkers, pigeon-dealers, dog-fanciers, and other men of that class. A great proportion of the children are those of worthless and drunken parents, and many others are the children of parents who, from their poverty, are too poor to pay even a penny a week for schooling.[1]

Though John Pounds of Portsmouth is often regarded as the originator of ragged schools for children of this type, this is by no means certain. In 1810, some ten years before he started his school, Thomas Cranfield of Camberwell was said to be teaching children who were unsuitable for the Sunday schools in the area. But John Pounds' school was important in that it evolved methods to be followed in subsequent ragged schools. He was aware that the child must be fed and clothed if it were to get any advantage from its teaching, and that some training for future employment must be given if it were not to return to the occupations of the streets. It was the painting of John Pounds, the cobbler, surrounded by his ragged and dirty children, which inspired Dr. Guthrie to introduce such schools in Edinburgh and Sheriff Watson in Aberdeen. In London, many arose as part of the work of the London City missioners. Their annual report for 1840 says that "during the year several schools have arisen out of their labours, and five have been formed exclusively for children raggedly clothed—one in the

---

[1] *Select Committee on the Education of Destitute Children*, evidence 6, Locke (Hon. Sec. of R.S.U.).

West, a second in Lambeth, a third in Rosemary Lane, a fourth in Bethnal Green and a fifth in Shoreditch at which 570 children are attending".[1]

Such schools would probably have remained isolated and unconnected in the poorer parts of London had it not been for the formation of the Ragged School Union in 1844, "to give permanence, regularity and vigour to the existing ragged schools and to promote the formation of new ones". The Union resulted from a meeting of teachers from the larger schools at St. Giles Ragged School, and was essentially an Evangelical organisation, its chairman being Lord Shaftesbury and its treasurer R. C. L. Bevan. Among the committee members were the Rev. Baptist Noel, who was closely connected with the London City Mission, Lord Kinnaird, the Rev. James Sharman of the Surrey Chapel, George Hitchcock of the Y.M.C.A., and John Macgregor who devoted his time to the welfare of boys, the Ragged School Union being linked in this way with many other forms of Evangelical social work. But the Ragged School movement was not entirely Evangelical. The Unitarians, under the influence of Mary Carpenter, opened schools, particularly around Bristol, and some were run in connection with the non-Evangelical Anglican churches.

The movement grew quickly. When the Ragged School Union was formed, sixteen schools were connected with it, but by 1861 their number had increased to 176. The schools in the provinces were independent of the Union, though a few of the larger cities, like Liverpool which had sixty-four schools in 1861 and Manchester which had seventeen, had unions of their own. Only the larger schools joined these unions, and there were many small ones which do not appear in these figures. Further, it is impossible to say how many children attended the schools, as so many only came intermittently, but the Ragged School Union reckoned that in the 1860's some 25,000 to 26,000 children came under its care in one way or another.

The distinguishing features of these schools were that they were entirely free, and they welcomed, and quite often sought out, the poor and neglected child:

[1] *London City Mission*, annual report 1840.

Here comes one of the little fellows. See how tattered, and patched is every garment he has on; his bare feet are brown with a covering of dirt of long standing; through the holes in his dress the winter blasts find full entrance; and by their means also, we see plainly enough the neglected, unwashed condition of his poor body which is scarcely comforted by a single rag of under linen. If his clothing and the state of his person are pitiable, so also are his features to all those who have learnt to interpret their lineaments. Dirty, pale and thin, it wants altogether the rosy bloom which God has appointed as the sweet ornament of healthy childhood, and the roundness that is the natural growth of sufficient and wholesome food.[1]

Such schools were held at the outset in barns, cowsheds, stables, covered-in railway arches or disused store-rooms, or if very small in a room in a workman's cottage. Often the neighbours would grow alarmed at the rowdiness, the landlord would close the doors, and the teachers be forced to find new accommodation. It was only as the schools grew in size, held regular weekday classes, and became more firmly established that they were able to rent their own premises, and occasionally to own them.

The teachers were usually Christian men and women whose initial purpose was to start a small Bible class for the children. Only when they had begun did they discover what the work involved and the varied needs which they would have to meet. Then they would call for volunteers from among their friends or from their church and for money to help provide the things that they required. Some were working men, but the majority were of the middle or upper classes, and among them were several well-known individuals—people such as Quintin Hogg, the Hon. Arthur Kinnaird, General Gordon, Dr. Barnardo, and Dr. Thomas Guthrie. Paid teachers would only be employed when the schools were very large, and then they were usually in a subordinate position to the voluntary teachers.

The apparent purpose for these schools was educational. At first they were held on Sunday nights, then in the afternoon or morning. But gradually they spread to week nights as well. The subjects taught were chiefly reading and writing, though some history and geography might be added for the more advanced scholars.

[1] George James Hall, *Sought and Saved*, a prize essay on Ragged Schools, 1855, pp. 20-21.

Equipment was extremely meagre. The children mostly sat on the floor; reading books, if available at all, had to be shared, and writing materials were only provided for the steadier pupils. They were therefore strongly criticised for their low standards, in particular by the Newcastle Commission which reported upon the "education of the independent poor" in 1861. Yet most people recognised that the standards of the ragged schools could not possibly reach those of the paying schools, since comparatively small finances were available, but, in spite of the pleas of Lord Shaftesbury and Mary Carpenter, the State would only provide a grant for one year—1866.

Nor was the Ragged School Union in favour of a high level of teaching, since its primary purpose was to reclaim and civilise the child and make him or her a useful member of the community. The uproar with which anyone visiting such a school would be greeted, the unsavoury remarks, the lewd jokes and the general atmosphere of low living would make the visitor immediately aware of this. In fact, many ragged school teachers opposed applying for a government grant on the grounds that it would hinder this aspect of their work, and the view of the secretary of the Ragged School Union on the matter was that "we think, if the government interfered, they would require a teacher of higher standard, and more attention would be paid to secular things". Therefore much of the work of the ragged schools had little to do with book learning. They concentrated upon what we should call today welfare services. They were particularly concerned with better food and clothing for their pupils, with providing lodging for those who had no home, with finding suitable work for those who had to support themselves, and with holding religious services for both the children and their families.

It was not long before ragged school teachers became aware of the desperate hunger of many of the children. Sheriff Watson, who had started ragged schools in Aberdeen in 1841, realised at the outset that children must be fed if they were to benefit at all from their education. The Scottish ragged schools, therefore, aimed at keeping the children all day, providing them with meals and sending them home at night. Thomas Guthrie's school in Edinburgh opened at 7 a.m. in the summer and 8 a.m. in the winter, started with a shower and then an hour's work, to be followed by a breakfast of oatmeal porridge, secular education, dinner at mid-day, religious education and industrial training, and finally a supper of porridge. Food was also available for them on Sundays.

In England the ragged schools rarely provided meals, possibly on the grounds that this was the duty of the parents. A London City missionary, however, in 1848, by persuading some local butchers and cookshops to help him, was able to give bread and soup occasionally at ½d. per head to numbers of starving children. But the City missionaries were not supposed to undertake such work, and it did not become general, though it is more than likely that teachers did help to feed the hungriest of their children.

The unemployment and consequent poverty of the sixties drew attention to the need. Emaciated children would accompany their parents to the soup kitchens which were opened at that time, and it was realised that many of them had no regular meals but existed on odd crusts of bread and cups of tea, sometimes with nothing from the previous evening until the following mid-day. In 1863 an article appeared in Punch entitled *Dinners for Poor Children Wanted*. Baroness Meyer de Rothschild responded by providing dinners for fifty children daily at the New Tothill Street ragged school in Westminster. The outcome was the Destitute Children's Dinner Society (1867), formed to give free meals to hungry children at the ragged schools and Christian missions.

Lord Shaftesbury, Lord Kinnaird and Lord Mount-Temple were officers of the Society and it quickly gained support from the public so that it became possible to subsidise meals of meat stew, vegetables and rice, and offer them to the children at 1d. per head, or free if necessary. The Society opened children's dining rooms under local committees in the buildings of the large ragged schools, National or British schools, and some of the Christian missions, where the children were admitted by presenting a ticket from their teacher, minister, or mission worker who knew something of their circumstances. Within a year of its establishment, the Society had thirty-seven dining rooms, and by 1888 sixty-four were in existence, serving some 17,000 to 18,000 dinners a week. After the 1870 Education Act the Society worked in close co-operation with the board schools, and many of the meals were provided there.

Many of the ragged schools provided Christmas dinners for their children, though this was more in the nature of a treat than a welfare service. Contributions were raised by appeals and the children given a party with a meal of roast beef and plum pudding. This became more general in the 1880's with the institution of "Robins' Dinners". The Rev. Charles Bullock, the editor of *Home Words*, had first introduced them by inserting an appeal in his paper one Christmas for all the hungry human "robins". A large fund was raised for the Ragged School Union to give yearly Christmas dinners at all their schools and missions.

One would have thought that the feeding of half-starved children would have met with no criticism. Yet there were those who deprecated it on the grounds that it was the duty of the boards of guardians to deal with permanent under-feeding; and others who said that as the children were accustomed to large hunks of bread, stew and rice would not ease their hunger. Their example, however, led the newly-formed school boards, first to co-operate with the Destitute Children's Dinner Society, and then to make their own arrangements for feeding school children, with the result that, by the Education (Provision of Meals) Act of 1906, local authorities were empowered to provide school meals for needy children on the days on which the schools were open. Thus the precedent was set for the present-day school meals service.

Similarly ragged school teachers were not slow in finding out that many of their children were so cramped together in the dirt and squalor of their homes that much of the good which the school achieved was undone; while others had nowhere to go when they left the school in the evening and so would be found sleeping under the cover of a disused cart or huddled together in the lee of a wall. A teacher in the Old Pye Street school, Westminster, writes in 1847:

> At nine o'clock the door was opened; they were dismissed, but we found that some of the boys had nowhere to go; they sat down on the cold stone; or upon the threshold of the open school door; and that fact forced itself upon the sympathy of their friends, and they arranged to put up a few hammocks across the schoolroom, in which

those boys slept during the night; and that led to the formation of a refuge.[1]

Therefore, unlike the Scottish ragged schools, which never housed their children, the Ragged School Union began to open refuges where children could spend the night. The earliest of these were night refuges or dormitories where homeless children could sleep and where some food was provided. At the Old Pye Street Refuge fourteen out of the fifty scholars were allowed to sleep in the schoolroom on straw mattresses provided they did the household chores before school began, and similar refuges were opened in connection with the schools at Field Lane, the Seven Dials and Whitechapel.

The second type of refuge to be opened was one where the children were entirely provided for, being housed, fed, clothed and taught a trade. They were intended for children likely to be perverted by evil companionship or home circumstances, and for whom entire charge was desirable. Several were started both for boys and for girls, but they were more on the lines of an industrial school, and when the Industrial Schools Act was passed in 1857, most of them were recognised for this purpose and came under the control of the Home Office.

A third type of refuge was intended for those who had grown too old for the ragged schools, who were either unemployed or in a very low-paid job. They were attached to most of the larger schools with the purpose of keeping in touch with the boys until they had found suitable employment. It was with this in mind that some of the schools provided industrial training for the older pupils, or found them temporary employment.

This need for training the children as well as teaching them to read and write was appreciated in particular by John Macgregor. A close friend of the Rev. Baptist Noel, he had taken an interest in ragged schools since his Cambridge days, both as a teacher and a member of the Ragged School Union committee. His particular concern was with the boy who, through lack of parental care and suitable occupation, tended to be led into delinquency. He therefore encouraged the ragged schools to teach such things as tailoring

[1] 460 of 1861, *op. cit.*, evidence 403, Gent.

and shoemaking, making and mending clothes, woodchopping, horsehair picking, carpentry, mat making, knitting fishermen's nets, paper bag printing, and leatherwork to the boys; and sewing, knitting and embroidery to the girls. Industrial classes of one or other of these types were to be found at some fifty of the schools in London, but they rarely proved very successful in training the pupils for a future job. As we shall see later, it was the teenager who was more likely to benefit from such training.

The ragged school child was in general too rough and dilapidated to be acceptable to the ordinary employer. He would have to resort to such part-time jobs as sweeping crossings, selling matches or newspapers, running messages, or scavenging in the sewers and river beds. The ragged school leaders were well aware of the need of more suitable employment for their pupils, and it was after a meeting held to discuss the matter at the Field Lane Institution in 1850 that John Macgregor suggested that the boys should be trained as shoeblacks, similar to those on the streets of Paris and Amsterdam. Lord Shaftesbury was approached and the first shoeblack society formed in connection with the ragged school where John Macgregor taught in York Place, Charing Cross.

The purpose of these shoeblack brigades was to discipline and smarten up the boys at a part-time occupation and at the same time to give them some education. They were expected to assemble at the brigade room in the ragged school at 7 a.m. for prayers, to change into their uniform, pick up their box, polish and brushes, and set off to their appropriate station, where they worked all day, being supervised by the shoeblack beadle who was in charge of several stations. At dusk they returned with their takings, a third of which they were allowed to keep, a third being banked for them, and the other third being retained by the society to cover costs. A meal followed, then evening lessons, after which they returned to their homes or to the ragged school refuge. By 1878 the Ragged School Union had nine of these brigades in London, each wearing a different uniform and covering a particular district.

They were much criticised on the grounds that they trained the boys for a blind alley occupation which would only last for a short time. But those who held this view failed to realise that the purpose of the brigade was not to teach the boys a trade, but to try to turn them into useful and industrious members of society. This, on the whole, they were successful in doing, and in some cases, as the boys grew older, their evening educational classes were replaced by learning a trade such as shoemaking and carpentering.

The Ragged School Union was also aware of the need to influence the parents if the children were to improve. They tried to do this by opening ragged churches to which those who were too dirty and dissipated to attend the ordinary church or mission meeting were invited. The first two of these churches were opened in Northampton and Aberdeen and the idea spread to London in the 1850's, so that by 1852 there were thirty-five ragged churches with an average attendance of 2,500. Many of them were at first connected with the London City Mission whose missionaries would conduct the services. Then, in 1853, the Ragged Church and Chapel Union was formed, with Lord Shaftesbury as its president, to co-ordinate their work and raise funds to rent rooms to be used for worship on Sundays and for adult education and recreation during the week. The more outstanding churches were run in connection with the ragged schools at Field Lane, Gray's Yard, Brewers' Court and the King Edward School. Each catered for more than a thousand persons, many of them beggars, thieves, broken-down gentlefolk, and starving men and women, and unlike those who attended the other missions, about three-quarters of them were men. The most important part of their work lay in the organised home visiting, when contact was made with many of the parents of ragged school pupils and help and advice given with regard to their care. Here is probably the earliest instance of the school care committee, and possibly of the parent–teacher association.

The Field Lane Institution is a good example of the comprehensive ragged school. It was started in 1841 by a gentleman, F.E.B., in a small back room in Caroline Court, Field Lane. Its equipment was a Bible, a prayer book, two stools, two short forms, a box for a table and some old iron candlesticks. On the first night five young women arrived and spent the time giggling; then five young men appeared and pandemonium reigned. After that the

weekday school was abandoned and, with the help of a neighbouring church, a Sunday school was started instead, which soon had
some fifty boys and girls drawn from the poorest classes. An
appeal appeared in *The Times* of February 1843, headed *The Field
Lane Ragged School*, and this was probably the first time that the
term "ragged school" was used. It attracted the attention of Lord
Shaftesbury, who eventually became its president, and of Charles
Dickens, who visited and wrote about the school. For some time
it only opened on Sundays and once or twice a week. Then in
1847 a free day school, working from 9 a.m. to 12 noon and 2 p.m.
to 4 p.m., was started with a paid teacher and some seventy
pupils. The next step was a boys' refuge where the homeless lads
slept in a dormitory and were taught tailoring and shoemaking.
This was followed by the opening of refuges for homeless men
and women, the ragged church, and an adult evening school. The
building of the Smithfield market in 1861 meant the removal to
new and larger premises, and there more specialised services could
be started. These included a day nursery for babies whose mothers
were at work, an infant school, industrial schools for boys and for
girls, and a training home for girls who were going into domestic
service. Then once again in 1877 a move had to be made and this
time the present buildings were erected in Vine Street and opened
by Lord Shaftesbury. Here most of the existing activities were
continued, and a working boys' hostel and a youths' institute were
added. By the 1880's it had become a model institution, with huge
Sunday and evening schools and the largest mothers' meeting in
London. And it is still in existence, though most of its activities
are now concerned with welfare services for the very poor.

Another interesting ragged school was the King Edward Street
School, Spitalfields. It started with some dozen scholars in 1845,
and by 1889 had over a thousand. This growth was due to the
efforts of Charles Montague, one of the original scholars, who became superintendent in 1864 and who drew most of his workers
from the working class. About £3,000 was spent annually, much
of it on welfare activities such as a holiday home for children and
the care of the sick and aged.

A third school which might be mentioned was The One Tun,
Duck Lane, in the area behind Westminster Abbey known as the

Devil's Acre. It had been started in the thirties by an old tinker, but was taken over by Adeline Cooper in 1858 when the lease of a public house, The One Tun, was obtained. Her special concern was with the men of the district for whom she started a large working men's club and boys' institute, and later acquired a block of buildings which were renovated to house some of the needy families.

An important activity carried out by some of these ragged schools was the opening of infant nurseries where mothers could leave their children while they were at work. The care of young children of working mothers obviously formed an important aspect of factory life. But it was also necessary in the cities where women were out all day at domestic and other similar jobs. In most cases it was essential that the women should earn, and so they were obliged to leave their young children in the care of an elder sister or neighbour or sometimes even to lock them up alone in the dwelling room. Infant nurseries, or crèches as they were called, were not unknown in the industrial areas of the North, but the first mention of one in London seems to be in 1866 in connection with the Field Lane Institution. By 1872 there were fourteen of them in London, all semi-charitable institutions, where the mother was asked to pay 2d. or 3d. per day.

A well-known one was Marie Hilton's crèche in the Stepney Causeway. She was a Quaker and closely connected with the work of the Bedford Institute. A visit to an infant nursery in Brussels gave her the idea of starting similar work in this country, and so with thirty cots and the offer of a building near the Friends' Meeting House in Stepney she opened her nursery in 1871. The children were cared for from 8 a.m. to 8 p.m. They were bathed on arrival, their clothes fumigated, and they were given a breakfast of bread and milk. Then the younger ones were placed in cots and the older ones taught to play. Lunch followed with meat stew and pudding for the older children, and after that a rest. They were allowed to play again in the afternoon and given their supper before being handed back to their mothers. For this the mothers paid 2d. per day and had to show that their circumstances made it necessary for them to work.

No doubt it was one of the best infant nurseries of that time, for the nurse girls received some training in the care of children, there was an isolation room for those who were unwell, and a temporary home in the country for any whose mothers were sick or in hospital. Princess Christian became its patroness and its methods were widely copied. Four years later a similar crèche was opened in Hartford, Connecticut, U.S.A., and many others appeared in this country. Sometimes they were started by women poor law guardians for the infants of widows on out-relief; but more often by the ragged schools and Christian missions. George Holland, at George Yard, Whitechapel, opened The Flowers of the Forest Nursery in 1876, and charged a 2d. fine for any child not fetched on time; and the Whitecross Street Mission used two of its upper rooms for the purpose with a young nurse in charge. But the closest to our modern methods of child care was the infant nursery run by the sisters of the Wesleyan West London Mission. Special diets were arranged, and the mother advised on the care of all her children, not only of those at the nursery.

Not all the infant nurseries reached the same standard of efficiency; in fact the Charity Organisation Society was somewhat sceptical about conditions in some of them, but they were usually nurseries run on a profit-making rather than a semi-charitable basis. The better ones, however, were the forerunners of the infant welfare movement of the end of the nineteenth century, and anticipated much of the work of Rachel Macmillan and her sister for young children.

The idea of organised holidays for school children also sprang from the ragged school movement. The most that any child of the slums got in the way of an outing was a day in Epping Forest or at the suburban house of one of the wealthy subscribers of a ragged school or mission. Then, in 1869, the well-known author for children, A.L.O.E. (Miss Tucker), who was also a teacher at the Saffron Hill Ragged School, arranged a short holiday in the country for some of the poorest children. The Rev. E. Canney, the vicar of the parish in which the school was situated, continued to send such children for three weeks in the summer to cottages in the country and from this there developed the Children's Fresh Air Mission (1882) which provided similar holidays for children from the ragged schools and Christian missions in the poorest districts of London.

Canon and Mrs. Barnett of Whitechapel copied this idea, when in 1884 they formed the Children's Country Holiday Fund for sending children from the board schools for a fortnight's holiday in the country or at the seaside. With the closing of the ragged schools in the last decade of the century, more and more children qualified for their holidays and so in 1921 the Children's Fresh Air Mission was incorporated with the Children's Country Holiday Fund, which still continues to send many children for an annual holiday.

A day's outing in the country or seaside for children from the ragged schools and missions was made possible by Pearson's Fresh Air Fund (1892), which now provides seaside holidays for children. But it was more usual at that time for the large ragged schools and missions to possess country or seaside homes of their own to which they would send their needy children, using these homes for convalescents in the winter months and for holidays in the spring and summer.

Rather more loosely connected with the ragged school movement was the National Society for the Prevention of Cruelty to Children. Those working in the ragged schools had realised from the outset that the parents of some of their children not only neglected them, but starved, beat and ill-used them. In most cases they could do nothing, for such children were not protected by the law and the general attitude of society was that the parent had the right to do what he liked with his offspring. Then, in 1881, two men, unknown to one another, took steps to bring such children to the public notice. One was the Rev. George Staite, the vicar of Ashton-Hayes in Cheshire, who wrote to the Liverpool Mercury and enlisted the help of Lord Shaftesbury. The other was Mr. T. F. A. Agnew, a Liverpool business man who on a visit to New York discovered that a society for the prevention of cruelty to children had just been formed there. The formation of a similar society in England was suggested at a Liverpool meeting of the R.S.P.C.A., which had protected animals from cruelty since 1822, and the following year the Liverpool Society for the Prevention of Cruelty to Children was formed. A national society was then

organised, with the Rev. Benjamin Waugh, a Congregational
minister, as its secretary, and among its committee members the
Earl of Aberdeen, Dr. Barnardo and E. de M. Rudolf, one of the
founders of the Waifs and Strays Society.

From the beginning the Society had two principal aims, to protect the child from cruelty, and to secure a change in the law which
should afford him some legal protection. The Society had gradually obtained the second of these with the passing of the pioneer
Act of 1889 and its amendments of 1894 and 1904 which made it an
offence to wilfully ill-treat, neglect, abandon or expose a child in
a manner likely to cause it unnecessary suffering or injury to its
health. It still continues, through its inspectors who call on parents
whenever a case of cruelty is reported to them, to try to prevent
cruelty and if necessary to take the case to court. As the Children's
branch of the Home Office stated in 1923:

> A large proportion of the cases which come before the courts are the
> result of proceedings taken by the Society, the very small number of
> discharges a testimony to the care with which cases are prepared. . . .
> Surely there are few societies, either in this or any other country,
> which have such a record of successful work to their credit.[1]

In spite of the benefits which the ragged school movement provided for very poor children, its educational work was brought to
a halt in 1870 with the passing of the Education Act which had no
place for ragged schools in its scheme of elementary education for
all children. This was not a surprise, for, as we have seen, the
authorities never favoured such schools on the grounds of poor
teaching, equipment and discipline. Furthermore it was said that
some parents, who could well afford to pay, sent their children to
the ragged school. But it must be remembered that they performed a very important function at a time when the state was
unable to provide free education for the children of the poor, and
many a waif was taught to read and write and thereby placed on
the first rung of the ladder of advancement.

John Macgregor was largely responsible for helping the ragged
schools to adapt themselves to the new situation. He accepted a
position on the London School Board and did his best to link the

---

[1] Home Office, *Children's Branch, report,* 1923, p. 70.

work of the ragged schools with the new board schools. Some of the schools were closed, others were converted into board schools, and the remaining schools temporarily directed their attention to those who were still unsuitable for the newly opened schools, or to those for whom places could not quickly be found.

Meanwhile the Ragged School Union had to reconsider its future function, and in this it was guided by Sir John Kirk, its new secretary. Changing its name to the Shaftesbury Society, by which it is well known today, it concentrated its activities upon the welfare of children, who for one reason or another, did not fit into the generally conceived plan; and it took over the work of several independent organisations which dealt with some aspect of the care of children.

Their first job was to deal with what were then called "drift" children, or children of the roughest and the poorest who had little chance of religious teaching or of contact with welfare organisations. For this purpose some of the ragged schools were converted into juvenile missions, among them the Children's Mission, Camberwell, the Juvenile Christian Mission, Clerkenwell, and the Millwall Juvenile Mission. These missions held Sunday services for such children, had clubs for them on weekday nights, and helped to feed and clothe the needy ones.

Most of the other ragged schools merely gave up their educational work, and concentrated upon their welfare activities, including the whole of the family within their scope. They would hold Sunday afternoon and evening services, Bible classes, and mothers' meetings; organise provident clubs; provide penny dinners for adults and free breakfasts for children, and arrange country holidays. Thus they began to resemble more closely the Christian mission.

The provision of clothing and shoes for elementary school children also became an important function. Baroness Burdett-Coutts had helped to provide clothing for ragged children when the board schools were first opened, and the Barefoot Mission had supplied boots and shoes. Both these services were taken over by the Shaftesbury Society at the end of the century, and the Society continues to help needy children in this way.

But the most important and lasting activity of the Shaftesbury

Society has been its work for crippled children. Their infirmity made it impossible for them to attend school, and they were just left at home, unwanted, and often unfed, in the dingiest of surroundings, with no chance of playing with other children. Their plight was well known to district visitors and mission workers, but no concerted effort was made to help them until Charles L. Boyer, an American visitor, conducted a small survey in an East End district in 1888 to discover how many of such school-age children there were. At first he formed a mission to arrange meals and treats for them, but he soon realised that such children were to be found in every poor district and needed help on a much larger scale than he could hope to provide. Therefore, in 1890, he asked the Shaftesbury Society to undertake it, and they appointed Miss Margaret Coles to organise a special department of the Society to deal with crippled children. Voluntary workers would visit the children in their homes to see that they were receiving some medical care, being properly fed and provided with some sort of occupation. So-called "cripples' parlours" were opened at most of the missions and schools in connection with the Shaftesbury Society, and those children who were fit enough were fetched daily and given some schooling and entertainment. The cripple department of the Shaftesbury Society still continues to care for such children in its residential schools. But its main work today takes place at its numerous branch missions in London, many of them successors of the old ragged schools and Christian missions. Here particular attention is still given to the needs of the poorest and most destitute children of the district. Holiday homes and camps are available for them, and a children's convalescent home at Beaconsfield.

Thus the ragged school movement, since the 1840's, has continuously served the interests of the poorest children. During the nineteenth century it was the only organisation to do so, and almost everything which was done for such children was connected with it in one way or another. Yet the movement had its critics, among them Henry Mayhew who gave figures to show that juvenile delinquency increased in line with the numbers of ragged schools. The reason for this, he said, was that the partial education provided by these schools served to quicken the intelligence and increase the powers for mischief of such children. Maybe this was so in some cases. But many other people were of the opposite opinion and considered that ragged schools were an important factor in preventing crime. The London City Missionary for the King's Cross district reported in 1848 that "one of the police told a teacher a few days ago that they had not half the trouble with the boys since the school had been opened, and he attributed the change to the instruction of the school".[1] Similarly Thomas Wright, the prison philanthropist, attributed the decline in the number of juveniles in the New Bailey Prison, Manchester, in the 1860's to the influence of the ragged schools in the area, since they cared "for the fatherless, friendless and orphan children" who were the chief source from which criminals were bred. Nor should the fact be overlooked that some 2,000 children were placed in employment by the Ragged School Union every year.

Perhaps Mary Carpenter put forward the best case in favour of the ragged school movement. She regarded it as the first step in the reduction of poverty and crime. In her evidence to the Newcastle Commission she stated:

> The fact is patent to all practically acquainted with the subject that until there is a very great change in the social conditions of our country, there is and must be a large proportion of the population who are, from whatever cause, barely above starvation, and whose precarious means scarcely suffice for their daily bread, without the power of providing decent clothing or other necessaries; also that the low moral, intellectual, and often physical condition of this class necessarily perpetuates the same state of things, unless a helping hand is held out to the children to aid them to rise to a higher and better life.[2]

This the ragged school movement did, and many children were first taught how to earn an honest living at these schools. When, as Mary Carpenter foresaw, social conditions improved and elementary education became available for all children, the need for ragged schools declined. Then the movement turned its attention to less pressing needs and became the source from which any needy child could receive help.

[1] *London City Mission Magazine*, May 1848.
[2] *Newcastle Commission Report*, 2794 (1861), pp. 392–3.

CHAPTER VI

Children's Homes and Orphanages

THE RAGGED school movement took into its care the child from the very poor and ineffective home. But many of the children of the poor had no home at all. They were either orphans or deserted by their parents, or they were illegitimate and unwanted by their mother. Jim Jarvis, the boy who first drew Dr. Barnardo's attention to "nobody's children" was no exception.

His mother had been dead for years, and he could not remember having seen his father. There was not a soul in the world to take care of him. He was only ten. But he was destitute. Upon his mother's death Jim had been placed in a workhouse; but from there he had escaped. Since then he had been obliged to sleep out-of-doors; and for that offence he had once been sent to prison. Night after night he slept in the gutter of a roof, under a tarpaulin in one of the markets, behind a street hoarding, in a barrel, or in any other refuge that might shield him from the worst of the weather and the watchful eye of the police.[1]

It was intended that such children should be cared for by the Poor Law authorities and the Elizabethan Statute of 1601 made provision for their accommodation and apprenticeship. But by the nineteenth century they were usually housed in the workhouse with the adult inmates, were mostly untaught and untrained, and rarely kept any employment which was found for them but continually returned, bringing with them fresh knowledge of immorality and crime.

The authorities were aware of this and during the nineteenth century made some attempts to improve these conditions, first by ensuring that the accommodation for children should as far as pos-

[1] Norman Wymer, *Father of Nobody's Children*, Arrow book, p. 42.

sible be separated from the workhouse itself and then by making some provision for their education and training. By 1873 they were so deeply concerned with the difficulties of trying to train, educate, and care for pauper children that they asked Mrs. Nassau Senior to report upon the conditions of Poor Law girls. The result was some improvement in their methods, learnt in certain cases from the voluntary institutions, but at the end of the century many children still lived in the adult workhouses and when they went out into the world still suffered from the taint of being "pauper children".

These workhouse children had either come into the workhouse with their parents, or their mother, having entered the workhouse for the birth of her baby, had left the child behind when she returned to a job. Others had been sent by relatives, neighbours, the clergy or the police because they had been abandoned. But there were numerous homeless children who, for one reason or another, did not claim such protection, and the Poor Law officers were under no obligation to go out into the streets and slums of the cities and bring them in. Thus there were large numbers of destitute children, like Jim Jarvis, who made the streets their home.

Private philanthropy had begun to look after such children in the eighteenth century, and institutions such as the Foundling Hospital (1739) for illegitimate children, the Marine Society (1756) for "destitute boys of good character", and the Orphan Working School (1758) for "orphans and other necessitous children" were founded. Several more were started in the early nineteenth century, but in the late forties their numbers began perceptibly to increase, reaching a peak in the sixties and thereafter gradually declining. Howe's Classified Directory for 1878 mentions fifty in the London area alone, and there were others in the big provincial centres. Some of these institutions resembled provident societies, being set up by groups of traders or members of a profession for their own orphans, but most were charitable organisations and, unlike the earlier orphanages, were frequently small in size, taking only a few children and lasting only for a short time. An important reason for the increase in their numbers was the publicity given to the needs of destitute children in the second half of the nineteenth century. The writings of Charles Dickens, the reports of workers in the ragged schools and missions, and the many descriptive accounts, especially those in books published for children, brought about both a genuine concern and a flow of donations, sometimes with little enquiry as to how they were used.

Most of the homes and orphanages set up by voluntary charity had some religious connection. The care of orphan children was frequently undertaken by the High Church sisterhoods, and one of the first duties of the Roman Catholic Church after its re-establishment in this country in 1850 was to look after any homeless Catholic children. But by far the greater number of homes and orphanages were under Evangelical direction. This was largely due to the close connection which such orphanages had with other forms of Evangelical social work. Workers with the different organisations very soon became aware of the many children having neither home nor parents who were forced to live entirely by their wits, and sometimes they would rent a house for them in connection with their organisation; at other times the care of homeless children became the main occupation of the organisation.

Some of the best known children's homes, such as the National Children's Home and the Waifs and Strays, arose in the first place in connection with a denominational church. The National Children's Home, which today cares for some 3,000 children, was started by the Rev. Thomas Bowman Stephenson, a young Wesleyan minister who was in charge of the Waterloo Road Chapel in the New Cut, Lambeth. Two close friends of his, who had been holding religious services in a thieves' kitchen near the Mint in Southwark, drew his attention to the homeless children who would gather round the fire there. A workman's cottage in Church Street, off the Waterloo Road, was rented in 1869 as The Children's Home and the first two boys received. One of these is immortalised in the following verse which appeared in an early appeal:

> Poor little scaramouch, homeless and sad,
> Ragged little scaramouch, dirty and bad,
> Father gone to prison, mother in her grave,
> Vice and crimes learnt betimes; who is there to save?
> "In the street all day, Sir"; yes, but where at night?

Where he goes no one knows; somewhere out of sight.
Stupid little scaramouch, neither reads nor writes,
Stands up for himself though, lies and swears and fights.[1]

As more children were taken, the Bonner Road premises in Bethnal Green were acquired and branch homes opened one by one to accommodate different types of children so that there are now some thirty-five branches and homes.

The Waifs and Strays Society, which is now called the Church of England Children's Society, started in a very different manner. Two brothers, Edward and Robert de Montjoie Rudolf, who were teachers in the St. Ann's Sunday School, South Lambeth, found in 1881 that two of their boys were missing from their classes. On making enquiries they discovered that their father had died and their mother, who had seven children, refused to enter the workhouse on account of the people with whom her children would have to mix. The children were starving and the two boys were begging for scraps from the men who worked at the nearby gasworks. On trying to get them admitted to a Church of England home, they found that there was no such home which would take them without payment or election by subscribers. They mentioned the matter to their friends, sent a circular letter to many clergy, and the outcome was the renting of 8 Stamford Villas, Friern Road, East Dulwich, as a home for destitute children of the Church of England. From these small beginnings branch homes were opened throughout the country so that now the family is some 5,000 strong.

Another similar denominational home was the Stockwell Orphanage, now known as Spurgeon's Orphan Homes. At a prayer meeting at the Metropolitan Tabernacle in 1867, Spurgeon had asked for some new work to do and the money to do it with. Almost at once a widow, Mrs. Anne Hillyard, offered £20,000 to found an orphan home "requiring neither votes nor patronage and especially one conducted upon simple Gospel principles". At first Spurgeon tried to persuade her to give the money to George Muller for his orphanage at Bristol, but she refused and after some consideration a site was bought in the Clapham Road, Stockwell,

[1] William Bradfield, *The Life of Thomas Bowman Stephenson*, 1913, p. 95.

and the home built. Destitute fatherless children from "Evangelical churches dissenting from the Church of England and not holding Unitarian or Socinian opinions" were accepted, and V. J. Charlesworth, the assistant minister at the Surrey Chapel, placed in charge. Though the organisation has not expanded in the same way as the other two societies, two homes still exist, at Reigate and Birchington.

Many other homes for small children were opened in connection with particular congregations, usually for children known to them through their social work. Two typical examples were Archibald Brown's Orphanage (1872) and the Brixton Orphanage (1876). The first accommodated some hundred destitute children, most of whom had been found by the workers of the East London Tabernacle of which Archibald Brown was pastor. He was a close friend of Dr. Barnardo, whose advice he frequently sought. The Brixton Orphanage had been started by Mrs. Montague for fatherless girls whom she came across in her social work in connection with the Metropolitan Tabernacle. To house them she erected a large building in the garden of her own home, and herself superintended the work. This home was eventually taken over by Spurgeon's Orphan Homes.

Other children's homes sprang from the Christian missions. The outstanding example of this is Dr. Barnardo's Homes. Dr. Barnardo had never intended to take up the care of orphan children. He had hoped to be a medical missionary, and it was while in training for this that he discovered the needs of destitute children. The story of Jim Jarvis and the ways in which he found this out are too familiar for repetition, but what is often forgotten is that his work for children was a part of much wider missionary work centred on The Edinburgh Castle, "a flourishing gin palace, with a well-lit and attractive frontage, and behind it a music hall of the most unenviable reputation" in the East End. This he converted into a church for the people, a coffee bar, and a centre for social work, living there himself for a time, and conducting many of the services almost up to the time of his death. At the same time his children's homes were an ever-open door for any needy child in the neighbourhood. It was only after his death that the work for orphans predominated.

Mr. Fegan followed similar lines in South London, with his home in the High Street, Deptford (1870), for destitute boys and his mission hall across the road. Like Dr. Barnardo, he too was a Plymouth Brother, and had also been drawn into Christian mission work through the mid-century revival meetings. His homes never reached the dimensions of those of Dr. Barnardo, but he is noteworthy for his boys' camps, taking a group of them for a camping holiday as early as 1881.

Another home arising from a Christian mission which still exists is the Home for Motherless Children (1896), opened by R. T. Smith, the superintendent of the Chiswick Mission, because he was unable to find any institution which would take motherless twins of a few weeks old whose father was alive but unable to keep them. His home broke new ground, for he accepted, not the destitute or starving motherless child, but the one whose father could not afford to pay for a happy home life.

As would be expected, many homes evolved from the ragged schools, usually starting as a refuge for homeless children and then being turned into a permanent orphanage. Two well-known homes of this type are the National Refuges for Homeless and Destitute Children, now known as the Shaftesbury Homes, and the Manchester and Salford Refuges. The Shaftesbury Homes sprang from a ragged school started by William Williams in 1843 in a hayloft over a cowshed in Streatham Street, St. Giles. It continued there until New Oxford Street was built and then united with Neal's Yard Ragged School at the Seven Dials. A gin palace at the corner of George Street was acquired as premises and the two upper floors converted into dormitories for about 100 children. Thus the first refuges came into being, the children living, receiving their schooling and some industrial training in the building. As numbers grew, it became necessary to take over other buildings in the vicinity, then to open homes in the country, until finally the present site in Shaftesbury Avenue was used as the central office, home and club for lads in local employment, the main homes for boys and girls now being in different parts of the country.

In a similar manner, the Manchester and Salford Refuges grew from a ragged school started in Queen Street, Deansgate, by

Leonard K. Shaw. The first refuge in connection with the school was opened in Quay Street in 1870. A dark room on the ground floor was the eating room, the front cellar was a living room by day and a school room at night, the back cellar was the bathroom and lavatory, and the sleeping accommodation was upstairs in hammocks, which were hung around the room at night but rolled up against the walls in the day so that the room could be used for other purposes. Very soon more accommodation became necessary and a home for little orphan children was opened, to be followed by five additional orphanages, each the gift of some interested individual or family. Now the Manchester and Salford Boys' and Girls' Welfare Society has several organisations for the young, including a children's garden village.

William Quarrier's Homes, now the Orphan Homes of Scotland, began in a similar way. One day in 1864, when William Quarrier, a shop owner, was passing along Jamaica Street, he met a ragged match seller in tears because he had been robbed of his matches and earnings. Quarrier replenished his stock and comforted him, at the same time deciding that this type of child was in urgent need of help. A ragged school was opened in Jamaica Street, and after two years moved to Irongate where lodging for twenty to thirty boys were available. The accommodation was gradually extended, a night refuge for children added, and in 1876 the City Orphan Home built. The quarters were still too small for all those who needed help, and at last Quarrier's dream of cottage homes in the country began to come true. A large site at Bridge of Weir in Renfrewshire was acquired, and one by one, as the money came in, cottages were built, until today there are many buildings on the site.

Much the same sort of work, though on a smaller scale, is still being carried out by Mrs. Smyly's Homes in Dublin. Mrs. Smyly had been moved with compassion for the barefooted, hungry, ragged children in the streets of the city, and so in 1852 opened a ragged school for them in Townsend Street. In a short time a dormitory was added where the homeless children could sleep, and out of this dormitory the homes grew. The first two were opened in 1861, and Dr. Barnardo, who spent his youth in Dublin, used to say that it was his friendship with Mrs. Smyly and his acquaintance with her work which first drew his attention to the needs of destitute children. As money was donated, other homes were built or acquired in and around Dublin, making nine at the beginning of this century, several of them being the gift of some close friend.

Circumstances sometimes encouraged the formation of children's homes, particularly the cholera epidemic of 1866 which led to an interesting group of homes started by the "three Catharines", Catharine Tait, the wife of the Bishop of London, Catharine Marsh, the author of *English Hearts and English Hands*, and Catharine Gladstone, the wife of the future prime minister. They had all worked together in the London Hospital during the 1866 epidemic and each assumed responsibility for certain groups of children who had become orphaned. Mrs. Tait opened a home at Fulham for orphaned girls, Mrs. Gladstone one at Clapton for boys, and Catharine Marsh took care of the younger children, at first in a temporary building in the grounds of Beckenham Rectory where she lived, and then at Nonington. Periods of revivalism had a similar effect. Miss Cole's Orphan Homes at Kilburn (1864) and Miss Mittendorf's Homes (1869) for abandoned infants were both inspired by the conditions which they found when visiting in connection with the mid-century revival. Moody, too, encouraged such work, having been instrumental in persuading William Quarrier to build his City Orphan Home, the Manchester and Salford Refuges to extend their work, and R. T. Smith to branch out with the care of the motherless child.

Not only did the Evangelicals control most of the children's homes of the nineteenth century, but they also had an important influence upon the methods of child care which were followed. The older orphan asylums of the eighteenth century had been large barracks-like buildings, where discipline was strict, ungainly uniform worn, and where the child was trained in a frugal and thrifty manner reckoned to be suitable to the humble station in life which he would later occupy. Admittance was gained, not according to the relative needs of the child, but upon personal recommendation or by a majority of votes at the periodic meetings of subscribers. Funds were raised by advertisement and the charity sermon in one of the larger London churches was frequently used for this purpose. The emphasis was upon making the orphanage a sound business undertaking for the charitably minded rather than a place of refuge available for any destitute child.

It was the German "Pietists" of the seventeenth century who led the way in giving priority to the needs of the child. They were a group in the Lutheran Church who insisted that Christian belief should be shown in everyday living. August Hermann Francke, one of their members and a professor at the University of Hallé, had started the Francke Orphanage in 1696. Any homeless and destitute child was admitted and given a sound education, and the necessary finances were raised by prayer, a box being placed outside the parsonage to receive what people were led to give. His orphanage throve, grew greatly in numbers, and secured widespread recognition.

His ideas were brought to England by George Muller, a native of Prussia, who had spent several months at the free lodgings for poor divinity students in connection with the orphanage at Hallé before settling in England. Having joined the Plymouth Brethren and gone to live in Bristol, he decided to introduce the same type of institution there. The Ashley Down Orphanage, or Muller's Orphan Homes as they are now called, was opened in 1836. It retained the characteristics of eighteenth century orphanages with its large barracks-like buildings, its strict discipline, its frugality, its use of the children for housework and mending, and its lack of training for any but the lowliest of jobs. But Muller was in entire charge, accepted any needy child born in wedlock, and "instead of canvassing the city and applying by letter or otherwise to the wealthy and benevolent inhabitants of Bristol, Clifton and the country at large, he addressed himself to God".

He prayed for money and for suitable people to care for the children, and the answer enabled him to rent and equip a house for thirty. He did the same not only for the building of the five large orphan homes on Ashley Down but for the everyday needs of the children. When he had insufficient money for the requirements of the coming day, the staff and even the children would start to pray. The answers to such prayers were in many cases remarkable, needs in exactly the size or form required appearing at the very moment when all supplies were exhausted. According to Muller, the advantages of this method were twofold. The children were taught from an early age to depend upon God for all their needs, and so learnt to follow this principle throughout life; and the public were given an example of faith in action, since Muller would make known his answers to prayer in frequent pamphlets and tracts, and by speaking at meetings up and down the country.

"Dependence upon faith" to a greater or lesser extent became characteristic of many of the Evangelical children's homes. Some small homes, like Miss Cole's Orphan Homes at Kilburn and Henry Toye's Orphanage at Greenwich, followed George Muller closely. Others, like Mrs. Smyly's Homes, Miss Sharman's Homes, and Mrs. Giniver's Home at Kilburn, copied Muller's methods in a modified form. D. L. Moody was strongly in favour of them and followed the same principles in his institutions at Northfield, Chicago, U.S.A., encouraging others, such as William Quarrier, to do so. Dr. Barnardo had been in correspondence with Muller before opening his own orphanage, and had started on similar lines. But he found that if he were to admit every homeless and destitute child who applied to him, he needed more businesslike methods. So, in addition to praying for his needs, he began to introduce his familiar advertising campaigns.

No doubt, if such methods were strictly followed, there might be times when the children would feel the pinch, and it would be very difficult to make any long-term plans for future development and improvements. But whether or not one agrees with Muller's way of raising funds, it did have an important effect upon methods of admission to children's homes. The fact that subscribers' meetings were not held, and the names and amounts given by particular donors were not made public, meant that the children were usually selected according to their need, or all who applied were admitted. Thus the system of voting was rarely found in the Evangelical children's homes, and this example gradually led to the abolition of the voting system altogether.

A second way in which the Evangelicals influenced the care of the deprived child was in the organisation of the institution. Again the impetus came from the German church—this time from the Lutheran Inner Mission which had been started in the late forties to counteract the materialism and secularism of the period. A leading figure in the Inner Mission was Dr. Wichern of Hamburg who had opened a home for destitute boys—the Rauhe Haus—which he organised on the family system. Some twelve to fourteen boys lived together as members of a family in a small house with a house father and mother. Then, as more children came under his care, he built additional cottages of a similar size, trained suitable men and women to be placed in charge, and erected central buildings to be used as a gymnasium, schoolrooms, and infirmary.

A knowledge of his methods began to reach this country in the sixties. Several of the founders of children's homes visited his work at Hamburg, among them W. H. Williams of the Farningham and Swanley Boys' Home, Dr. Stephenson of the National Children's Home, and committee members of the Leominster Orphan Homes; others read about his methods which were described in popular books such as Fleming Stevenson's *Praying and Working*. The result was that the family system, either in the form of "cottage" homes, which were usually built together on an estate, or "scattered homes" in different parts of some town, began to be the form which English children's homes followed.

The first of the Evangelical institutions to adopt "cottage homes" was the Farningham and Swanley Homes for Boys when they moved from Tottenham to Farningham in 1867. They had been founded in the first place for little boys who were often too young for acceptance at the ordinary orphanages, and the aim of the founders had been to provide conditions which should be as much like home as possible. A description of one of the "cottage" homes appears in the annual report of 1877:

> In the house are the "father and mother", for at the head of each of the ten families of thirty boys into which the institution is divided are a Christian man and his wife who seek to do all they can to make the little ones at home, and to train them for future life. In these homes all that pertains to home life is carried out. Each family begins and ends the day with family prayer; they sit down to their family meals; they form their family groups in separate playgrounds; and in families they go up, like the Israelites of old, to the house of God.[1]

After hearing foul language among the girls in one of his large orphanages, Dr. Barnardo decided to follow similar methods in

[1] Education of Children (Poor) No. 1. *Return of the Local Government Board to House of Commons*, July 15, 285 of 1878, p. 4.

some of his institutions, and the foundation stone of the first fourteen of his village homes at Ilford was laid in 1875. William Quarrier followed the same policy when in 1878 his first cottages were built at Bridge of Weir; and Spurgeon did the same at the Stockwell Orphanage, though here, and at the National Children's Home, the children only slept in their cottages, but met together for meals, schooling and recreation.

The "scattered homes" used by the Waifs and Strays Society and by some of Dr. Barnardo's institutions were similar, although instead of forming a compact group, the cottages were scattered throughout a town. The children went to the nearest school and church, and so only met together for social occasions. Thus they were far more closely integrated into the community, and people rarely knew that they were "orphanage" children.

But whichever variant of the family system was followed, an entirely new atmosphere was created in the institution. The children could choose their own clothes, could visit the homes of other children and have their own outside friends. It was possible to check undesirable habits and to deal with difficult temperaments without having to resort to the strong discipline which had been necessary in the larger groups, and the character of each child could receive individual attention. Furthermore, it enabled homes to be started without an enormous outlay, and to expand gradually as the money came in. Thus the "children's home" replaced the asylum or orphanage, and the needs and interests of the child had become predominant.

Evangelical examples such as these indirectly affected the workhouse child. For some time the authorities had been dissatisfied with the large district schools. Mrs. Nassau Senior, in particular, had concluded in 1873 that while they might be suitable for boys, they were in no way desirable for girls. The success of the cottage homes at Farningham and Swanley prompted them to try a similar method. A village, with cottages, workshop, schools and a hospital, was erected at Marston Green for children from the Birmingham area, and the Banstead schools built for those from the Kensington and Chelsea Poor Law districts. By 1894 this had become a usual way of dealing with workhouse children.

The authorities also used "scattered" homes on similar lines to those established by Evangelical societies, though they did not regard these as so suitable as the cottage homes for it was more difficult to arrange for the children's training. Nevertheless, the so called "barracks" schools were, in most cases, replaced by smaller homes under the care of a "fostermother" whose duty was to make conditions as home-like as possible. Boarding-out was sometimes followed, and in this they copied the example of the Scottish authorities rather than the Evangelicals, since few of the voluntary organisations, except Dr. Barnardo and the Waifs and Strays Society, boarded-out suitable orphans and young children.

Similarly, the Evangelical homes had little to teach the authorities in the way of training the children, except perhaps in preparing them for the Merchant Navy, since the industrial training at the Poor Law institutions was probably better than that provided by these homes. A few homes, such as the Gordon Boys' Home, which had been founded in 1885 to commemorate the death of General Gordon who had worked for several years among the street urchins at Gravesend, and the Farningham Homes, did, however, keep the lads until seventeen or eighteen and gave them a thorough vocational training in a variety of crafts.

The National Refuges were the first to train boys for the Merchant Service. With the help of Lord Shaftesbury, the *Chichester* was loaned from the Admiralty in 1866 as a training ship, and fifty selected boys placed on board. In 1872 the *Indefatigable*, moored in the Mersey, was used for the same purpose by the Manchester and Salford Refuges, and William Quarrier introduced such training for suitable boys in 1887. This type of training and occupation proved most successful in the case of the rough, semi-delinquent boy, and was sanctioned by the Poor Law authorities for their boys in 1871, but as they had only one training ship of their own they sent most of their boys to those of the voluntary societies.

Special arrangements for the handicapped child were first instituted by an Evangelical home, Mrs. Giniver's Home at Kilburn, now known as the Kingsdown Home for Girls. Soon after her husband's death in 1874 she began to take orphan girls into her own home, and finding that some of those who applied had been refused at other homes because they were handicapped, she decided in 1877 to open a special home for them where they could

receive more individual treatment and be helped to lead a normal
life. They were taught needlework and plain sewing, and those
who might benefit from sea air were sent to a branch house at
Broadstairs. As many as possible were placed in employment, but
those who were unable to work were kept in the home and given
small household jobs to do. Today this would hardly be regarded
as ideal, but it did recognise the fact that handicapped children
needed special care and protection, and it set the example for similar specialised treatment, which was copied a decade later by the
larger children's homes. The Waifs and Strays opened a home for
cripples in 1888; the Manchester and Salford Refuge in 1890; and
both Dr. Barnardo and William Quarrier had special homes for
consumptives and epileptics by the end of the century.

Thus most of the characteristics of the modern children's home
are to be found in these nineteenth-century Evangelical homes.
They led the way in accepting each child according to his need, in
providing him with a happy family life whatever his circumstances
or handicaps, and in trying to fit him to make his way in the world
on an equality with other children. Of course, some of these
Evangelical homes were not up to standard, particularly those
which were small and relatively unknown, and the children in
such institutions were outside the control of any authority. But
most homes were well regarded and it was the policy of the
authorities to place Poor Law children in them when they could
not themselves offer suitable accommodation. Even in 1925 the
Children's branch of the Home Office stated with regard to these
homes that

> thousands of children have been rescued from lives of want, neglect,
> misery and even prostitution, and at little or no expense to the State,
> and have been given an excellent start in life.[1]

An alternative solution to the problem of the homeless and
destitute child was emigration. This had the advantage of removing the child entirely from its sordid surroundings and providing
no opportunity for the parents to fetch it back when it was of an
age to work. But it had its drawbacks. Suitable safeguards were
necessary in the emigrating country and an assurance that the

[1] Home Office, *Children's Branch, report,* 1925, p. 34.

child would be accepted on an equality with the other children there. This meant adequate supervision to see that the child was not exploited.

In the early years of the nineteenth century some children had gone to the colonies with their parents as part of one of the family emigration schemes. A few had been sent by the Philanthropic Society or one of the early reformatories; and the Children's Friend Society had made a rather half-hearted attempt, between 1830 and 1833, to train and despatch boys to the Cape and Canada. A clause in the Poor Law Act of 1834 made it possible for parishes to use the Poor rates to assist such emigration, and Lord Shaftesbury had persuaded the government to send 150 ragged school children to South Australia in 1849. But comparatively few children were sent abroad, and there was no concerted plan to help the deprived child in this way until two Evangelical ladies, Maria Rye and Annie Macpherson, started their schemes of child emigration in the last three decades of the century.

Maria Rye, a prominent leader in the women's movement, was the first to devise a scheme for enabling children to emigrate to Canada. She had already had experience of adult emigration through her connection with the Female Middle Class Emigration Society, and it was while taking a group of such emigrants to Canada in the 1860's that she became aware of the keen demand there for the services of boys and girls. As a result she began to make arrangements for sending workhouse and other destitute girls to Canada. They were given three months' training in domestic work at her Little Gutter Girls' Home in Avenue Road, Peckham, and then sent to Our Western Home at Niagara, from which they were hired out to Canadian families. When she retired in 1896 her work was taken over by the Waifs and Strays Society, and by this time 4,000 children had gone out under her care.

Annie Macpherson was drawn into such work through her knowledge of the desperate conditions of the children who sought shelter at her Home of Industry in the Commercial Road. She had already visited America in 1866, sending some fifty poor families to Canada in 1869, but the difficulty of finding employment for the children under her care led her to concentrate upon child, rather than family emigration. Enlisting the help of her two sisters and their husbands, Mr. and Mrs. Merry and Mr. and Mrs. Birt, she began to organise such emigration, the first party of boys being taken to Canada in 1870. The shipping company would only provide plank beds and roughly cooked food, so she had to take all her own bedding and cooking utensils. Rumours spread in Canada that she was bringing a hundred wild street arabs from London and the immigration officers had orders to make strict inspection. But when they arrived such fears were dispelled and the Government of Ontario placed a house at Belleville at her disposal, which became her main distributing centre. After this several parties went over every year, each being conducted by a member of the Macpherson family.

At first the children were trained at the Home of Industry until in 1874 her training home at London Fields, Hackney, was opened. Here they spent three to six months learning such things as simple carpentry, farm and stable work which was intended to give them some idea of life in the countryside. The arrangements in Canada were similar to those of Maria Rye. Applicants for their hire had to give two references, and a legal document was drawn up for each child stating the terms of adoption and apprenticeship. There were eventually three receiving homes, at Belleville, Galt and Knowlton, to which the children went on arrival, and those who took over parties of children would, before their return, visit all the children already there and bring back photographs and records of their careers so that these could be displayed at the Home of Industry.

Both Maria Rye and Annie Macpherson sent three types of children to Canada: pauper children who were sent at the expense of the rates, homeless and destitute children who had been brought to her by various members of the public such as the clergy, district visitors, and even the police, and sometimes children whom the superintendents of orphanages thought might benefit from emigration. But in Canada no distinction was made between them. They were all either "Miss Rye's" or "Miss Macpherson's" children.

Though their efforts were welcomed at first by the Poor Law Board which recommended that "the guardians in dealing with the emigration of children will avail themselves of the means

which the active benevolence of these ladies has provided for promoting the welfare of the children", they were strongly criticised
in 1874 for a lack of knowledge of the character of the children
they sent, for too little training, for the bad conditions of the distributing homes, and for the inadequate supervision of those
boarded out. In consequence the further emigration of pauper
children by them was prohibited until 1883. But this did not affect
the emigration of children who were not in the care of the authorities, and therefore had little influence upon the work of Annie
Macpherson who only sent a very small number of pauper children. It is difficult to judge to what extent such criticism was justified, but it is probable that by this time adequate supervision was
becoming difficult. As Andrew Doyle, the local government inspector who made the adverse report, pointed out, "the work was
on much too large a scale for two ladies, and a handful of helpers
who had little prior experience. It was amazing that they accomplished so much, and that so many children were placed in better
conditions than they experienced at home."[1] The publicity which
this report brought, however, had the effect of increasing the interest in child emigration, and thereby not only caused the public
to keep a watchful eye, but also encouraged Annie Macpherson
and others to extend the work.

Meanwhile, Annie Macpherson had visited Edinburgh in 1871
and been instrumental in the opening of two training homes there
for the emigration of boys and girls. The same year she persuaded
William Quarrier to send some of his children to Canada and
placed her receiving home at Belleville at his disposal. In 1873
some Liverpool shipowners asked her to arrange for the emigration of children from that city. She sent Mr. and Mrs. Birt to
organise this and the Liverpool Sheltering Homes, which amalgamated with Dr. Barnardo's Homes in 1896, were opened in
Myrtle Street on similar lines to the Home of Industry. At first
the children were sent to Nova Scotia, but eventually she took
over the receiving home at Knowlton. Meanwhile Mr. and Mrs.
Merry had been placed in charge of the emigration work at the
Home of Industry to free Annie for supervisory duties.

Thus the Macpherson family had widespread control over child

[1] Andrew Doyle's report, *House of Commons Sessional Papers*, 1875, vol. lxiii, p. 29.

emigration in the later decades of the nineteenth century. They were also indirectly responsible for the starting of most other agencies which sent children abroad at that time. Many of the orphanages and children's homes, including the Manchester and Salford Refuges, the Waifs and Strays Society, the National Children's Home and Mrs. Smyly's Homes, used the Macpherson agencies until they could provide their own. Dr. Barnardo, who was responsible for the emigration of almost twice the number of children of any other agency and whose "boys", according to Professor Carless, formed 1 per cent of Canada's population in the early twentieth century, was first taught the methods of emigrating children by Annie Macpherson at her Home of Industry. The Catholic Emigration Society was started at the suggestion of two of the Liverpool Sheltering Homes' Committee. The only societies of any size which appear to have no connection with the Macphersons are John Middlemore's Emigration Homes at Birmingham, and Mr. Fegan's arrangements in Toronto.

The importance of these Evangelical pioneers in child emigration lies in their determination to do their best for the child by removing him from undesirable circumstances and placing him in surroundings where he has the opportunity of making good. This has remained the basic principle on which child emigration is still carried on. Methods have improved since the Macphersons sent their children to Canada. On the one hand commonwealth governments have made arrangements for their supervision and welfare and so relieved the societies of their most difficult work. On the other, new societies have tried out improved methods of handling the emigrants, particularly in relation to giving them an adequate training in farming and other occupations in which they can find lucrative employment. But the benefit of the child, and its establishment in a new and better environment which the Macpherson family regarded of primary importance, continues to be the purpose of these twentieth-century societies.

The growing sensitiveness of public opinion to the needs of the child and the development of an interest in its welfare which has taken place in the last one hundred years owes a great deal to the Evangelicals. When large numbers of children were without care, and when the State only dealt with a small proportion of them, these Evangelical homes and emigration societies gave them a new chance in life and made it possible for them to take their place in the community like any other person. In doing this they developed a pattern of care which has been closely followed in more recent years.

Most deprived children are now placed with foster parents or adopted, but there are a certain number for whom this treatment is not suitable, usually those who are placed "in care" for only a short period, or whose temperaments are awkward. Institutional facilities are still available for them, and it is the large nineteenth century Evangelical societies—the National Children's Home, the Church of England Children's Society and Dr. Barnardo's Homes —which still provide most of this care. They still follow the basic principles which they adopted then, of family units, of personal care and of an interest in the welfare of each individual child.

CHAPTER VII

The Teenager

THE TEENAGER today, looking back at the teenager one hundred years ago, would be struck by the small amount which he earned, the hours he had to work, and his lack of leisure. James Doyle told the Children's Employment Commission of 1863:

> I am thirteen. My father is an Irishman. I do not know how long I have worked. I wedge clay for a thrower. I come at 6. At Baker's I used sometimes to come at 5.30 a.m. About two or three days a week I used to come at 5.30. I sometimes give over at 6.30; sometimes at 7 or 8. It was 8 last night. I came at 6 yesterday morning. I go to dinner at 1. I always go home to dinner. I come back at 2. I get 4/6 a week. I can't read. I go to school sometimes on Sundays.[1]

James was fortunate in living at home. Many boys of his status in society would have to find their own lodgings, pay for their meals, and amuse themselves as best they could in their free time.

Little notice was taken of the adolescent in the early nineteenth century. Directly he was old enough to work he was regarded as grown up, and it was not thought necessary to help him to find suitable employment, to look for lodgings for him in a strange city, or to provide him with somewhere to go in his spare time. The only aspect of his life to which any attention was paid was that of education, and here the motive was not so much a personal one as to make him more efficient at his work. The modern change in outlook owes much to the great revivalist, D. L. Moody, who throughout his evangelistic campaigns claimed that the period of adolescence was of supreme importance in the later development of men and women, and one in which help should be given to enable the individual to take his place in the

[1] Children's Employment Commission, 1st report, 1863, evidence, pp. 16–17.

life of the community. From him and his associates in this country can be traced the first determined effort to deal with the needs of youth. He became the inspiration of a small group of Evangelicals who knew one another well, who were already engaged in various forms of philanthropy, and who were all closely connected with the origins of many of the modern services for youth. Among them were the Kinnairds, the Hoggs, and the Hon. T. H. Pelham. Lady Mary Jane Kinnaird had, in the mid-century, taken a personal interest in young people of all classes, and two of her children, the Hon. Arthur and the Hon. Emily, were closely connected with various aspects of youth work in the later decades. Arthur Kinnaird and Quintin Hogg had been at Eton together, and with T. H. Pelham they had taught in the York Place ragged school, Charing Cross, and later at the school in Long Acre. The women of their families were interested in similar work for girls, and together they formed the nucleus of the group from which much of the youth work of the 1870's and 1880's arose. On his visits to London, Moody would stay with one or other of these families, and they would help in his evangelistic campaigns, and carry out his suggestions when he left.

Another great friend was Henry Drummond, a lecturer in Natural Science at the Free Church Theological College in Glasgow and author of *Natural Law in the Spiritual World*. He undertook Moody's young people's meetings in the different campaigns in this country, and in Moody's absence devoted much time to drawing attention to the needs of adolescents and in arranging social work for them. Moody and his friends were responsible for giving a definite objective to the scattered threads of Evangelical social work for boys and girls, and in helping to direct such work along lines which would meet the various needs of young people.

Prior to this the only provision made for the working class boy or girl was the "institute". Some ideas of how such an institute was conducted can be gathered from the following contemporary account:

> The ordinary furniture of the day school is removed every evening by seven o'clock. The space is occupied with small tables covered with red cloth on which are placed various games, chess, draughts,

spelicans and the like. A large table at the end has some thirty newspapers and periodicals suited to young men's tastes; and another
table in a quiet corner has all necessary materials for letter writing. At
7 p.m. a collect is said by the gentleman on duty for the evening, and
about an hour is given to reading, games and chat. By 8.30 education
is going on in from three to five different rooms. About thirty-five
classes are held during the week.[1]

The institute developed from two sources, the Bands of Hope
which in the 1850's began to extend their meetings to boys and
girls who had left school, and the ragged schools which started
classes for older children at this time. But they copied their
methods from the young men's societies which came into being
in the eighteenth century, and which were fostered by David
Nasmith, the founder of the city missions, who frequently
established "mutual improvement societies" in connection with
his missions, for men of good moral character between the ages
of fourteen and thirty-five to meet "periodically under the superintendence of a pious and experienced president" for the purpose
of "mutual improvement and benevolent exertions".

By the 1870's these institutes had become the chief means of
providing leisure occupations for the poorer working boy or
girl, and were to be found in connection with most of the
Christian missions. The Field Lane Institution opened a large
youths' institute in 1866, the Mildmay Lads' Institute was started
the next year, and the Tower Hamlets Mission Institute in 1869.
Churches, not only of the Evangelical type, introduced them as
one of their social activities and many were still conducting them
at the turn of the century. Some of the most successful ones were
run by maiden ladies. Two such ladies had started the Red,
White and Blue Christian Institute in 1888 at Pentonville which
had a membership of 120, and another lady organised the thriving
football and cricket clubs in connection with the Working Lads'
Institute at Wandsworth (1883).

Their rapid development at this time was largely due to a
lecture given by Professor Leone Levi, of King's College, London,
to business men at the Mansion House in 1876. He had expressed

[1] London Diocesan Conference, *Committee on the Welfare of Young Men*, 1883–4.

the view that these institutes were an important means of preventing juvenile delinquency, and the Drapers' Company and the Ragged School Union straightway took him at his word. The Drapers' Company helped Henry Hill, a well-known Evangelical social worker, to open several large institutes in the East End, among them the Whitechapel Institute, which had a reading room, library, a large refreshment room, a gymnasium and two dormitories for those who needed living accommodation. The membership fee was 6d. per week, and classes in shorthand, French; and drawing were available. The Ragged School Union did not attempt anything as pretentious. They recommended that their schools should open free institutes for lads from fourteen to eighteen years where the activities should be both educational and recreational. It was from one of these, the Long Acre school, that the Regent Street Polytechnic sprang.

At the same time as these institutes were providing leisure occupations for the poorer working boy, the young apprentice was being catered for by the Y.M.C.A. George Williams, an apprentice with a drapery firm, Messrs. Hitchcock and Rogers of Ludgate Hill, had started the Association in 1844 for the benefit of his colleagues who, like himself, lived on the premises and had nothing to do in their free time. At first it took the form of a Bible study, then of weekly meetings held with apprentices from other drapery stores in the City at St. Martin's Coffee House, Radley's Hotel or Sergeant's Inn, and finally it became a world-wide association to help young men of all types.

Yet it was 1855 before recreational and social activities were included in its programme and only at the international conference at Paris in that year was it decided that the objective of the Association should be redefined as "Christian discipleship developed through a programme of religious, educational, social and physical activities".[1] This was largely due to American influence, where, from, the first the Y.M.C.A. had shown concern for all aspects of the personal well-being of young men. It was about this time that Moody became closely connected with the Chicago Y.M.C.A., which came to that city as a result of the 1857 revival, and throughout his career he made the Y.M.C.A.

[1] *One Hundred Years, the Story of the Y.M.C.A.*, 1844–1944, p. 16.

the centre for his activities. He made great use of the Y.M.C.A. during his visits to this country, and its subsequent development here owed much to him. Whenever possible, he had his headquarters at the local branch, the Aldersgate Y.M.C.A. being the centre on his first visit to London in 1867, and the Y.M.C.A. at York being the starting point of his second campaign in 1873. He did this in order to gain the support of the Christian young men of the district, and made them the pivot for his work among young people in the area. Every effort was made to increase its membership, the branches were encouraged to provide various leisure activities for their members, and often hostel and holiday accommodation as well. Moody's popularity helped to increase their funds, and the purchase of Exeter Hall in 1881 as the central headquarters of the Association was made possible through his backing. Since then the Y.M.C.A. has catered for increasing numbers of young men, among them the servicemen of the two world wars who spent much of their free time in the recreation tents of the Association.

Moody was also aware of the many lads who liked to spend their free time on the streets and wanted something more exciting than the indoor games, the talks, and the magazine reading provided by the Y.M.C.A. and the institutes, and it was he who inspired William Smith to start the Boys' Brigade. William Smith had come under the influence of Moody in 1874, and as a result had started a class for older boys at the North Woodside Road Mission in Glasgow. But, as in so many senior Sunday school classes, he found discipline poor, and he had little use for the customary method of pleading for conversion among lads of that age. Therefore he decided to introduce some of the military methods of the volunteer movement which had captured the imagination of so many of the young men of the period. In 1883 he provided his boys with a military cap, dummy rifle, leather belt and white haversack, and taught them drill, physical exercises, obedience to the word of command, punctuality and cleanliness. At the same time he made a point of getting to know each lad personally, and of setting before them the Christian way of life. Henry Drummond supported him from the start, and it was largely as a result of his support that the movement spread from

Scotland to England, the first boys' brigade in London being formed at St. John's Wood Presbyterian Church. By 1893 there were some 22,000 boys and 1,100 officers in the movement in England, and following a visit from Henry Drummond to America, it also became popular there. In an address at Harvard University, he points to the main features of the brigade:

> You get a dozen boys together, and instead of forming them into a class, you get them into some little hall, and put upon every boy's head a little military cap that costs in our country something like 20 cents, and you put around his waist a little belt that costs about the same sum, and you call him a soldier. . . . You have his obedience, punctuality, intelligence and attention. . . . The Brigade inculcates a martial, but not a warlike spirit. . . . This is the outward machinery; but it is a mere take-in. . . . The real object of the Brigade is to win that boy for Christianity.[1]

The movement appealed to the churches as a means of keeping in touch with lads who had outgrown the Sunday schools, and the Church of England adopted a similar scheme in 1890 when the Church Lads' Brigade was formed. This was followed by the Catholic Lads' Brigade and the Jewish Lads' Brigade. But there was quite a large group in the community who thought that it fostered the spirit of militarism and, led by J. B. Paton in 1889, they encouraged the formation of the Boys' Life Brigade which should emphasise discipline but should do so by teaching the boys life-saving instead of military methods of destruction. Since 1926 the boys' brigades and the life brigades have joined forces, but their membership has never been large and most of them are at present run in connection with the churches.

It was, however, the Boys' Brigade which first inspired Baden-Powell to start the Boy Scout movement. He had always been an ardent supporter of the boys' brigades, had sought the advice of William Smith before starting his own movement, and written *Scouting for Boys* with the brigades in mind. But he found their strict Evangelical principles too confining, and while retaining their ideals of physical development and a disciplined life, adopted a more modified religious outlook which could be adapted to all

[1] Henry Drummond, *One Way to Help Boys*, an address to young men in Harvard University, April 1893.

shades of religious opinion. Thus the Scout movement has flourished in all walks of life, both in this country and abroad.

The brigades were rarely successful in reaching lads who did not attend Sunday school or chapel. It was largely this type of boy that the boys' clubs had in mind. They differed from the brigades in encouraging the team spirit rather than using the discipline of military methods. Organised games were the centre of their activities, and through democratic leadership they hoped to teach a sense of responsibility. Many such clubs were formed, often, as would be expected, in close connection with the public school missions and the settlements, and they varied greatly in type, ranging from those for the better type of boy to those which were merely intended to keep the boy off the street.

The Evangelicals did not take much part in the boys' club movement, though the Hon. T. H. Pelham was instrumental in helping to form the Federation of Working Boys' Clubs in 1886. They favoured the small club where a personal interest was taken in each boy and where the club leader exercised a firm control, whereas the general tendency was towards the larger club, organised on efficient business principles with much of the control in the hands of the boys themselves. Yet many of the institutes began to introduce games and outdoor activities, and the churches and missions would have their youths' club evening once or twice a week.

The need for girls' institutes and clubs was less urgent because many girls were employed in resident domestic service and had their appropriate organisations, and others were cared for by the preventive societies which existed to keep girls off the streets. Nevertheless there were girls, particularly those employed in business or the shops, who lived in, and those working in the factories, who required some form of evening occupation.

Lady Mary Jane Kinnaird had, in 1855, invited some West End shop girls to spend their leisure time in a room in her house in Pall Mall East and, after the Crimean War, when her lodging house for nurses returning from overseas was closed, she re-opened it as a home for working girls, most of whom were employed in the dress trade. This was followed by several other homes and some forty girls' institutes were eventually set up in the City,

Holloway, Kensington, Southwark and Greenwich, where girls could spend the evening. At the same time, unknown to her, Miss Emma Robarts, who lived in Barnet and was a close friend of Mrs. Pennefather, had started a prayer circle with branches throughout the United Kingdom to link together those who were engaged in social work for girls. Mrs. Pennefather was responsible for bringing these two organisations together in 1877 as the Y.W.C.A., which was the name that Emma Robarts had used for her prayer union.

The organisation of this prayer union, with its many branches throughout the United Kingdom, became the structure of the Y.W.C.A. Lord Shaftesbury was invited to become president, with Lady Kinnaird as vice-president of the London branches and Mrs. Pennefather of the provincial branches, and the central offices were, until 1884, at the Mildmay Institution. Institutes on the lines of those of Lady Kinnaird were opened at most of the branches in England, and they provided rooms where working girls could spend their spare time and where they could get the advice and help of an older person who lived on the premises. Some of them had a dormitory where those out of a job could sleep, a few in London opened restaurants where working girls could get a hot mid-day meal, and there were several homes for convalescents and those needing a holiday.

The Hon. Emily Kinnaird, Lady Kinnaird's daughter, became honorary secretary in 1881, and in 1885 the Association moved to larger headquarters. It then became possible to extend the social work to cover special categories of working girls, such as nurses, teachers, those who were blind or deaf and factory girls. The Time and Talents department was formed to encourage educated girls to help those who were less well off, and the Travellers' Aid department to meet working girls who were coming to London for the first time. Both of these have since become independent organisations. Thus by the late eighties the Y.W.C.A. covered the needs of most working girls.

There were, in addition, a certain number of independent girls' institutes, most of them connected with churches and missions, but they usually consisted of little more than a room set aside in the evenings where the girls could learn to sew, knit and sing.

The Cloudesley Institute in Islington and the Percy Institute in the West Central area of London are interesting, for they were both started on the instigation of Moody at the time of his meetings at the Agricultural Hall in 1876. He was particularly concerned by the numbers of factory and other working girls who had no evening occupation and these institutes were opened for those with whom he had come into contact. They were still flourishing at the end of the century with some 200 members apiece.

With this more elaborate organisation for the leisure needs of working girls and the fact that in general girls are rarely as "clubbably-minded" as boys, there was not the same need for brigades and clubs. Some of these were formed however. The counterpart of the Boys' Brigade, the Girls' Guildry, was started in 1900 but was mostly confined to Scotland, the Girls' Life Brigade being more popular in England. They substituted first aid, nursing and hygiene for the more regimented activities of the boys and were usually run in connection with a church or chapel. In spite of their small membership, they served an important purpose in teaching things which were useful in the home. This was very necessary when little in this way was being taught in the schools and when the help of health visitors was unknown.

Similarly girls' clubs were insignificant in comparison with those for boys. The first ones are said to have been formed among the mill girls of Liverpool and Manchester at the time of the cotton famine of the 1860's, but their activities resembled those of an institute, and they were clubs in name rather than function. The Factory Helper's Union of the Y.W.C.A. started some girls' clubs in the East End for this type of girl, and from them there grew the short-lived Federation of Working Girls' Clubs. Like the boys' clubs, it was in connection with the settlements that the more successful girls' clubs were started, and here Evangelical influence was slight. It was only as the "forward movement" in the churches gained impetus that Evangelical girls' clubs were formed. The Wesleyans were particularly successful in this respect, having girls' clubs at most of their central missions, and the Quakers provided an interesting example with their

Frideswide Girls' Club in Drury Lane, called after a little Saxon girl who, 1,000 years before, had started a friendship club for neighbours. The Frideswide Club was opened in 1893, the girls were encouraged to organise their own activities, and to recruit their members from the most needy in the district around.

If leisure occupation was regarded as the most important need of the nineteenth century teenager, hostel accommodation was a close second. Not all teenagers required it since many lived at home, but there were two main groups of boys for whom some form of accommodation was necessary—boys from the country who came to work in the towns, and boys brought up in institutions. At some of the workshops, factories and business houses dormitories were available, though this usually meant sleeping quarters with no living room or meals; only a very few of the boys' orphanages made any arrangements for lodging those who went out to work, and the Poor Law authorities made none. The boy was therefore faced with paying 3/– to 4/– per week for the meanest of lodgings, or finding a bed in one of the common lodging houses.

One of the earliest hostels for boys is described in the memoirs of the Rev. David King. It was kept by a widow in his parish in Glasgow where, in 1834, she had taken half a dozen homeless boys to live with her on condition that they went out to work and brought home to her their earnings. In return she housed and fed them and gave them pocket money. Other similar examples could probably be found, but it was the mid-century revival which first drew attention to the urgency of the need and led to the founding of several boys' hostels. Among them were the Carter Boys' Home, opened in 1860 for homeless and destitute lads who came to William Carter's evangelistic meetings in South London; and the Youths' Christian Association and Home in Marylebone Road which was for boys from the country and was supported by the Rev. Pennefather and other Anglican clergy who had taken part in the revival. The ragged schools, as well, began to provide dormitories for boys who had gone out to work, charging 1/– per week for a hammock bed with meals at cost price. The Youths' Homes in Brook Street and Maida Vale were examples of these. The Field Lane Institution also had a hostel for boys from their industrial school who had been placed in their first job.

The orphanages were far slower in making arrangements for their boys. The Newsboys' Home in Gray's Inn Road, connected with the National Refuges, and opened in 1871 for sixty to seventy boys, was the first of these. It was followed by William Quarrier in Glasgow, by the Manchester and Salford Refuges, and by Dr. Barnardo with his Working Lads' Home in Stepney Causeway which housed both boys in employment and those who were seeking work. A few of the smaller orphanages, such as the Boys' Home, Barnsbury, found first jobs for their boys locally and provided a special dormitory for them in the home.

Some of the Christian Missions, among them the Tower Hamlets Mission and St. Giles Christian Mission, had accommodation for working boys. In the former the home was used as a testing place, and if the boys showed an inclination to stick to their first job they were apprenticed for a skilled trade. The Factory Lads' Christian Home in Kentish Town, in connection with the St. Giles Mission, housed lads employed in the local factories. Similarly some of the Youths' Institutes had some accommodation for their members, though in this case it was a slightly higher class of lad who was taken. Two shillings per week was charged for a private cubicle and cheap meals were available. The Working Lads' Home, connected with the Whitechapel Institute, with its large curtained dormitories and spacious living rooms, was an outstanding example of these, and is still in existence.

But the capacity of these hostels was not nearly enough for the number of lads who required respectable lodgings. A very general estimate at that time put the number of such lads in London as over 200,000. It was to try to fill this gap that the Homes for Working Boys were opened in 1870. Their exact origin is obscure, though it seems that the immediate cause was the difficulty experienced by A. O. Charles, the Secretary of the Farningham Homes, in finding suitable accommodation for his boys when they were placed in employment in London. He contacted other persons interested in the welfare of teenagers, among them Quintin Hogg and the Hon. Arthur Kinnaird, and in January 1870 the first home was opened in Spital Square. The Earl of Aberdeen, R. C. L. Bevan, C. E. Tritton and many other Evangelicals gave their help, and the Hon. T. H. Pelham was, for some time, the honorary secretary, thus emphasising the close connection of these homes with other Evangelical organisations for young people.

The main purpose was to place homes in different parts of London so that no area should be completely inaccessible to one. The home in the City was followed by one in the East End and then by others at Southwark, Holborn, Spitalfields, Woolwich and Long Acre. These seven homes, with some 400 beds, remained the average accommodation for the next fifty years. One shilling to 2/6 per week was charged for residence and 3/6 for meals, most of the lads earning between 5/- and 7/6 per week. The boys were left to do very much as they liked, though technical and other classes were available in the evenings, and all were expected to join the sick club at 1d. per week which gave them free medical attention and 1/- per day when they were ill.

A characteristic of these hostels was their homely atmosphere. Each was named after a member of the committee or some interested person who was expected to visit the home and get to know the boys, and who was often instrumental in finding them work in some well-established occupation. At first most of the boys were from the country or important orphanages such as Dr. Barnardo's, the Orphan Working School, or the National Children's Home, but as such boys received more care they tended to come from the Poor Law institutions and the industrial schools. None could stay after the age of eighteen, and for a time the society had a home for older boys at Kings Cross, though more usually suitable lodgings were found for them. Most of the hostels for boys have gradually been closed, but the Homes for Working Boys still remain as one of the organisations which provide lodging for juveniles working in London. This is one of the branches of welfare work in which the Evangelicals not only set the pattern, but carried out the greater part of the work until well into the present century.

The need for lodgings for working girls was less urgent since

7. William Quarrier

8. Quintin Hogg

9. Mrs Smyly

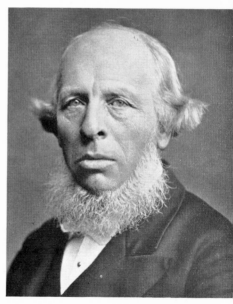

10. Edward William Thomas

Some Leaders in Youth Work

the majority of the girls from the orphanages and Poor Law institutions entered resident domestic service, and the better shops like Whiteleys and many of the business houses provided their own lodgings for their female staff. Those who had to make their own arrangements were chiefly assistants in the poorer class shops, dressmakers' "hands", and workers in the factories. As was the case with the boys, the earliest hostels for girls were opened by Evangelicals at the time of the mid-century revival. Lady Kinnaird had set the precedent in 1857 when she converted her home for nurses at Upper Charlotte Street, Fitzroy Square, into the North London Home for Girls who were employed in business, to be followed by a second hostel in Mount Street for shop girls. After this the Y.W.C.A. continued to provide hostel accommodation for the better type of shop and business girls both in London and the provinces. Mrs. Ranyard made similar provision, though she was concerned with the poorly paid seamstresses, shirt-makers and tailoresses with whom she came in contact through her Biblewomen's Mission. Her first dormitory for girls was opened in Dudley Street, St. Giles, in 1859, to be followed by a second in Parker Street, Holborn.

The founding of several other hostels can be traced to the direct influence of the mid-century revival. Miss Bramwell and her sister, Miss Augusta Bramwell, were prompted by this to start what they called at first the Revival Homes. They consisted of two hostels for business girls, one in the West End and the other in Blackfriars Road, with a home at Ham Common for any who were convalescing or might be in need of a rest. This was followed, in 1862, by Lady Rowley's Home in Spital Square, Bishopsgate, for young needlewomen. When their founders died, all these homes came under the control of the Y.W.C.A.

Little other provision was made for young women employed in the workshops and factories, and only a very few of an estimated 250,000 in the seventies were boarded by their employers. This led John Shrimpton to bring the matter before the committee of the Homes for Working Boys, and in 1878 it was decided to start similar homes for girls. Under the presidency of Samuel Morley and with the aid of the Hon.

Arthur Kinnaird and the Hon. T. H. W. Pelham, the society was formed and the first hostel opened in St. John Street, West Smithfield. There were eventually eight of these homes, taking 350 girls of thirteen to eighteen. They paid 2/6 to 4/– per week for residence and 4/6 for meals and, like the boys, had to put 1d. per week into the sick fund. There was a very close connection with the Homes for Working Boys, some people being on the committee of both, and they were well in advance of their times in holding combined social evenings with the boys' homes. Like the boys' homes, their capacity was small in comparison with the need, but they appear to have awakened an interest in the provision of lodgings for working girls in America, Sweden and some of the Commonwealth countries, and they set a precedent for the schemes of approved lodgings which is the more usual way, today, of housing girls working in factories and business establishments. They still provide the greater part of the hostel accommodation for juveniles in London.

For the working girl in a resident job two societies were formed in 1875, the M.A.B.Y.S. (the Metropolitan Association for Befriending Young Servants) and the G.F.S. (the Girls' Friendly Society). Neither of these societies was distinctively Evangelical in origin, though many of their workers were Evangelicals and they co-operated closely with the missions and churches. Both societies owed their origin to Mrs. Nassau Senior, who for a short time was an assistant inspector of pauper schools. Impressed by local experiments for befriending workhouse girls in the early sixties, she had recommended their wider adoption. When the M.A.B.Y.S. was contemplated, she suggested the lines on which it should be formed, and was also present at the meeting at Lambeth Palace at which the formation of the G.F.S. was discussed.

The M.A.B.Y.S. confined its activities entirely to the domestic servant in London, but the G.F.S. covered the provinces as well and helped not only domestic servants but girls working in factories and workshops. They followed similar methods in placing each girl in touch with an associate of the society whose function was to act as a friend, but while the M.A.B.Y.S. visited the girl at her place of work the G.F.S. organised leisure time activities for her, providing clubs at the different "lodges" and sometimes hostels where she could stay when out of work. One of the rules of the G.F.S. was only to admit to membership girls of unblemished character, and in order not to make this rigid distinction, an Evangelical society, the Young Women's Help Society, was formed by Mrs. Papillon in 1879. It was designed to meet the needs of any type of girl from the superior shop girl to the servant girl and the rough factory hand. Its branches were organised to suit the district, though all had club facilities and registry offices for domestic and other situations and some had temporary sleeping accommodation as well. The only one of these societies which remains is the G.F.S., which today is an important source of hostel accommodation, recreational facilities and holiday homes for the working girl.

Classes of one sort or another were frequently held in connection both with these organisations providing leisure activities for teenagers, and also with the hostels. They usually supplied some form of elementary education, for, until 1870, few children of the poorer classes spent more than two or three years at school and many only attended very intermittently. But few of them taught any technical subjects. The only means of learning these was to attend one of the older established mechanics' institutes, or the more recent Artisans' Institute, set up by Henry Solly, the champion of working men's clubs, in 1874. Yet these attracted comparatively few working class lads because their theoretical approach was not understood by most of them.

It was at Quintin Hogg's Youths' Christian Institute in Long Acre in 1879 that trade subjects were first taught in a practical manner to the working class lad. In his experience of ragged school work, first at York Place, Charing Cross, and then at Long Acre, Quintin Hogg found that as his boys grew up they needed something more than the usual Bible study and elementary education. His visits to the continent had shown him how the youths there were learning various trade subjects and were getting a far more liberal education than was the practice in England. At this juncture one of his former ragged school pupils, Robert Mitchell, became secretary of the Institute. The latter knew from his own experience how urgent was the need for technical and trade education and, although he had no academic qualifications, he began to teach the lads the elements of building. This proved highly popular and was followed by other technical subjects. The boys attended from 7 to 8 a.m. for 1d. a day, which included breakfast at the end of the class. They then set out for their own job.

The premises in Long Acre soon became too small and Quintin Hogg began to look around for larger ones. In 1882 the building in Regent Street, which had been used since the thirties for the advancement of practical science in connection with agriculture, art and trade, became vacant, and he immediately bought it and adapted it to meet the needs of his boys. Robert Mitchell drew up a syllabus of technical subjects, and within twelve months there were 100 classes going with some 5,000 students. Most of the courses lasted seven months, fees of 2/6 to 4/- were charged to Institute members and double for outsiders, and those who liked could take the City and Guilds examinations.

The next step was to introduce day as well as evening and early morning classes. This was done in 1886, with the intention of giving younger boys a basic education so that when they went to work they could continue as evening students. In the meantime, Mrs. Hogg, whose interests coincided with those of her husband, had started a sister institute for girls in Langham Place which developed in a similar manner, though the main subjects were cookery, dressmaking and domestic economy. Eventually they combined to form the Regent Street Polytechnic.

Quintin Hogg's aim was to develop not only the educational but all aspects of the character of his lads. Moody's influence is to be found here, for it was after one of Moody's visits, when he stayed with the Hoggs, that he began to introduce organised sport and planned holidays. Prior to this, the most that was provided for working class people was a holiday at the seaside, but in 1886 Quintin Hogg took his first party to Switzerland, and so began the Polytechnic Holiday Tours which have enabled many poorer people to travel abroad. At the same time a gymnasium was equipped on the Regent Street premises and football, cycling, rowing and cricket clubs were started. Behind all this, as T. H. Pelham tells us, lay the influence of the Bible class:

The public did not understand that the real secret of success from the beginning was the Sunday afternoon Bible class, which formed a bond of union and Christian fellowship for those engaged in working the various departments of the Institute. Q.H. used often to say that quite apart from direct spiritual results the Bible class was the keystone of success for all boys' clubs and institutes.[1]

Yet the boys were not allowed to forget their duties to others less fortunate than themselves. They organised their own mission among the very poor, ran a club for street boys, and saved their pence to send them for a short holiday.

It was Quintin Hogg's intention to start other polytechnics on similar lines, and for this purpose the National Association for the Promotion of Technical and Secondary Education was formed in 1883, with the Earl of Meath and Quintin Hogg as vice-presidents. But the only one of the new polytechnics, opened in the late nineteenth century, which followed the ideals of Quintin Hogg was the Woolwich Polytechnic which was supported in the first instance by the Hon. Arthur Kinnaird, T. A. and E. M. Denny and John Cory. Quintin Hogg was far too busy to spare the time for the intimate contact which he had with the Regent Street Polytechnic, and with a change in superintendent the connection was lost. The other polytechnics copied Quintin Hogg only from the educational aspect.

Yet he played a very important part in the development of technical education in this country. It was as the result of a visit of the Charity Commissioners to the Regent Street Polytechnic that the decision was reached that much of the funds freed for education under the City Parochial Charities Act of 1883 should be used to start other polytechnics. This was followed by the 1d. education rate in 1889 and by the application of part of the tax on beer and spirits—the so-called "whisky money"—in 1890. The result was that by the end of the century there were twelve technical colleges, most of them still functioning, and technical education had become an important part of our educational system. Full-time day trade schools were started in the London area, many of them organised, as had been done at the Regent

[1] Hon. T. H. W. Pelham, *Recollections of the Pre-Historic Days of the Polytechnic*, 1914, p. 19.

Street Polytechnic, within the existing local technical college, and in 1913 it became possible to establish junior technical schools for boys and girls of thirteen to fourteen. Thus the example of Quintin Hogg, coming as it did at a time of relative trade depression and foreign competition, enabled this country to improve its technical skills and led to the inclusion of technical subjects in future educational plans.

It is also possible to trace some seeds of secondary modern education to the example of nineteenth century Evangelicals, in particular to J. B. Paton, a progressive Congregational minister in Nottingham, who was already known for his social service union in that city. To attract the teenager who was not so interested in advanced technical subjects he opened, in 1883, recreative evening schools where languages and subjects of general interest were combined with games and other forms of recreation. When the ban on State grants to schools teaching anything other than educational subjects was withdrawn at the end of the century, these became increasingly popular and the local school premises were frequently used for the purpose after school hours. Paton followed this by the National Home Reading Union (1889) which encouraged the formation of reading circles both within these schools and elsewhere, and which prepared reading lists for them, supplied explanatory notes, loaned books and prints, and conducted correspondence with groups which were isolated.

The influence of the Evangelicals can therefore be traced in all aspects of youth service—in the educational sphere, in the organisation of leisure activities and in the provision of hostels for those at work—and in many cases their influence predominated. Much of this work, as would be expected, sprang in the first instance from the ragged school movement which had cared for the boy and girl of school age and so made some attempts to continue this care. It was the ragged school which started many of the early institutes, which opened most of the first hostels for both boys and girls, and from which the polytechnic movement sprang.

As we have seen, the most striking aspect of the progress of this youth work in the nineteenth century was its close connection with revivalism, particularly with the work of D. L. Moody. Many of the early hostels had their origins in the social work which arose from the mid-century revival, and the influence of Moody and his friends was particularly apparent in the 1870's and 1880's. The underlying motive for this was the revivalists' recognition of the importance to convert the youth of the community if there was to be a widespread religious awakening. This was first demonstrated in the 1859 revival when a concern for child conversion led to the formation of the Children's Special Service Mission. It was expressed again by Moody and Henry Drummond, who paid particular attention to the linking of the Sunday school with full Church membership and who supported all those who showed any inclination to work with youth. They encouraged the social as well as the religious aspects and it was this furtherance of social work for youth by Moody and his friends which developed the widespread scope of the Y's, which led to the large-scale opening of hostels for working boys and girls, and which initiated the polytechnics.

The Evangelicals realised the need for friendship, and provided it through their Bible classes and their social evenings. They used the brigades to teach their members discipline and how to exercise authority, and the increasing importance of recreational activities at the institutes and clubs indicates a growing concern for the physical welfare and wellbeing of the adolescent. Though today there is a demand for more democratic leadership, and for a far greater freedom on the part of youth, the principles and methods of this small group of nineteenth century youth leaders—the Kinnairds, the Hoggs and the Hon. T. H. Pelham—still prevail.

CHAPTER VIII

Gospel Temperance

THE VICTORIANS did not usually think that adults needed help unless they failed to conform to the accepted manner of life. Drunkenness, prostitution and crime were the chief causes of this lack of conformity, and so it was generally accepted that help should be given to those who succumbed in these ways. Drunkenness and prostitution were not always legal offences, while proven crime was. There was, therefore, far greater freedom to help the drunkard and the prostitute than there was to help the criminal, since the latter was usually in prison under the control of the authorities.

Drunkenness was by no means uncommon in England, and there were periods in her history when it was far greater than during the nineteenth century. But in this century there was a noticeable increase in drunkenness among the labouring classes of the manufacturing towns, particularly among the women and children. A witness to a Select Committee in 1854 states

> that he lately visited in the evening the whole of the public houses in the New Cut, from Blackfriars Road, numbering about sixteen. They are full of people drinking; in one house he counted fifty persons drinking; they were serving as fast as they could. Amongst the numbers were women with children in their arms; upon one butt there was an infant fast asleep, and the father and mother were drunk by one side; against the counter was a little child, about four years old, fast asleep. At one house the police were obliged to stand with their staves to prevent the people from pushing the doors in, as the publican and his servants drove them out to prevent their getting more drunk and to enable the public house to be closed at the time prescribed by the Act of Parliament.[1]

[1] *Select Committee of the House of Lords on Public Houses*, report, 313 of 1854, p. xiv.

There were several reasons for this state of affairs. Overcrowded and uncomfortable conditions of living made the public house appear cheerful, warm and attractive, and leisure occupations and counter-attractions were few, so most members of the family would resort there in the evenings. Dire poverty led some to forget their needs in the happiness of intoxication, while to others the price of tea or coffee was prohibitive, and the supply of drinking water quite inadequate. Furthermore, social customs encouraged "drinking". Wages were frequently paid in the public house on a Saturday afternoon, and meetings of the friendly and benefit societies held there. The beginning and end of apprenticeship, changes of employment, weddings, christenings and funerals were invariably accompanied by a drinking party; and alcohol was usually prescribed in illness and provided for those who were undertaking strenuous and heavy work. The organisation of the liquor trade also encouraged the sale of drink. The "tied house" system, whereby the publican received from the brewer a percentage of the profits on the beer sold, encouraged him to keep his premises open at all hours, and to sell to everyone, whether sober or not; and the Beerhouse Act of 1830, which allowed any retailer to sell beer, nearly doubled the number of places where alcoholic drink could be obtained. Some modification was brought about by the Licensing Acts of 1872 and 1874, but by the end of the century there were still many more licensed premises than requirements warranted.

Except for the vested interests, most people were in favour of trying to improve this situation. But there were various opinions as to how this could be done. Some thought that legislation should be passed to control the sale of liquor: others that people should be persuaded not to take "strong drink". There were a few who suggested that alternatives should be found for the public house and every encouragement given to the supply of soft drinks. One of the strongest influences was "gospel temperance". It linked together the preaching of the gospel and refraining from "strong drink", and is to be found in connection with most efforts made to reduce drunkenness.

The seeds of the nineteenth century temperance movement can be traced to John Wesley who, in 1743, advised his followers to avoid buying and selling spiritous liquors and drinking them except in extreme necessity; and to Dr. Benjamin Rush of Philadelphia who, in the early nineteenth century, advocated moderation in the drinking of spirits on the grounds of bodily health. Wesley's example influenced many Evangelicals and led directly to the early temperance societies, and the writings of Dr. Rush gave an impetus to the American temperance movement which in its turn affected the nature of our movement.

These early temperance societies were started in the late 1820's in the North and Midlands. They were mostly local in character, with little connection between them, though many owed their origin to Quakers and Primitive Methodists. Their chief characteristic was their method of "suasion" which involved persuading others to give up drink and asking them to sign the "pledge" which was a promise not to touch alcohol for a definite period. To keep in touch with one another and to exercise some degree of control, members met periodically, and this was often turned into a social occasion. But these societies had no religious connection. Their arguments were largely moral and based upon the harmful effects of liquor upon the individual and his family. Total abstinence, or "teetotalism" as it was now called, also began to find a place in the sphere of mutual help, since it was realised that intoxication was frequently an indirect cause of claims upon the benefit societies. Two American societies, the Independent Order of Rechabites and the Sons of Temperance, opened branches in this country in the thirties, which combined the pledge of total abstinence with mutual assistance to one another.

Thus by the fifties the temperance movement had become well established and two national societies were formed to develop its different aspects. The United Kingdom Alliance was started in 1853 to encourage the passage of all forms of legislation which should restrict the liquor traffic. Its founders were a Quaker, Nathaniel Card, and a Baptist minister, Dr. Dawson Burns, and it had some Evangelical support but was by no means an Evangelical society. The National Temperance League was organised in 1856 to co-ordinate the work of the suasionist societies which were already formed into local associations, and was more closely connected with Evangelical work. Its president was the Quaker,

Samuel Bowly, its secretary Robert Rae, and it counted among its supporters the Earl of Aberdeen, Lord Mount-Temple, Lord Kinnaird and C. H. Spurgeon. It organised lectures to teach the public the physiological effects of alcohol, it had its own publishing house under the management of William Tweedie, it held meetings wherever there were large gatherings of people for some particular purpose and made special appeals to scripture readers, city missionaries and other social workers to teach temperance to those among whom they worked. Much of the temperance work of the second half of the century can be traced to the efforts of this society, which took steps to adapt its methods to such diverse groups as the medical profession, the army and navy, and the churches.

It was at this stage that "gospel temperance" began to take a hold upon the English temperance movement. The religious motive for temperance had been dominant in the American movement since the thirties, and was closely connected with the hard drinking of the frontier states. The following extract from the annual report of the American Temperance Society for 1832 gives some indication of this:

> Ardent spirit destroys the soul . . . to use it is an immorality, a violation of the will of God . . . the use of ardent spirit tends strongly to hinder the moral and spiritual illumination of men; and thus to prevent their salvation, and bring upon them the horrors of the second death, who, were it not for this, might live for ever.[1]

Here can be seen not only the extent to which the religious motive had eclipsed the moral, but also the confusion which had arisen between "total abstinence" and "salvation". A similar confusion is to be found in the later stages of the "gospel temperance" movement in England, where "conversion" was not regarded as authentic unless accompanied by the pledge.

America experienced three waves of gospel temperance, the Washingtonian movement of the 1840's, the Blue Ribbon reform clubs of the early 1870's and the Women's Crusade of 1873; and each of them had their influence upon the English temperance movement. The first had been started by six "old topers" of

---

[1] Herbert Asbury, *The Great Illusion, a History of Prohibition*, N.Y., 1950, p. 40.

Baltimore who had been persuaded by a temperance lecturer to give up "drink" and who subsequently spent their time telling others to do the same. The second occurred in the state of Maine, where in 1870 Francis Murphy began to introduce gospel preaching to the meetings of the moral suasionist societies. It was followed almost immediately by a sensational campaign against the sale of drink started by the women of Hillsboro', Ohio, in December 1873. A well-known temperance lecturer, Dio Lewis, had suggested that the ladies of his audience might do something practical to stop the widespread sale of drink in the town. The next day, Mrs. Eliza Jane Thompson, the daughter of the governor, led a band of women from the Presbyterian Church to the saloons and hotels of the town. They called upon the proprietors and asked them to give up the sale of drink. If any refused they gathered on the pavement outside his saloon to sing hymns and to pray, and this was repeated day after day, until he finally capitulated. The astounding thing was that the pressure of opinion was such that in the end all the drinking saloons in the town were closed. Frances Willard, the leader of the movement in its later days, describes it in these words:

> The whirlwind of the Lord began in the little town of Hillsboro' on the 23rd of December, 1873. There the Pentecost of God descended and seventy women, without the slightest preconceived plan, lifted their hands as silent witnesses when asked by the good minister and famous lecturer if they were willing to go out from their homes and pray in the places where their husbands and brothers were tempted to their ruin. Then the Crusade psalm was read; a rallying cry "Give to the winds thy fears" was sung; and the first silent prayerful procession of women and mothers moved along the Ohio street.[1]

The fire of enthusiasm spread, and was soon taken up in other areas, among them Springfield, Ohio, where "Mother" Stewart, who later brought the movement to England, was the leader.

There was a close link between this and the Murphy movement. Both had the same basic principle of making temperance a religious issue and frequently worked together in their campaigns. They followed the custom of wearing a ribbon on the lapel of their coats to indicate their allegiance to the temperance move-

[1] Eliza Thompson, *Hillsboro' Crusade, Sketches and Family Records*, Cincinnatti, pp. 195–6.

ment—a blue ribbon for the followers of Francis Murphy and a white one for the women. D. L. Moody took a great interest in both groups, and made gospel temperance a prominent feature of his campaigns. For a time he was helped by Frances Willard, but they parted company over disagreement as to the prominence which temperance should have in his revivalist meetings. It was, however, Moody who encouraged the formation of the Ladies' Temperance Prayer Union in Glasgow, which invited "Mother" Stewart to come to Britain in 1874 as an advocate of the women's temperance movement in England.

Meanwhile there was growing up in this country a consensus of opinion which felt that some definite attitude needed to be taken with regard to "drink" by those who were engaged in social work. Mrs. Wightman, the wife of the vicar of St. Alkmond's, Shrewsbury, had written to Catharine Marsh in 1857 explaining that in her contacts with working men in the parish she found the public and beer houses the chief hindrance. "The landlords lay such snares and plots to catch the wages of the working men . . . men find that they cannot stop at the first half pint—they cannot drink moderately". Miss Marsh replied that in her work with navvies at the Crystal Palace she had tried a six months' pledge with success, and therefore she advised its use at Shrewsbury.

Mrs. Wightman was to become the leader in the gospel temperance movement in this country, and her book, *Haste to the Rescue* (1859), which described the devastating effects of drink in the homes of the poor, had an issue of 26,000 copies in its first fourteen months. The visits of J. B. Gough to this country in 1853 and again in 1857–60 had first drawn her attention to the matter, and he was the only temperance advocate she would allow to plead her cause "because of the thoroughly religious tone of his spirit". An Englishman by birth, he had emigrated to America in his early youth, had come into contact with the Washingtonian movement, and in 1843 begun to lecture for it. He gave to the movement a strong religious bias, and can be regarded as the first of the exponents of "gospel temperance" in this country. Mrs. Wightman followed his approach in her total abstinence society at Shrewsbury which became the model for the temperance societies which were to become attached to almost every charitable organisation in England. All the members of her working men's club were asked to join, and if they did so had to promise "by the help of God, to refrain from all intoxicating drinks, except when ordered by a doctor, or when taken at the Lord's Supper". Weekly prayer meetings were held to keep up the fervour of the members, and they were expected to pay into a savings bank the money which they saved by not drinking. Mrs. Wightman was one of the first to take the pledge, as she felt that only thus could she expect others to do so.

She was also indirectly responsible for the beginnings of temperance work in the Church of England. Unlike America, where many denominations encouraged the temperance movement from the first, the churches of England, except for the Primitive Methodists and the Bible Christians, stoutly refused to take any action until the latter part of the century. Therefore, at the suggestion of the National Temperance League a copy of Mrs. Wightman's *Haste to the Rescue* was sent to every clergyman and theological college in the country, and this resulted in the introduction of temperance work in many parishes and in the formation of the Church of England Total Abstinence Society in 1862. Ten years later this Society was re-constituted as the Church of England Temperance Society, which admitted to its membership moderate drinkers as well as abstainers, and which directed much of the social work of the Church at that time.

Gospel temperance was carried a step further by William Noble, also a friend of J. B. Gough and a co-worker for a time of Francis Murphy in America. He returned from his visit to America in 1878 with the purpose of introducing the "blue ribbon" movement in this country, and was successful in gaining the financial support of W. I. Palmer, the well-known biscuit manufacturer of Reading, who made it possible for him to take the Shoreditch theatre for his initial meetings, and then to concentrate the work at the Hoxton Hall. For the first time in England, the preaching of the Gospel and advocacy of temperance were inextricably combined. Those who professed "conversion" were straightway asked to sign the pledge, and were then presented with a blue ribbon which they were expected to display at all times. It became a movement for all social classes. Francis Murphy and his two sons, Edward and William, came over from America to appeal to the workers. They toured the country, holding missions and forming gospel temperance societies in all the places they visited. "Help-one-another" groups were formed in connection with the societies for the mutual encouragement of members to improve conditions in their homes and to take better care of their children. Richard Booth was invited over to appeal to the wealthier members of the community. He was in great demand at religious conferences, speaking at such eminent gatherings as that at Broadlands, the home of Lord Mount-Temple, and was frequently to be found on the platform of the religious meetings of all denominations. The movement was well organised from Hoxton Hall. A list was kept of all who took the "ribbon" and care taken to see that they joined a local group.

The "blue ribbon" movement gained widespread adherence. It was supported by the National Temperance League and the Good Templars. Samuel Bowly and Frederick Sessions of the Quakers were prominent advocates; the Rev. Charles Garrett of the Wesleyans and C. H. Spurgeon and F. B. Meyer of the Baptists were staunch supporters; and many leaders in social work followed the example of Dr. Barnardo in wearing the "ribbon". By November 1882, 6,000 to 7,000 persons had signed the pledge for the first time, and more than a million had taken the "blue ribbon" to show that they were both Christians and total abstainers. It was worn by ordinary people going about their work; was seen on the coats of bishops and lords; and was even tied to the carriages of families who had joined the movement. It became a familiar sight for most people on the platform of public meetings to display the "ribbon" and it was quite common for many of those attending important functions to refuse to "drink".

The effect of gospel temperance was to change the issue from a moral to a spiritual one. Total abstinence became usual for most Evangelicals and many members of other persuasions, though some of the older school, like Lord Shaftesbury, refused to change their views. For the younger generation it became a matter of principle, and for all zealous Christians, a necessity. Temperance societies were to be found in connection with practically all charitable and religious organisations, and numbers of the poor came under the influence of their temperance activities. Furthermore, since these societies also encouraged thrift, they had a beneficial effect upon the ways in which the poor spent their earnings and so led to some improvement in their manner of living. Therefore, whether or not one agrees with the principle, it must be admitted that gospel temperance gave zest to the temperance movement as a whole, and so helped many families to lead better and happier lives.

This was particularly true of the impact of the movement upon working class women. They had not been encouraged to join the men's societies, and so it was only with the formation of the British Women's Temperance Association in 1876 that any direct influence was brought to bear upon them. As already mentioned, this had a close connection with the women's crusade in America and several of its leaders came over to organise the movement here. But the methods of the British women were not as eccentric as those of the leaders of the so-called "Whisky War" in America. They concentrated upon helping women in their daily living rather than on stopping the sale of drink. At the local branches lectures were given on home management and the effects of "drink" in the home. Coffee stalls were set up near the factories where women worked and clubs opened for single women. Under the presidency of Lady Henry Somerset, the Association tried to help, as well, those who were addicted to drunkenness. The police court cells were visited, women were met on release at the prison gates, and homes were started for confirmed drunkards and for girls who had become prostitutes as the result of excessive drinking.

Closely allied with the B.W.T.A. was the Temperance Union of Christian Workers (1875) whose purpose was to suggest ways in which social workers should teach temperate habits to those among whom they worked, and so try to make some improvement in the homes of the poor. Its members included many leading Evangelicals, among them Charlotte Mason of the Home of Rest for Christian Workers, Anne Cole of the Mount Hermon Orphanage, Miss Weston of the Sailors' Rests and Annie Macpherson of the Home of Industry. They usually copied the

11. The Drunkard's Children in the Gin Shop *by Cruikshank*

12. The Drunkard at the Bar *by Cruikshank*

methods of Mrs. Wightman and did much to extend the work which she had begun in the fifties.

Children, too, were included in this temperance movement. In fact in many cases work among children was begun before that among adults, and often proved more acceptable to the public. Lord Shaftesbury, who had no use for adult total abstinence societies, supported the work for children from its beginning. The children suffered in two ways. They would often visit the public house with their parents or be sent to fetch liquor home and so would acquire a liking for "drink" at an early age. On one occasion, when a publican told a boy not to drink any of the beer he was carrying home, the pert rejoinder was "I will fill it up at the water tap before I get there". Indirectly the children suffered from the wretchedness of their poverty-stricken homes and the neglect and cruelty of their parents. The following gives some idea of the home of a child of drunken parents:

> The windows are broken and stuffed with rags; the walls are filthy, the floors are filthy, the beds, where there are any at all, are filthy and rotten; the odour of the room makes a visitor to them sick and faint. The place is not fit for a dog. On the floor lies somebody drunk. On the table lies a beer can; around it half-naked children stand perplexed, pale, hungry and ill. They would be in tears were they ordinary children, but tears in them have long since dried up. Their skin is alive with vermin. Their heads are sore with festerings. There is no food in the cupboard, and what is worse, there is no water.[1]

It was the sight of drunken children which first led to organised temperance work among them. Mrs. Carlile, one of the founders of the Band of Hope and the widow of a Presbyterian minister, was shocked to find that the child of a woman prisoner, whom she had adopted, was licking up some whisky which had been spilt on the floor. At the age of seventy-two she began to tour the British Isles and address meetings on behalf of temperance work among children. On her third visit to England, she met in Leeds a young Baptist minister, Jabez Tunnicliff, and in 1847 they together formed the first temperance society for children. Looking down from the platform at the eager, bright faces of the young

[1] *The Children and Drink*, an enquiry conducted by a committee under the Bishop of Hereford, 1901, p. 111.

children, she remarked to the person next to her "I think we ought to call the present meeting a Band of Hope". The movement spread throughout England as the result of Mrs. Carlile's visits which she carried out with whirlwind speed until 1854. The organiser in London was John Easterbrook. He, too, had been first drawn to the movement by the numbers of drunken children whom he came across in his district visiting, and this led him to start a Band of Hope in Walworth in 1848. Within the year he had formed ninety-three societies in London with 4,000 members. A similar growth was taking place in some of the Northern cities, and so it was decided to ask John B. Gough to come and address a children's meeting, under the chairmanship of Lord Shaftesbury in St. Martin's Hall. The outcome was the formation of the United Kingdom Band of Hope Union (1855) to unite these societies, and by the end of the century the Union had some 26,000 bands with over three million registered members.

The principles of the Bands of Hope were those of Gospel temperance. Many of them were attached to the churches and all held a weekly evangelistic meeting with much hymn singing, at which children, with the consent of their parents, were asked to sign the pledge. But scientific lectures with examinations and prizes were also given to show children the physiological effects of alcohol, and many of the day schools in the nineties included them in their syllabus. This led to a section for children in connection with many of the adult societies, among them the Rechabites, the Sons of Temperance and the Good Templars, to the "Y" branches of the B.W.T.A., and the Young Abstainers' Union for middle class children. Thus few children in the later decades of the century, failed to come into contact with one or other of the juvenile societies, and most were aware of the effects of excessive drinking.

There is little doubt that this played an important part in reducing the amount of drunkenness among children. But it cannot be separated from other aspects of the temperance movement. The adult societies obviously had some effect in improving the home conditions and in persuading parents to let their children belong to bands of hope. Similarly the legislation of 1872 for-

bade the sale of spirits to any child under sixteen for consumption
on the premises and included all forms of liquor in 1886, though
it was not until 1908 that children under fourteen were prohibited
from entering the bar of licensed premises and so debarred from
being "child messengers". The effect of these combined efforts
was to improve the plight of such children and to put temptation
out of their way.

Considering the effects of Gospel temperance as a whole, it can
be said that it did something to reduce excessive drinking in the
later decades of the nineteenth century, though to what extent
is questionable. Henry Carter, the historian of the "suasionist
societies", claims that it did a great deal, but some other writers
do not agree. What can be said in favour of Gospel temperance
is that it reached the lower classes and did help to make some
improvements in the homes of the poor. But its effects would
probably have been transitory had it not been for those in the
movement who took a positive approach in providing counter
attractions to the public house and so played a part in altering
the customary pattern of drinking.

Early in the nineteenth century it was difficult for the working
man to find any place of relaxation where beer and spirits were
not sold. The coffee houses of the eighteenth century had either
been converted into clubs or eating houses for the middle class,
or become dingy and dirty coffee rooms which were decidedly
unattractive. There were some so-called "temperance" hotels
where drinks could only be brought in from outside, but the
teashop or café for the worker, so familiar in the present century,
was virtually unknown. The working man or woman had
usually to visit the public house when refreshment was needed,
when somewhere warm or comfortable was required for spare
time or when he wanted to meet his friends or discuss matters
of interest.

An awareness of this coincided with the beginnings of Gospel
temperance in the 1850's. The first coffee house was opened in
Dundee in 1854, and Lord Kinnaird tells how

> it was at the suggestion of some earnest and intelligent working-men
> in Dundee, who represented to me that if they met a friend in the
> street they had no place to retire to for a quiet chat or where they

could spend the evening innocently and profitably, and they had no convenient place where they could obtain a meal cheaply—a very important consideration in a large town where the homes of working men are often situated at a great distance from their work.[1]

A second coffee house was opened in Edinburgh by J. Burns Murdoch in 1855, and a third at Lichfield by the Rev. J. Erskine Clarke. The Rev. Pennefather started one in connection with his work at Barnet in 1856, several temporary coffee huts were provided for navvies at places of railway construction, and they gradually became customary wherever large numbers of working men were gathered. At most of such coffee rooms, coffee, tea, or soup with bread and butter were sold for 1d., a room available for reading or writing, and sometimes games were provided in the evenings. A typical example were the coffee rooms opened by Lady Hope (Elizabeth R. Cotton) in Dorking in 1873. She had started by providing coffee at certain times for the men attending her Bible study. Then, when others asked to come, she hired a room in the town hall where meals and snacks were served from 5 a.m. to 10 p.m., and where night school was held every evening, with weekly socials for the wives. Her methods are described in *Lines on a Dark Ground* (1879), which had a very wide circulation, and it was largely due to this that some 3,000 coffee rooms were opened throughout the country. Many of them were in connection with the local temperance society, and some, like that of Mrs. Wightman, served full-scale meals on days when large numbers of people were likely to be in the town.

Mobile coffee stalls, barrows and vans also began to be provided for workers who were travelling to or from their work or who were engaged on some heavy job. John Pearce's Gutter Hotel on Holborn Hill in the seventies was a popular one. He had attended William Carter's mission at Southwark, become an ardent supporter, and when William Carter became overworked, took to drink and died, decided to do what he could to prevent this happening to others. He built a double-decker stall with an ornamental canopy, painted in red with "Gutter Hotel" on the side, and sold hot coffee with bread and cakes which he

[1] E. Hepple Hall, *Coffee Taverns, Cocoa Houses and Coffee Palaces*, n.d., pp. 26-7.

baked himself. His success was immediate, and with the profits which he made he built other stalls and set them up at strategic places. Others copied him, among them the Church of England Temperance Society which sent coffee vans to the factory areas, and the Billingsgate Market Christian Mission which had a permanent stall for the workers in the fish market. In 1879, the Select Committee on Intemperance reported that

> coffee carts are now often seen at the entrance to great works, factories and dockyards, supplying workmen with breakfasts, and furnishing pleasant additions to their portable victuals; thus relieving them of the temptation of visiting the public houses. Some of them ply their work all night for the benefit of those whose calling keeps them out at a very late, or takes them home at an early hour.[1]

Though workers of all types would frequent the coffee stalls, it was usually only those with some temperance connections who would go to the coffee rooms. Therefore Mrs. Hind-Smith, the wife of the secretary of the Leeds Y.M.C.A., decided to open premises, similar to those of the public house, which would provide non-intoxicating drinks in surroundings which were familiar to the ordinary man and woman. In 1867 she acquired an old public house and put the following notice in the window:

> A public house without the drink,
> Where men can sit, talk, read and think,
>   Then safely home return;
> A stepping stone this house you'll find,
> Consent to leave your beer behind,
>   And truer pleasures learn.[2]

and offered cheap meals and refreshments in warmth and comfort. Its success led to the opening of several more, so that by 1871 there were fifteen in Leeds and the idea had spread to other provincial centres. It reached London the next year when Miss M. A. Mariage opened one in Curtain Lane, Shoreditch. By this time they had become known as "British Workmen". A large lamp and sign to this effect would hang over the door, most were open from 4 or 5 a.m. to 10 p.m., the larger ones made

---

[1] *Select Committee of the House of Lords on Intemperance*, report, 113 of 1879, par. 66.
[2] Hepple Hall, *op. cit.*, p. 35.

provision for games and other evening activities, and they were usually managed by a local committee with a salaried man and his wife in charge.

Since few of them paid their way and had to be supplemented by voluntary contributions, it was decided to form companies to control all those in particular areas. This idea seems to have sprung from a conference held to discuss how to help the masses, at the time of Moody's visit to Liverpool in 1875, at which the Rev. Charles Garrett pointed out that "drink" was the main difficulty, and that some 20,000 men working at the docks had nowhere but the public house to go to during meal times or when unemployed. The formation of the Liverpool British Workman Public House Company was suggested, and the first house opened in 1875. Within six months five houses were in operation and four others being fitted up, and by the end of the first year the company was declaring a dividend of 10 per cent. In Glasgow, the next year, a company was formed on similar lines and this became the usual method of setting up "British Workmen" in the principal towns, so that by the eighties there were few large towns which did not possess several of them.

Still it was found that they did not appeal to some workmen, chiefly because they all displayed a pledge book, many had texts on their walls and some held mission meetings. Coffee palaces and taverns, therefore, began to appear which had all the gaudy fittings, bright lighting and plate glass windows of the up-to-date public houses, and which had no obvious religious connections. Dr. Barnardo was responsible for two of the earliest coffee palaces, the Edinburgh Castle (1873) and the Dublin Castle (1876), both of which had previously been prominent public houses. They formed a part of his East End Mission, and among their trustees were R. C. Morgan, the Hon. T. H. Pelham, and Lord Kinnaird. A third coffee palace was The Rose and Crown (1876) opposite the barracks at Knightsbridge which had on its committee Ernest Trotter and R. C. Bevan. All offered good meals and refreshments and provided games and current newspapers, and one or two had dormitories for artisans, shopmen and junior clerks.

The coffee taverns, as the name indicates, were smaller in size, but they catered for all ages and both sexes, were open from 3 a.m. to midnight, provided light meals and refreshments at all times and were frequently used for the meetings of friendly and benefit societies. Probably the first in London was The Red Star on Clerkenwell Green. The Lively Duck came to grief through bad management, but a third in Bell Street, off the Edgware Road, met with better fortune. Like the British Workmen, the company method of financing was adopted at an early stage. The Coffee Tavern Company (1876) under the presidency of the Hon. W. F. Cowper-Temple, opened twenty-seven houses, twelve of them in the provinces. The Coffee Public House Association (1877) in which Samuel Morley and F. A. Bevan took a leading part, gave loans to those who wished to start such organisations, and both the London and Provincial Coffee Palace Company and the United Kingdom Coffee Taverns Company set up houses throughout the country. By 1882 there were over a hundred of these companies as well as a large number of private speculations.

Thus by the later decades of the century every town of any size had its coffee rooms, British Workmen and probably coffee palace or tavern. The Select Committee of 1879

observed with great satisfaction the efforts which are being made in many parts of the country, and especially in London, Liverpool and the larger towns, to provide on a scale far more extensive, and in a form much more attractive than hitherto, for the physical refreshment and rational recreation of the working class. . . . It is only lately that direct rivalry with the public house by means of coffee-taverns, cocoa houses and other places of entertainment has been attempted on a large scale and in an effective form. These new establishments are usually more roomy, more cheerful and better provided with general refreshments and with the means of agreeable relaxation than the generality of the public houses. Most of them provide all the materials for a good meal at very moderate rates and supply coffee, cocoa, tea and other refreshing drinks to those who prefer to bring their own solid food. The best of them are brightly lit and neatly decorated and furnished with mirrors, prints and maps; they are well supplied with newspapers; the use of tobacco is not prohibited; and chess, draughts and dominoes are provided.[1]

[1] 113 of 1879, *op. cit.*, par. 66.

As the towns grew in size, and better and cheaper transport facilities became available, workers began to live at a greater distance from their work, and this made it necessary for them to purchase a mid-day meal. Dining rooms for workers, where a complete meal could be bought for a very low price, had existed for some time in certain industrial towns. Mrs. Wightman had visited the Irwell Dining Rooms in Manchester to learn institutional cooking, and Mr. Corbet had opened some thirteen cooking depots in Glasgow in 1860, but they offered plain and unvarying dishes which could be made in bulk at as low a cost as 1d. per helping.

John Pearce decided to provide better facilities in London in the 1880's. His Gutter Hotel was followed by a coffee bar in Aldersgate Street and then by a dining room in Farringdon Street where he served 3,000 meals a day between twelve and 3 p.m. There was a self-service choice of meat pudding, chops, steak or sausages, with tea or coffee. He called his dining rooms "Pearce and Plenty" and by a careful arrangement of mirrors at the entrance and exit made his customers appear thin on entry and fat on leaving. This was followed by the British Tea Table in Aldersgate for clerks, and in the nineties J.P. Restaurants began to appear, the first in Holborn, Newgate and Fetter Lane. These proved popular for business men, and many were to be found in different parts of London and were still running, on commercial lines, until well into the twentieth century when they were taken over in the late twenties by the Aerated Bread Company. Pearce was one of Moody's personal friends, and there is little doubt that Moody encouraged him in the provision of eating places, conducted on temperance principles, for workers of different income levels.

Again Moody's influence is to be found in the provision of lighter meals and snacks for the poorer workman. One of his staunch supporters, Robert Lockhart, the chairman of the British Workman Public House Company in Liverpool, had opened a cocoa room near the new North Docks for the men employed there, where cocoa, tea and coffee with cheese snacks, hot pot and sausages could be obtained. It proved very popular, others were started and soon "Lockhart's Cocoa Rooms", as they were called, were to be found in the poorer parts of London and other provincial cities. They became recognised as places where a cheap |meal ,could be obtained in clean and decent surroundings and were recommended by social workers to those new to a place. St. Giles Christian Mission issued a 2/6 book of tickets to ex-prisoners for use at Lockhart's and some of the hostels made arrangements for their teenagers to eat their mid-day meal there. The man and his wife, who were placed in charge, were people able to help any who were in need and to place them in contact with the appropriate agency.

Cafés also began to be opened by the People's Café Company, under the presidency of Lord Shaftesbury and the direction of Samuel Morley, in 1874. The first was in Whitecross Street, St. Luke's, a second in the Whitechapel Road, and a third was opened for office workers in Ludgate Circus. Like many of the cheaper cafés today, they had marble table tops, used thick white china, and sold hot and cold joints, entrées, soups, fish, cakes and bread, with tea and coffee as well as the new American effervescing drinks, "Sparkling Hygeia" and "Sparkling Phosphad". Thus, in their provision of cheap, clean, well-served meals with a choice of non-alcoholic drinks, these cafés were the forerunners of the great modern teashop "chains" of London.

These "People's Cafés" made some provision for working women as well, a room upstairs usually being reserved for them. Until then dining rooms for women were very rare. There was one in Marsham Street, Westminster, and another in Jewin Street, Aldersgate, where 4d. and 6d. dinners could be bought; and the Y.W.C.A. had two restaurants and several small dining rooms for business girls. But otherwise there were few places where respectable working women could get a meal. The example of the People's Cafés made it general for the teashops of the 1890's to accommodate both men and women and so began the modern custom of restaurants catering for both sexes.

Another modern custom—that of not selling alcoholic drinks in the auditorium of theatres—also had its beginnings at this time. The music hall was a place where intoxicating liquor was consumed in large quantities, since drinks were sold in the hall itself during the whole of the performance and frequently were of

as much attraction as the show itself. Emma Cons, a colleague of
Octavia Hill, had the idea of opening a music hall with all the
usual "turns" but without drink. Lord Mount-Temple was
approached and together they formed the Coffee Tavern Music
Halls Company, opening the first of such music halls—the Old
Vic—on Boxing Day, 1880. With the help of John Pearce, who
did the catering, coffee and light refreshments were provided in
the intervals instead of the usual alcoholic drinks. When Samuel
Morley joined the executive committee in 1884, the Old Vic
gained a new lease of life, first with variety shows, then excerpts
from opera and finally Shakespeare, Morley himself being com-
memorated in Morley College, which for a time shared the
same buildings as the Old Vic.

Thus the coffee public house movement had widespread reper-
cussions. Not only did it offer alternatives to the existing "pubs",
but as the Select Committee stated:

> It may be mentioned as a proof that the work is telling on the former
> customers of the public houses that many of them now advertise hot
> coffee from 6 to 9 a.m., and in some of them better accommodation
> and better refreshments are provided.[1]

There was now no longer any necessity for those who did not
want to "drink" to do so. Soft drinks could easily be obtained,
and snacks or larger meals, at the dining rooms and cafés which
were rapidly being opened. Even the public houses began to offer
such forms of refreshment. This state of affairs acted as a direct
complement to the Gospel temperance societies. Leaders in the
coffee public house movement were frequently prominent
Gospel temperance enthusiasts, though this was not always the
case, and many of the coffee public houses were linked with
temperance societies. This meant that if a man signed the pledge
there were now plenty of places where he could get refreshment
without being coaxed by his friends to drink, and no reason for
his having to enter a public house.

But neither the work of the temperance reformers nor the
coffee public houses could touch the inveterate drinker, in whom
the craving was so strong that everything else was sacrificed.

---

[1] 113 of 1879, *op. cit.*, p. lxxxix.

Some of them found themselves in the police courts, others were regarded as insane, and many were in and out of the workhouse. Little was done for them until the passing of legislation—the Habitual Drunkards Act of 1879 which allowed for the provision of retreats to which inebriates could go on the signature of a "request for reception", and the Inebriates Act of 1898 which encouraged the setting up of certified reformatories for those convicted of offences caused or contributed to by drink. The majority of the retreats and reformatories which were opened in compliance with these acts were connected with groups of Evangelicals. The C.E.T.S. and the B.W.T.A. both had retreats in connection with their police court work, the Church and the Salvation Armies and the Wesleyans had several small homes. Reformatories were few in number, but of these, the National Institute for Inebriates, started by the Rev. H. N. Burden, a former police court missionary, accounted for five. For female inebriates, Lady Henry Somerset purchased Duxhurst Manor, near Reigate, in 1895, housing the paying patients in the manor house, and the others in cottages on the estate. But unlike the other retreats which enforced close confinement and total abstinence, she gave them the full run of the grounds, encouraged them to do gardening and keep poultry and only slowly deprived them of drink. Women convicted of frequent moral lapses due to drink, were sent to her by the Home Office, and her treatment was often successful. She was well ahead of her time in recognising that alcoholism was a form of illness and in providing therapeutic care. But probably the most important contribution which the Evangelicals made to the treatment of alcoholism was their emphasis on after-care. They realised that the most difficult time was when the patient left the institution, and they made elaborate provision for this. In 1901 the Inebriates Reformatories and After-Care Association was formed in connection with the Reformatory and Refuge Union, which had agents throughout the country who would keep in touch with those who had undergone treatment and do their best, through friendly help, to prevent a recurrence.

Thus the Evangelicals were dominant in most aspects of the nineteenth century endeavour to reduce drunkenness. Gospel temperance became the prevailing force among the "suasionist" societies; the coffee public house movement not only made provision for those who wanted refreshment other than at the public house, but it changed the whole character of the catering trade; and many of the later efforts to deal with alcoholism stem from the Evangelicals. In particular the influence of Moody should be noticed, for it was his encouragement which led to the development of both the Gospel temperance and the coffee public house movements, and his campaigns were periods when these developments forged ahead. The only sphere in which the Evangelicals took little part was in gaining the passage of legislation. At first sight this may seem strange, for in the American temperance movement this formed an important part of their endeavours. But in England prohibition was never a strong cause, and the demands for the control of licensing were in the hands of other groups in the community. The Evangelicals, therefore, concentrated upon the preventive side, and tried to persuade men and women that "strong drink" was both unnecessary and undesirable. Their activating motive in this was the poverty and degradation caused by drink which they found in their contacts with the poorer people, and their deduction that only by weaning the working man and woman away from it could any improvement be expected.

The effect of their work needs to be measured against the other factors which led to the decline in drunkenness at the turn of the century. The Royal Commission on Licensing reported in 1931 that since 1899

> a marked decrease in the consumption of intoxicants has been accompanied by a marked decrease in insobriety ... which is particularly noticeable among young people.[1]

and gave as the principal reasons the legislation in relation to licensing hours and taxation, and such social factors as the marked growth in counter-attractions, the better housing conditions and the improvement in education, all of which helped to change the attitude towards "drinking", and so to moderate the extent to which alcohol was consumed by the individual person. There is

[1] *Royal Commission on Licensing*, 1929–31, report, Cmd. 3988, pars. 33 and 35.

no doubt that these factors, particularly legislation and the opportunity for sport, travel and more varied amusements, were highly important, especially in reducing insobriety among young people. But the effect of these factors would have been far less pronounced had they not been accompanied by a change in outlook towards the need for drinking, which the Evangelicals were responsible for keeping alive, and had not the various forms of refreshment houses and the example of the Old Vic, which they encouraged, made such a change possible.

CHAPTER IX

The Reform of the Prostitute

UNLIKE THE temperance movement which was almost entirely Evangelical, the efforts which were made to reform the prostitute were undertaken by both the Evangelicals and the High Church. The latter has been reasonably well documented, but much of what the Evangelicals did, and of the example which they set, has so far been overlooked.

One of the things which greatly concerned contemporary opinion in the nineteenth century was the extent of prostitution. William Acton gave a candid and detailed account of it in 1857 in his book *Prostitution considered in its Moral, Social and Sanitary Aspects*; Henry Mayhew described some of the forms which it took in his fourth volume of *London Labour and the London Poor*; and foreign observers, such as Taine, were astounded by the debauchery which they found in this country. As Taine remarked, when visiting Shadwell:

> All the houses, except one or two, are evidently inhabited by harlots. . . . Every hundred steps one jostles twenty harlots; some of them ask for a glass of gin; others say "Sir, it is to pay my lodgings". This is not debauchery which flaunts itself, but destitution—and such destitution.[1]

Undoubtedly much of this prostitution was connected with poverty. The low level of wages in certain trades, and seasonal employment in occupations connected with fashion and dress were important factors. Other occupations, such as domestic service, were particularly open to temptation, and in some the surroundings fostered immorality. According to the findings of the prison chaplain, G. P. Merrick, half the prostitutes eventually

[1] H. Taine, *Notes on England*, 1872, pp. 34 and 36.

sentenced were domestic servants, one tenth had been laundresses, charwomen, factory hands and seamstresses, another large contingent barmaids, and a few described themselves as governesses. Contributory factors were often a bad home environment, lack of parental control, parental example and occasionally incest. Overcrowded dwellings and open profligacy in the streets would lead to promiscuity, and the common lodging houses and workhouses, where the prostitute mingled with young unmarried girls, were sources of much loose living.

Until well into the nineteenth century the attitude towards the prostitute was one of censure. Her mode of life was wrong, and all that could be done was to "rescue" her from it. It was to offer help of this nature that the Magdalen Hospital had been founded in 1758 for "penitent prostitutes", a small refuge opened in connection with the Lock Hospital a few years later, and the London Female Penitentiary Society and the Guardian Society formed in the early years of the nineteenth century. Except for the Guardian Society, these early institutions were long-stay homes where every effort was made to induce penitence. Her cropped hair and her dismal uniform constantly reminded the prostitute of her wrong-doing. She was expected to ask for admission and to be prepared to atone for her sin by a time of humiliation and strict discipline. During her two years' stay she graduated from disciplinary probation to training in laundry, domestic work and cooking and after this was sent out to domestic service.

It was on these lines that the High Church sisterhoods started their homes in the 1850's. Houses of refuge were established in the towns for "the immediate reception of such fallen women as, desirous of forsaking their sin, knock at the door for admission" and houses of mercy were opened in the country where such girls could "undergo a longer course of discipline and training and thus be prepared, by God's help, to return to the world". The only difference between these houses of mercy and the early penitentiaries was the increased emphasis upon the character of the girl. The sisters hoped by prayer and example so to transform her that she might either enter upon a similar life of dedication or earn an honest living in the world. As the Church Penitentiary

Association, which was formed in 1852 to link together these institutions, expressed it: "the mission of the Association is to rescue individual souls".[1]

The Evangelicals, however, laid less stress on the penitentiary aspect. The women were sought out, offered the chance of a different sort of life, and if willing were taken to homes where they were kindly treated and taught to become respected members of society. Dickens indicates this in his description of Urania Cottage opened by the Baroness Burdett-Coutts at Shepherds Bush:

> There is a lady in this town, who from the window of her house has seen such as you go past at night, and has felt her heart bleed at the sight. . . . She has resolved to open at her own expense, a place of refuge very near London, for a small home for females, who without such help are lost forever; and to make it a HOME for them. . . . In this Home, which stands in a pleasant country lane, and where each may have her little flower-garden, if she pleases, they will be treated with the greatest kindliness; will lead an active, cheerful, healthy life; will learn many things it is profitable and good to know; and being entirely removed from all who have knowledge of their past career, will begin life afresh, and be able to win a good name and character.[2]

A small group of Evangelicals, among them the Hon. and Rev. Baptist Noel, Theophilus Smith and Lieutenant J. Blackmore, were responsible for this policy. The Rev. Baptist Noel, when vicar of St. John's, Bedford Row, had written in 1835 to the Bishop of London deploring the numbers of dissolute women to be seen on the streets, and as a result the London City Mission agreed to do something about. The London Female Mission, later known as the Female Aid Society, was started with a home for women in White Lion Square, Islington, and from this developed most of the moral welfare work of the Evangelicals.

Although a few small societies were started for this purpose in the thirties, it was the late fifties before any serious attempt was made to combat the evil, and then it was closely bound up with the mid-century revival. Those visiting in connection with

---

[1] *Church Penitentiary Association*, annual report, 1862–3.
[2] Clara Burdett Patterson, *Baroness Burdett-Coutts and the Victorians*, 1953, p. 161.

the revival were astounded by the debauchery they saw; the revivalists often suggested rescuing these girls as a useful form of social work, and frequently the girls were among their converts.

Three large Evangelical societies were formed at this time, the Rescue Society (1853), the London Female Preventive and Reformatory Institute (1857) and the Homes of Hope (1860), the first two of which are still in existence. Their respective super-intendents, Daniel Cooper, E. W. Thomas, and W. Hornibrook were to play an important part both in the development of moral welfare work and in the campaigns for legal reform which were waged in the later decades. The Preventive and Reformatory Institute grew out of some earlier homes which Lieutenant Blackmore had opened in the late thirties, the Rescue Society, with Lord Shaftesbury as its president, concentrated upon young girls who were new to the streets, and the Homes of Hope were opened specially for those who had been influenced by the revival. The co-ordinating link between these societies and other smaller ones which appeared at this time was the Reformatory and Refuge Union (1856), now the Children's Aid Society, which had some sixty homes on its books, and stood in a similar relation to the Evangelical societies as did the Church Penitentiary Association to those of the High Church.

Instead of waiting for the girls to call, as had been the case with the penitentiaries, many were brought to these homes by people who had specifically sought them out. Lieutenant Blackmore, E. W. Thomas and two ragged school teachers in the late forties had started what they picturesquely called the London by Moon-light Mission. They would meet at the house of E. W. Thomas for prayer, would then go out into the streets of London, give tracts to girls who were obviously waiting for custom, and plead with them to change their ways. Those who wanted to do so were then taken to one of the homes. Philip Magnus describes how Mr. Gladstone, in his young days, would walk the streets alone at night, armed with a stout stick, and persuade prostitutes to return home with him, where his wife would give them food and shelter.

It was not until the Midnight Movement was started in 1860, however, that this became a recognised part of moral welfare work. This movement was led by Theophilus Smith, then secretary of the Female Aid Society, and had the full support of the superintendents of the other large Evangelical societies. It is probable that the Rev. Baptist Noel was its chief supporter, as he took a leading part in its organisation and frequently addressed the meetings. The first of these meetings was held at St. James' Restaurant, Piccadilly, on February 8, 1860. Some 500 invitations were distributed, and about half that number came, of whom sixteen were sent to different homes. The conduct of this meeting and of the many subsequent ones, was similar. Cards worded "Madam, will you favour a few friends with your company at the above address. Refreshment is provided" were distributed a day or so beforehand. On the night itself those who came were entertained at small tables, at each of which sat one of the voluntary lady workers who attempted to get to know the ten or dozen girls sitting with her. Light refreshments were followed by a short address after which an invitation to any persons willing to change their way of life was given. Each one, on leaving, received, in an envelope, the address of the worker at her table, whom she was asked to visit if she so desired.

Nineteen meetings were held in London in the first year, with an attendance of about 4,000, and this continued for the next five or six years, with meetings as well in the large provincial centres such as Glasgow, Manchester, Nottingham, Liverpool and Cardiff. Among the speakers were well-known figures such as Dr. Brock of the Bloomsbury Chapel, the Rev. Newman Hall of the Surrey Chapel, the Rev. Daniel Wilson of Islington, and Catharine Booth of the Salvation Army. After 1866 the pace began to slacken, though the Movement continued to operate both in London and the provinces on a gradually diminishing scale until 1912 when it was incorporated with the work of the Preventive and Reformatory Institute, now known as the London Haven for Women and Girls.

As would be expected, the Movement was not without its critics, and two main criticisms were raised against these activities. Many thought that the work offended Victorian modesty and that the reports of it, which regularly appeared in the Revival, were far too outspoken. It is likely that this was the first real break in the so-called "conspiracy of silence" which shrouded such subjects in Victorian times, though reading these reports today one is struck by their reticence. Other critics scathingly referred to it as "The Tea and Toast Movement" and said that the meetings provided too much excitement and so did little permanent good. But emotionalism was a characteristic of Victorian society, and though on an average only some twenty-five out of perhaps two hundred girls would ask for help, this is by no means a small proportion in work of this kind. The sixties was a decade of economic difficulties and many of these girls were ones who had only taken to the streets through financial necessity. No doubt Mayhew realised this, since he was in the habit of directing girls whom he found wandering in the streets to the nearest meeting. Such methods obviously helped many more girls than would have been the case had they been left to come to the homes of their own accord, and they were useful at a time when societies had no other means of outdoor work.

The Female Mission to the Fallen, which was started in 1858 as a sub-committee of the Reformatory and Refuge Union, was the first society specifically to employ outdoor workers. It was sometimes known as the "Women's Mission to Women" as, contrary to the practice at that time, only women were employed in its work. One of its initial objects was "to go out into the streets at night to distribute tracts and seek to lead the fallen to a better life", and by 1871 nine districts in London had an outdoor worker who lived in the area. She visited the lock wards of the hospitals, the brothels, the police courts and the lodging houses, getting to know the girls and their circumstances and distributing tracts with the address of her home at the bottom. Those who called upon her were offered a temporary shelter while the facts were being checked, and then were either returned to their relatives, found employment or placed in suitable homes.

This Midnight Meeting Movement plus the outdoor work of the Female Mission to the Fallen anticipated by some fifteen years the use of similar methods by the High Church societies. It was 1874 before the London Mission, conducted by the High Church, followed a similar pattern of midnight services at St. Thomas's, Regent Street, St. Peter's, Eaton Square, and St.

Gabriel's and St. Barnabas, Pimlico, and the Church Mission to the Fallen, whose women workers began for the first time to seek out girls in the streets, workhouses, hospitals and brothels, was not formed until 1880. Their methods of opening a shelter in Mayfair and the division of London into districts, each under an outdoor worker, described by the Rev. Arthur Brinckman in *Notes on Rescue Work* (1885), closely resemble what had already been started by the Evangelicals. Therefore, although it was from the work of the High Church that much of the modern moral welfare work is directly descended, it was the Evangelicals who set the precedent in the mid-century and who first used the outdoor worker.

From the 1860's onwards many small Evangelical rescue homes for girls were opened. It is difficult to discover much about them, for as Mrs. Ranyard explains with typical Victorian reticence, when asked about these activities in connection with her Bible-women's Mission, "the work is secret and cannot reach the public ear". But we do know that there were several rescue and training homes in the early sixties, among them Mrs. Vicars' work at Brighton and the Home for the Friendless and Fallen at York, which preceded the work started by Josephine Butler in Liverpool in 1866. By the seventies and eighties it had become usual for the Christian Missions to make some arrangements for helping these girls. Most of them were linked with one of the societies specialising in such work, but some of the larger missions had their own shelter and training home, as, for example, St. Giles' Christian Mission which had shelters at the Seven Dials and Drury Lane and a training home in Kentish Town, and the Mildmay Institution which controlled "The Haven" in the Borough.

Similarly, both the Salvation and the Church Armies had from the first helped these girls. Ever since Catharine Booth had taken part in the Midnight Meeting Movement such work had been carried on quietly by Salvation Army officers, and in 1877 Major Catharine Reynolds began outdoor work in Whitechapel, and three years later Mrs. Cadman opened a training home in Newcastle. Moral welfare work then became a part of the official policy of the Salvation Army, and has remained so ever since. By the end of the century outdoor work was well established in

London, Aldershot and Chatham with two receiving homes and sixteen training homes in all. There was a maternity hospital and a day nursery in Hackney and an enquiry bureau to which relatives could send details of missing girls. In the same way, one of the earliest duties of the Church Army sisters, when they were first recruited in 1887, had been to help girls in the Charing Cross area, and it is reported in 1889 that their job was "to scour the streets round the Edgware Road and Lisson Grove at midnight, to hold meetings and approach individuals". Their work for women was on a much smaller scale than that of the Salvation Army, but, as in the case of their work for the homeless and the destitute, only the most deserving were chosen and then they were given careful and lengthy treatment.

These Evangelical homes had certain characteristics in common. The majority of them cultivated a homely atmosphere where the girls were allowed, as far as possible, to develop their own personalities, and some of them like the Church Army homes, were organised as family groups under the care of a house-mother, each girl having her own cubicle and her possessions around her. Though the inevitable laundry and domestic work were their chief occupations, it is possible to find instances where this was not so, as for example in the case of Mrs. Wilkes' needlework shop in Kerley Street, Poplar. She had rented a house with a shop front and workroom behind, and invited the girls to come and live with her. She offered them paid employment in the workroom and sold the articles which they made in the shop. Princess Louise became her patron and some four hundred girls passed through her care betwen 1878 and 1882.

In the larger societies attempts were made to classify the different types of girls. Most had a shelter or receiving home to which they came in the first instance, before they were sent to an appropriate training home. The Preventive and Reformatory Institute, the Rescue Society and the Homes of Hope had several specialised training homes, and the Reformatory and Refuge Union encouraged this policy by asking managers of training homes to concentrate upon a single type of girl so that they might direct cases which were referred to the Union to the appropriate homes. By the 1880's the Union had opened its own shelters at Peckham, Richmond and Spitalfields from which the girls were placed in training homes. Thus the beginning of many of the characteristics of modern moral welfare work can be traced to these Evangelical societies.

Evangelical societies also gave the lead in making arrangements for the confinement of the unmarried mother and for the care of her child after birth. A few hospitals, such as Queen Charlotte's and the General Lying-in Hospital, had small wards for unmarried mothers expecting their first child, but most unmarried mothers had to go to the workhouse infirmary. The Anchorage Mission (1882) was probably the first society to make private arrangements for this purpose. Its founder, Colonel Stuart-Wortley, was a convert of Moody and a close friend of the Rev. Pennefather. He was particularly concerned about the mingling of the young girl with the dissolute women of the streets in the infirmary wards. With the help of his wife who had been a Mildmay deaconess, expectant mothers were accepted at the Mission, private arrangements were made for the confinement and the mother and child were kept for several months afterwards. The Mission worked in close contact with The Haven, which was the centre for Mildmay rescue work, and mostly helped girls who had been seduced and were obviously anxious to start life afresh. It was taken over by the Children's Aid Society in 1923. Josephine Butler also opened a small maternity home near her rescue home at Winchester in 1884, and similar maternity homes were started by the Rescue Society and the Salvation Army in the early 1890's.

Before the sixties, few training homes accepted both the mother and baby and it was usual either for the child to be left in the workhouse to be brought up by the State, or to be "farmed out" with some person for payment, in which case it stood the chance of severe neglect or even death. During the 1860's the Evangelicals opened several homes which took both mother and child. Two of these appeared in 1864, one connected with the Homes of Hope to which the Marylebone board of guardians frequently sent mother and child, and the other, the Refuge for Deserted Mothers at 35 Coram Street which was in close contact with the Mildmay Institution. This latter home, which was under the control of Mrs. Main of Barnet, is noteworthy as an early experiment in placing the child in the care of foster parents and encouraging the mother to contribute towards its keep. It was the method which the Charity Organisation Society copied when workhouse girls' aid committees were set up in 1880. The girl would be placed in a suitable job, and the child sent to foster parents. A member of the committee would then keep an eye on the child and demand contributions for its keep from the mother, relatives, or the putative father.

But the more usual method followed at that time by Evangelical societies, and one which is customary today, was to keep the mother and child together in the home, the mother going out to daily work and returning at night to take over the care of her child. Two homes, opened in the 1880's, which followed this method were Mrs. Ransome Wallis's Babies Home at Walthamstow and Mrs. Harrier's Home at Brixton. Miss Broughton's Home in Cumberland Street was less satisfactory since the children were sent to a branch home at Thornton Heath, the mother to a residential job, and only on rare occasions was she able to visit her child. Yet the Lambeth guardians favoured her home and often paid for their children to be accommodated there.

It can therefore be seen that many of the methods used in moral welfare work today had their origins in the Evangelical societies of the later nineteenth century. The use of the outdoor worker can be traced to their societies in the fifties. They made a careful distinction between the shelter or short-stay home and the training home, and introduced specialised homes for different types of girls. They were aware of the basic needs of the unmarried mother and her child, and for this purpose started maternity homes and mother and baby hostels. All these things now form part of the pattern of work which is carried on by the diocesan organisations of the Church of England, by the Salvation Army and by the various other organisations which take part in such work.

Despite all their efforts, these societies were able to bring about little diminution in the amount of prostitution in the later nineteenth century. The Howard Association in 1881 expressed the view that the different societies did not do much to mitigate the evil, but were only able to "take out spoonfuls as it passed". This was because they concentrated entirely upon the individual and made no attempt to get to the root of the problem. They made little enquiry into the causes of prostitution and offered no suggestions as to ways in which it might be prevented. This had to await the work of Ellice Hopkins. Born and brought up in Cambridge, she had come under the influence of Annie Macpherson and had helped her with her mission for working men in that town. Moving to Brighton in 1866, she began to work with Mrs. Vicars, one of the more enlightened of the moral welfare workers of that period, who had already begun to organise some preventive work in connection with her rescue home. Her friendship with James Hinton, a medical specialist and philosopher who had been much concerned over the degradation of women whom he saw on the streets of London, and his appeal to her on his deathbed in 1875 to carry out the work which he had been unable to do led her to make strenuous efforts in the following thirteen years to encourage preventive work in its different forms.

As Ellice Hopkins pointed out in 1880:

> The rank and file of those who pass through our penitentiaries are for the most part very young girls—sometimes mere children in years, generally the victims of bad conditions presented by our large over-crowded towns . . . girls whose original fault has been nothing greater than unruliness, the idleness, the silly birdlike vanity, and reckless love of fun, that we sometimes have to contend with in our own girls, during the difficult ages of fifteen to seventeen. . . . Add to this a certain number of victims of love basely betrayed, and I think my audience will agree with me that it is the standing disgrace of the Church that these masses of young girls should be in a great measure practically abandoned in the midst of our Christian civilisation, the vile haunts where they herd as a rule unvisited, and no systematic Christian influence brought to bear on them.[1]

She attempted to deal with the situation in three ways. Since the children brought up in brothels nearly always followed their mother's profession, she encouraged those who were already helping such children; she set in motion the formation of societies to protect the young girl from evil; and she spoke out strongly against the attitude of many men to prostitution.

The problems of children in immoral surroundings had been

[1] Ellice Hopkins, *On Penitentiary Work*, 1880, pp. 203.

realised by James Talbot as early as 1835 when he helped to form the London Society for the Prevention of Juvenile Prostitution which later opened the Princess Louise Home at Wanstead; and the Mildmay Institution, the Reformatory and Refuge Union and other societies also had small homes for such children. Yet in 1880 a metropolitan inspector reported that there were some 10,000 children being brought up in brothels in London. At this juncture Ellice Hopkins intervened. She was so successful in rousing public opinion that a clause was inserted in the Industrial Schools Amendment Act of that year which made it necessary for certified industrial schools to accept any child committed to them by a magistrate for being found in a brothel or in the company of abandoned women. This was a step in the right direction, but magistrates were slow to commit for the purpose and therefore she pursued a second line of action—the opening of homes which would voluntarily accept such children. This was difficult for not only did the children have to be tracked down, but the mother had to be persuaded to give them up.

The methods she suggested were followed by Miss Steer at the Bridge of Hope Mission, opened in the Ratcliffe Highway in 1880. Taking a house in Princes Square, one of the worst localities, she started a club for women. This enabled her to get friendly with many of those living in the brothels, and so persuade them to let her look after their children. Lady Ashburton provided her with a house in Stepney and eventually eight cottages were acquired at Chingford where the children could live an ordinary home life. A special home was reserved for those who were diseased, and another certified under the Industrial Schools Acts to receive any children committed from the courts. As a result, some of the orphanages were persuaded to make special arrangement for such children. Dr. Barnado set aside one of his homes for the purpose, and the Waifs and Strays opened a special home at Ashurst in 1884.

Ellice Hopkins' main concern, however, was with the girl in her teens, who, although not yet committed to an immoral life, was too rough to meet the standards required by societies such as the G.F.S., the Y.W.C.A. and the Young Women's Help Society. A few societies already existed for this type of girl. As early as the thirties, the Female Aid Society had opened a home for "friendless young females of good character", and in the early seventies Miss Cobbe and Miss Elliot had started their Prevention Mission at Bristol. But Ellice Hopkins realised that little would be achieved in reducing potential prostitution unless such societies were available in every town of any size. The type of girl whom she particularly wanted to help was the wild, undisciplined girl from poor home surroundings whose schooling was over but who had not yet settled down into any suitable job. From 1878 to 1888 she travelled throughout Britain speaking to groups of women and pleading with them to help such girls. She had the power of inspiring others, and her meetings usually resulted in the formation of a local organisation. Their first step was to organise a committee of ladies who would collect funds and rent a house in a suitable district which would take from eight to ten girls with a matron in charge. Here, for about three months, they would be taught the rudiments of domestic service, then be provided with an outfit and placed in a job. They were expected to pay the cost of their outfit from the wages which they received in the first few months, and this would be collected by a lady visitor who would make such visits an occasion for seeing that the girl was well and happy and attending a club on her days out. When out of work the girl was encouraged to return to the home until another job could be found for her.

The larger of these "associations for friendless girls", as they were called, developed a very wide range of activities. They would run girls' clubs, provide lectures for young mothers on the care of children, arrange for unmarried mothers in the work-house to enter a home and board out her baby while she was away, urge the greater legal protection of young girls and see that the local authorities were not overlooking any illegalities. A few of the associations had their own rescue home and might arrange for the emigration of suitable girls. Each association was allowed to be completely autonomous so that it could more easily be adapted to the needs of the particular neighbourhood. Since her ultimate purpose was to raise the moral standards of such girls, Ellice Hopkins refused to form the associations into a national society, but encouraged the girls to join one of the existing women's organisations when they were acceptable, and closed her own associations when the need for them no longer existed.

Her example led other Evangelicals to start such work, and many preventive homes of varying quality were opened in the eighties. A few were criticised for exploiting the girls, in particular those which employed them in a steam laundry where they worked for very long hours in sultry conditions. But on the whole such homes did consider the welfare of the girls. Some offered a training of up to two years in housewifery, cooking, needlework and laundry work; others in districts where there were large numbers of factory workers arranged for the girls to be visited in their lodgings, and for a nurse to attend them when they were sick; and all had free employment agencies which were very necessary at a time when such places were frequently used to obtain girls for immoral purposes.

There is no doubt that these "associations for friendless girls" did help to keep many of the younger ones off the streets, especially those who through inability to find work might have been led into bad ways. They mostly catered for girls who would have been unacceptable to the other organisations for women and girls and so filled in a gap in the contemporary pattern of services for young people. But the most outstanding contribution which they made to the social services was to emphasise the preventive aspect of moral welfare work. From the eighties onwards, the importance of this became increasingly recognised by all groups undertaking such work, and this was largely due to the understanding and foresight of Ellice Hopkins who left no stone unturned in her endeavour to help the girl on the verge of immorality.

It became increasingly evident that if preventive work among girls was to be successful, the men must be reached as well. The "double standard"—the toleration of sexual licence to men which was not permitted to chaste women—was much in evidence at this time, and an important cause of illicit sexual relationships between the different social classes. The Rev. Baptist Noel had recognised this, when as part of the Midnight Meeting Movement of the early sixties he had addressed meetings for young gentlemen attending the music halls and dancing saloons, to point out that the blame for much of the "social evil" lay with them, and Josephine Butler was forever urging the need for the same standard of purity among men as among women, writing for the purpose in 1882 *The Hour before Dawn*, in which she showed that it was the duty of men both to live and to allow women to live in purity. The result was that men's preventive societies began to be formed which imposed a standard of purity upon their members.

Once again Ellice Hopkins was the perpetuator rather than the originator of the movement. The Social Purity Alliance had been started in 1874 by several Unitarians, and organisations on these lines were recommended by Ellice Hopkins at the places which she visited in connection with her associations for friendless girls. Then, as a result of her visit to Bishop Auckland in 1883, the White Cross Army was formed which, though intended at first to be interdenominational, was later united with the Church of England Purity Society to become the White Cross League which remained the Church's organisation for work among men until in 1939 it was linked with the Church of England Moral Welfare Council. Indirectly this had led to similar organisations in connection with the other denominations whose purpose was

> to treat all women with respect and to endeavour to protect them from wrong and degradation, to endeavour to put down all indecent language and coarse jests, to maintain the law of purity as equally binding to men and women, to endeavour to spread these principles among friends and companions, and to use every possible means to fulfil the command "to keep thyself pure".[1]

Ellice Hopkins was of the opinion that something more than leagues of men prepared to maintain a single standard of purity was needed. Mothers of all social groups should be encouraged to teach their children about sexual matters. Thus she held drawing room meetings for middle-class mothers at which they were asked to bring up their boys with equal respect for all women, and mothers' meetings for working-class mothers to help them to overcome the lack of privacy in their crowded dwellings, since this was an important cause of immorality. It was this two-fold

[1] Rosa M. Barrett, *Ellice Hopkins, a memoir*, 1907, p. 157.

approach which led her to give strong support to the Gospel Purity Association (1884), under the leadership of a Salvationist, J. G. Wookey, which included all Evangelicals. The Association had both men and women members, the men's group pledging themselves to purity, and the girls' groups, known as "Snowdrop Bands", promising to offer no enticement to men. Branches of this Association, at which lectures were given on elementary physiology and the training of children, were started by most Christian missions and other Evangelical societies in the last decades of the century, and they were extraordinarily useful in reaching all social groups in the community, both rich and poor.

Though the purity movement helped to bring about more equal standards of morality, its chief success lay in the ways in which it managed to break through the "conspiracy of silence" on sexual matters which prevented such things being mentioned in polite Victorian society. Thackeray had written to Elizabeth Browning in 1861 with regard to a poem which she was offering for publication:

> There are things my squeamish public will not hear on Monday, though on Sunday they listen to them without scruple. . . . Though you write pure doctrine with real modesty and pure ethics, I am sure our readers would make an outcry.[1]

Yet Ellice Hopkins talked about such things to her audience of both men and women in a simple, straightforward manner which rarely met with any opposition and made it far easier for others to do the same.

Another reason for the large number of young prostitutes was the lack of protection of young girls under the English legal system. The age of consent was fixed at twelve in 1861 and although brothels were illegal it was necessary for the complaint of two ratepayers before any action could be taken in relation to any suspected house. Thus it was relatively easy for young girls to be decoyed and either housed in brothels in this country or sent abroad. This situation was well known to leaders in moral welfare work several decades before the 1880's, but it was not until then that any action was taken.

[1] *Transactions of the International Congress on the White Slave Trade*, 1899, p. 146.

In the course of the campaign for the repeal of the Contagious Diseases Acts which Josephine Butler and her friends had conducted in the 1860's and 1870's, definite evidence had been found of an organised market in procuration and sale of young girls which was carried on without any fear of legal action. A *placeur* in London wrote to a brothel-keeper in the Hague in 1880:

> I have now two beautiful English girls, one fair, the other dark. The fair one speaks French a little. You will be very well satisfied with these two charming girls, I am sure. You say that you do not wish to come to London; that it is too dangerous. There is no danger. They can do nothing to you in London.[1]

Josephine Butler provided proof of traffic between England and Belgium in 1879 and a government agent, T. W. Snagge, had reported that

> the *placeur* plies his trade with impunity in the streets of London, and finds a plentiful supply of the commodity in which he deals, not only among the class of women who have already adopted a dissolute life, but also among the multitude of young, thoughtless and ignorant girls belonging to a class of persons who need all the protection that the law can secure for them.[2]

Though the facts were sufficiently evident, action was unduly slow. The Press refused to publish accounts of meetings held by groups concerned with such things; the government would give no publicity to the cases brought before their notice; and the churches were loth to take any active part. Josephine Butler writes of the more correct Evangelicals:

> They don't *want* to know of it. . . . The godly people have numerous conferences for the deepening of the spiritual life, from which they come away gorged with spiritual foodstuff. What is the use of these conferences when they result in nothing and leave the hell around as bad as ever?[3]

Therefore, as in the case of the "repeal" campaign, Josephine Butler and her friends decided to supply this publicity, and

---

[1] *Select Committee of the House of Lords on the Law relating to the Protection of Young Girls*, 448 of 1881, Appendix A, Mr. Snagge's paper, p. 145.

[2] *Ibid., loc. cit.*

[3] A. S. G. Butler, *Portrait of Josephine Butler*, 1953, pp. 210–11.

approached W. T. Stead, the editor the *Pall Mall Gazette* for the purpose. He, with the help of Bramwell Booth of the Salvation Army, proved, by taking part in a definite procuration, that a girl under the age of consent could be bought, taken to a brothel, be employed there, and then despatched to the Continent, all without the interference of the authorities. He then published an exact account of how this was done in the next issue of the *Pall Mall Gazette*.

This publicity had the desired effect. Within a few hours the issue of the gazette was sold out. Its details were then investigated by Cardinal Manning, the Bishop of London and Samuel Morley, and a monster petition of some 343,000 signatures was sent to the House of Commons. Within a short time the Criminal Law Amendment Act (1885) was passed which raised the age of consent to sixteen, made it an offence for anyone to procure a girl under the age of twenty-one, and penalised parents for placing girls in a position of moral danger. But there still remained the need to see that the law was enforced. Two public demonstrations were held, the first in St. James Hall, Piccadilly, on August 21, 1885, which suggested an extension of the different forms of vigilance work already being carried out; and the second in Hyde Park the next day which passed a resolution that

> this meeting pledges itself to assist and stimulate the public authori-
> ties in the vigorous enforcement of the Criminal Law Amendment
> Act, and to support any strengthening of the law which may be
> found necessary for the protection of young girls; that it is the duty
> of all good citizens to face resolutely the evils, social and moral, in
> which the crimes against girls have their roots, in order that their
> extirpation may be secured.[1]

The outcome was the formation of the National Vigilance Association (1885) at the offices of the Reformatory and Refuge Union. Its secretary was an Evangelical of deep religious convictions, W. A. Coote, who was convinced of the missionary character of the work which he and his colleagues were performing.

In spite of the work of the Association which was concerned

---

[1] W. A. Coote, *A Romance of Philanthropy, the History of the National Vigilance Association*, 1916, p. 13.

particularly with the suppression of houses of ill-fame, the control of obscene and indecent literature, the registration of servants' agencies, the meeting and accommodation of travellers, and the placing of women matrons at the police courts, its effectiveness was hindered by the international traffic in women. William Coote gained first-hand evidence of this when Canon Wilberforce asked him to trace a missing girl in whom his wife was interested. Haunted by the stories of deception and fraud which he heard when he eventually found her in a hospital in a Continental city, he determined to rouse public opinion in favour of international control of this traffic in women.

A principle of the National Vigilance Association was that no new project should be entered into until the necessary finances were obtained. He therefore prayed for £200 to enable him to visit the chief European capitals, and when the exact sum arrived, regarded it as a sign that the work should commence. In the spring of 1895 he set forth and found that several European governments were willing to send representatives to an official conference. The conference was convened in 1899 and resulted in diplomatic action to which the international acts for the suppression of the white slave traffic of 1904 and 1910 owe their origin. Voluntary committees for the suppression of the traffic were formed in all the principal European countries to see that the law was enforced, and the copious information which they provided with regard to the traffic led the League of Nations to take up the matter. Article 23 of its covenant entrusted the League with the general supervision over the execution of the agreements with regard to the traffic in women and girls. Thus from the voluntary work of the National Vigilance Association there eventually developed the official advisory committee of the League of Nations on the traffic in women and children which consisted of both official delegates and representatives from voluntary organisations. This co-operation between official and unofficial activities has succeeded in reducing to a very large extent this international trade in women and girls.

In these different ways of dealing with the problem of prostitution, the influence of Josephine Butler cannot be overlooked. Although one hesitates to classify her as an Evangelical, much of

13. The Hon. and Rev. Baptist Noel addresses a Midnight Meeting for prostitutes

her fighting spirit and the methods which she used were derived from her father who, with Clarkson and Wilberforce, had helped to promote the abolition of slavery; and her religious approach bears the stamp of her early contact with Methodist preaching in Northumberland. She is known chiefly for her campaign to secure the repeal of the Contagious Diseases Acts, but her influence was, in fact, far wider than this. During the seventies, when there was a lull in her crusade, much of her time was occupied in discovering details about the international traffic in women, and the National Vigilance Society was greatly indebted to her for this. She had herself experimented in moral welfare work, and was in close touch with the different groups of moral welfare workers of the period. The resulting interchange of ideas did much to improve the methods which were followed in the later years of the century.

By the end of the century a great change in attitude had occurred. The "conspiracy of silence" was broken and sexual matters were beginning to be discussed with greater freedom. This, too, had its effect upon moral welfare work. The more understanding and kindly attitude towards the prostitute, which had been introduced by the Evangelicals, became a common approach. This is well described by the following impression of a man returning to this country in 1883 after ten years' absence to find his brother's wife engaged in moral welfare work:

> She and her friend Aimée visit the houses of ill-fame in the daytime, try to reach the inmates separately, and when they have got them out, which they accomplish mainly by winning their affections, deal with each case singly as the special circumstances require.
>
> She has often told me that when she made for herself the discovery that these nameless ones were her sisters, made of her own flesh and blood, only poor, only weak, only ignorant, only ground into a foul serfdom by the tender mercies of our Christian civilisation, it revolutionised her life. She had been taught that it was wrong to know of their existence. When the scales fell from her eyes she saw that in that teaching lay the root of half their wrong.[1]

In dealing with such cases the method which the Evangelicals had formulated—the outdoor worker, the short-and long-stay homes,

---

[1] *The New Godiva*, 1883, pamphlet, pp. 6 and 14.

and the mother and baby hostel—became more usual and still predominate today. It was gradually realised that social and economic pressures were important causes of prostitution. Hence the support which Ellice Hopkins was able to gain for her preventive measures in the 1880's, and the growing awareness that preventive work was of greater importance than that of the rescue societies.

By the early twentieth century prostitution had declined and the state of the streets described by the mid-century observers had greatly improved. This was due, in part, to the higher level of wages, particularly in industries which were previously "sweated", the chance of more regular employment, less overcrowding and improved living quarters, and the change in the drinking habits which made it less usual for prostitution to be associated with intemperance. But it owed a great deal to the Evangelicals who combined preventive with rescue work, and who were successful in bringing about a far closer control over the traffic in women.

CHAPTER X

Help for the Prisoner

THE PRISONS, in the mid-nineteenth century, consisted of the short sentence gaols, some fifty-six of them in the chief counties and boroughs, and Holloway, Coldbath Fields, Tothill Fields and the Wandsworth gaols in London; the convict prisons of Pentonville, Millbank, Brixton and several other gang labour establishments; and, in London, separate detentional prisons for those awaiting trial at Clerkenwell, Newgate and the Horsemonger Lane gaol. John Howard had brought the deplorable conditions of the prisons to the public notice in 1777, but the long period of the Napoleonic wars had interrupted reform and except for the fantastic "panopticon" of Jeremy Bentham, little was accomplished until 1835 when the first step towards uniformity between the different prisons was taken by the creation of the office of prison inspectors who, in their first report in 1836, again described the disgraceful conditions in many of the prisons. The remedy seemed to be a closer centralised control, and this was achieved by the Prison Act of 1865 which amalgamated the gaols and the houses of correction into local prisons and laid down a code of regulations to be followed in all the prisons; and by the Prison Act of 1877 which placed the control of all prisons in the hands of the Prison Commissioners.

Though Howard had also recommended the separation of prisoners, this too did not become common practice until the mid-century when the substitution of penal service for transportation involved the accommodation of long sentence prisoners in the English prisons. The prisoner was now confined to his cell for the greater part of the day, only meeting the other prisoners at exercise or chapel. Employment, or "hard labour", was entirely unproductive, and usually consisted of work on the cranks, treadmill, shot-gun or stone breaking. There was some slight modification in this when the "marks" system was introduced, since it meant that the well-behaved prisoner was granted certain privileges, but during the second half of the nineteenth century the main purpose was to segregate the prisoner from his companions and from outside contacts. This was particularly noticeable after 1878 when Sir Edmund Du Cane was appointed chairman of the Prison Commission.

The conditions under which the prisoner carried out his sentence varied from one prison to another, and depended to a large extent upon the personalities of the governor and the chaplain. They were in control of all the details of his daily life and, except for contacts with warders and any prison visitors who might be permitted, were the only persons with whom he had any dealings. It is difficult to discover when chaplains were first officially appointed to the prisons, though Howard reports in 1780, "I had the pleasure to find a chaplain appointed to most of the county gaols".[1] By the middle of the nineteenth century at least one was attached to every prison, but all were priests of the Church of England and it was the end of the century before dissenting ministers were allowed to visit except on the invitation of the prison chaplain. Since the duty of the governor only extended as far as seeing that the prisoner's sentence was duly and properly carried out, it was the chaplain who performed what welfare work was done in the prison. Where there was no schoolmaster the chaplain would teach those who wanted to learn; the library was under his control; and his permission with that of the governor was required for all visitors. As the administration of the prison became more strict in the later decades of the century, so the position of the chaplain became increasingly important from the point of view of the prisoner. Since most chaplains had the care of very large numbers of prisoners it is surprising to find the great extent to which they did attend to the personal welfare of the prisoner and demand the reform of prison conditions.

Mayhew speaks of the goodness of the chaplains at Brixton prison who knew all the prisoners and members of their families;

[1] John Howard, *The State of the Prisons in England and Wales*, 1784, p. 28.

but we know most about the work of the Rev. John Clay through the memoirs published by his son. As Chaplain of the Preston gaol from 1821 to 1858 he saw every prisoner admitted, and would bring news to them from their homes and write or take messages back. He would secure interviews between prisoners and their friends if he thought good would result, and if a prisoner were badly treated he frequently asked for mitigation of sentence. Instead of the usual loquacious dissertation, his annual report, produced consecutively from 1824 until his retirement, contained a series of carefully worded case histories, which were widely read and often used as the basis for reform. Other chaplains copied his methods, and these reports helped to bring together those who were concerned with the welfare of prisoners.

The prison chaplain sometimes encountered disapproval from the authorities, and this was frequently the case when he advocated reforms. Dr. Morrison, for instance, chaplain of Wakefield and later of Wandsworth, voiced the views of many of the younger prison officials with regard to the inhumanity of the regime of Sir Edmund Du Cane. His dismissal for doing so enabled him to conduct a campaign for reform which eventually led to the Gladstone Report of 1895 and the changes introduced by Sir Evelyn Ruggles-Brise. Lord Haldane, writing to him at the time, said:

> Now that we have reported I cannot let the opportunity pass without saying how deeply I think that not only the prison committee, but the whole English public are in your debt. You have been the real instrument in bringing about what I hope will be a very great change for the better.[1]

The prison visitor was often more acceptable to the prisoner than the chaplain because there was no direct official connection. The beginning of systematic prison visiting can probably be traced to the Methodists. The Holy Club at Oxford visited in the Castle Gaol in 1730 and for some subsequent years Whitefield, Wesley and his followers "prayed, preached and distributed alms in all gaols, bridewells and bedlams within the circuits" until a storm of unpopularity arose; "so", said Wesley, "we are

[1] Shane Leslie, *Sir Evelyn Ruggles-Brise*, 1938, p. 89.

forbidden to go to Newgate for fear of making them wicked, and to Bedlam for fear of making them mad".[1]

Elizabeth Fry provided the pattern for modern prison visiting when she penetrated to the women's section of the Newgate prison in 1813. At first her intention was to bring comfort and spiritual help to these women, but by the 1820's she had organised prison visiting to both male and female prisoners throughout the country. If her instructions to prison visitors are interpreted in modern terms, they could well be followed today:

> They will take their turns in visiting the prison daily; they will read the Scriptures with the prisoners; they will instruct the ignorant, and will find employment for the idle . . . they will make themselves intimately acquainted with the disposition and circumstances of every prisoner; and they will endeavour to procure for him such an establishment in life as will afford him an opportunity of maintenance, respectable for himself and unoffensive to his neighbour.[2]

Prison visiting continued on these lines until the middle of the century, when restrictions on outside contacts were tightened and only justices of the peace allowed to visit regularly. From then until the end of the century private visiting was very rare, though it did take place in those prisons where the chaplain or governor permitted it. Among such visitors were Mrs. Carlile, Catharine Marsh, Sarah Robinson and Charles Cook of the Hyde Park Christian Mission. It became one of the chief tasks of the Howard Association to get the privilege of regular visiting restored.

The Howard Association, now the Howard League, had been formed in 1866 to carry on the work of prison reform which John Howard had started. Its secretary, William Tallack, and many of its supporters were Quakers, and it was the chief source of publicity for the needs of the imprisoned in the later decades of the nineteenth century. In 1872 the Association had drawn attention to the beneficial effects of the visiting of convicts in the state of Pennsylvania, U.S.A., in Holland and several other countries, and at the International Prison Congress of 1885 William Tallack had pleaded for efficient visitors in this country

[1] W. L. Clay, *The Prison Chaplain*, 1861 p. 35.

[2] Joseph John Gurney, *Notes on a Visit made to some of the Prisons in Scotland and the North of England, in company with Elizabeth Fry*, 1819, pp. 146–7.

to be sought for, or accepted if suitable when they offer themselves, and if on experience they are found to possess the great gift of power over the heart and lives of criminals, they should receive the utmost encouragement at the hands of the authorities.[1]

Results were slow, but by 1892 two or more voluntary visitors were allowed at each of the convict prisons and lady visitors for the female prisoners at about half the other prisons. Though the Association for Lady Visitors to the female prisons had been formed in 1901, men visitors to all the men's prisons were not appointed until 1922, and only in 1924 were women visitors allowed to see both boys and girls. Thus it was the 1920's before prison visiting was restored to the state at which Elizabeth Fry had left it, and only recently has the National Association for Prison Visitors had a branch at every prison.

Much more could be done for the prisoner on release, since once he had walked out of the prison gates the authorities no longer had any hold over him. In fact the authorities encouraged work of this nature by recognising it and frequently giving small grants towards it. Furthermore, the care of the prisoner after his release was in many ways more important than while he was in confinement. He was returning to a society from which he had been cut off for some time and whose ways of life he might have forgotten. It was essential that he should find employment, and for this he needed recommendation and frequently training. Suitable friends and relatives might help him, but he had probably lost contact with them and in the meantime had to find somewhere to stay, clothes to wear and food to eat. Thus he was a ready prey to any undesirable contacts he had made in the past and to the gangs of ne'er-do-wells who gathered near the prison gates each day at the time of release.

In the early days of the nineteenth century the after-care of the prisoner was usually left to the prison visitor, who at that time was able to get to know him and his family long before release, and so could arrange for his training while in prison and recommend him to suitable employers when he left. Sarah Martin, a poor dressmaker of Great Yarmouth, had helped the prisoners in

[1] *Howard Association*, annual report, September 1885.

the local gaol. The first report of the prison inspectors in 1836 describes her work:

> Many of the prisoners have been taught to read and write, of which very satisfactory examples were produced; and the men are instructed and employed in binding books, and cutting out of bone stilettoes, salt spoons, wafer stamps and similar articles, which are disposed of for their benefit. The females are supplied with work according to their several abilities, and their earnings are paid to them on discharge; in several instances they have earned sufficient to put themselves in decent apparel, and be fit for service. After their discharge, they are, by the same means, provided with work, until enabled to procure it for themselves.[1]

Thomas Wright had rendered similar services to the male prisoners from the Manchester gaol in the 1840's.

Those who had nowhere else to go to were housed with other destitute people in refuges, and this was feasible at a time when persons were imprisoned for very minor offences. The Quaker, Peter Bedford, opened the first of these, the Refuge for the Destitute at Hoxton, in 1805, and the government gave it an annual grant. Elizabeth Fry recognised that it was far better to restrict such refuges to ex-prisoners, and so she opened a refuge at Westminster for female ex-prisoners from the Tothill Fields Prison in 1822, and a School of Discipline for young girls at Chelsea. After her death the Elizabeth Fry Refuge was opened in her memory for female ex-prisoners who had been convicted for small offences.

When, in 1841, a halt was called to transportation as a means of punishment, it became necessary to rehabilitate on their release the long-sentence prisoners who were now incarcerated in the English prisons. Again the authorities helped, and the London Reformatory for Adult Criminals (1848) was started in Westminster for men, and for women the Fulham Refuge in connection with Brixton Prison and the Carlile Refuge at Winchester. But relatively few passed through these refuges and there was a crying need for more to be done.

Mrs. Meredith became aware of this when she began visiting at the Brixton Prison in the early sixties. She already had some

---

[1] L. W. Fox, *The English Prison and Borstal Systems*, Appendix B, p. 421.

experience of prison work since her father had been governor of
the county gaol at Cork. Her attention at that time had been
directed to finding employment for the Irish poor in the depression of the late forties and fifties, and this had brought her into
touch with the women's movement, so that when she came to
England she was very soon appointed one of the governors of
the Royal Free Hospital. She was also a fervent Evangelical,
though, unlike some who were justifiably accused of other-
worldliness, she was convinced that the careful organisation of
social work was as important as its religious approach, and that
a scientific outlook needed to be introduced if beneficial results
were to be achieved. These attributes gained for her the respect
of the prison authorities, who allowed her to work among
prisoners at a time when most voluntary workers were strongly
discouraged.

Her primary concern was with finding employment for
the woman prisoner on her release. Furthermore, though
Elizabeth Fry had obtained separate quarters for female prisoners under the supervision of a matron, and in the larger
prisons there was a nursery for the very young children who
stayed with their mothers, there still remained the problem of
what to do about the rest of the family when their mother was
in prison. Mrs. Meredith started by renting a small room outside
the gate of the Tothill Fields Prison where women could come
for breakfast directly they were released. Then in 1867 she opened
her Prison Mission in connection with her work at Clapham to
provide work for those who wanted to reform. Instead of keeping
the women in comparative seclusion, as was done by the refuges,
she placed them in carefully chosen lodgings near her medical
mission at Nine Elms, Battersea, and employed them from 8 a.m.
to 7 p.m. on laundry work, paying them 1s. per day with free
meals. If, after a month or so, their work and behaviour were
satisfactory, they were found suitable employment. This enabled
Mrs. Meredith to single out those who were most likely to
succeed on their own, and to keep the others under temporary
supervision but with gradual freedom from restraint. The prison
authorities were not slow to realise the worth of her mission, and
in 1868 made it a recognised discharged prisoners' aid society

for women convicts, sending suitable women direct from the prisons to her. Her mission continued to employ some two hundred ex-prisoners until the end of the century by which time other societies had also become engaged in the work.

From her contact with these women she learnt about the plight of their older girls who were left at home to fend for themselves and in order to do so were frequently forced to steal or take to the streets. In 1870 she sent a few of such children to a cottage in the country and this developed into "Mrs. Meredith's Prison Mission School" at Addlestone, Surrey, where the children of long-sentence prisoners were sent. They lived in small cottages, each under a house mother, and were educated, trained for domestic work and then placed in a job. Her difficulty at first was to persuade those who were nominally looking after such girls to let them come, and therefore she had her home certified as an industrial school, which made it possible for the magistrate to send children to her when the parent was in prison. Her homes are the first instance of any special provision for the female children of those in prison, and they found favour with Queen Mary when she was Princess Mary of Teck. She allowed them to be called Princess Mary's Village Homes, and, as a junior approved school, they still carry this name.

Another problem was to find some way of getting into touch with women in solitary confinement in the convict prisons, for although she was sometimes allowed to visit short-sentence women prisoners she was never permitted inside the quarters of the convicts. Therefore, on Christmas Day, 1881, she started her "Letters to Prisoners" by sending twelve letters, written by herself and her friends, to women in the Millbank Prison. Each was written by hand, addressed personally to the prisoner, super-scribed "a Christmas Letter to you" and contained a short Christian message and Christmas greeting. She gradually gained the permission of the governors and chaplains of other women's prisons and of some of the men's prisons to send such letters, and they are still being sent by the "Christmas Letters to Prisoners" to prisons all over the world. To the convicts of the later nineteenth century they were usually the only contact which they had with persons outside the prison, and they still provide a memento of Christmas to those who are cut off from their families.

Mrs. Meredith holds an important place in the line of prison philanthropists and reformers in this country, which has been greatly overlooked. She continued the work which Elizabeth Fry had started for the female prisoner, by caring not only for the woman when she was in prison, but by making adequate arrangements for after-care and for rehabilitation, and by helping to look after other members of the family when the mother was absent. These are distinctive forms of welfare work for the prisoner which are performed, often in a similar manner, today.

Other offenders for whom some special provision was urgently needed were the young lads in their late 'teens who were too old to be sent to the reformatories and, until the Borstal system was started, had to mingle with more hardened criminals in the adult prisons. The Colony of Stretton in Warwickshire (1815) and a few other discharged prisoners' aid societies helped such lads on release, but they did not really adapt themselves to the special problems of this age-group. The attention of William Wheatley, a worker with the St. Giles Christian Mission, was first drawn to such lads by the chaplain at Newgate, who told him of many first offenders being caught almost immediately on release for stealing or embezzlement and returned to the Coldbath Fields Prison. Therefore, when William Wheatley was placed in charge of the work for discharged prisoners which the Mission decided to start in 1877, he took particular care to follow up such cases, to find employment for them, to visit them regularly and to do his best to keep them straight.

His chance came ten years later when his friend, Howard Vincent, managed to get the First Offenders' Act passed which made it possible for the court to place on probation any lad, not previously convicted, who was charged with larceny or false pretences. The Act remained largely inoperative because there were few persons suitable to supervise those on probation, but William Wheatley was one who could do so, and several magistrates committed lads to his care. His method was to visit the courts, select the more hopeful cases and suggest that they should be placed in his charge. The boys came for one or two years, and after a short period of trial were sent to jobs found specially for them. In the evenings classes or organised recreation were provided for them, and they had to pay part of their wages for board and lodging. Few of the lads who passed through his homes committed fresh offences, and by the first decade of the twentieth century this had become the usual way of dealing with them. In this work he anticipated methods such as a congenial atmosphere with strict discipline, organised occupation for all free time, and training in an honest way of living, which were later incorporated by Sir Evelyn Ruggles-Brise in his Borstal system. His homes are also suggestive of the approved hostels of today to which lads on probation, who have unsatisfactory home surroundings, are sent.

The needs of discharged prisoners had been recognised for some time. They were included in some of the charitable trusts for those in prison, and since 1792 societies had been formed to help them. The State encouraged this form of help throughout the nineteenth century, the Discharged Prisoners' Aid Act of 1862 empowering justices to pay a small sum of money to each ex-prisoner helped by a society. But there were certain gaps in the organisation. Nothing was done for long-sentence prisoners and convicts, nor were there any societies in connection with the London prisons. These gaps the Evangelicals filled.

The long-term prisoner had not previously received any aid because he was given a gratuity, according to his conduct, when he left prison, and this was intended to enable him to find employment. But it was often used for quite different purposes. The Royal Society for Discharged Prisoners, which was set up at Charing Cross in 1857 with the aid of Lord Kinnaird, was intended to help these men either to return to their families and find a local job, or to emigrate. Convicts had to inform the prison governor if they wished to avail themselves of the services of the Society. Their particulars were then sent to its agents, the gratuity paid direct to the Society, and any difference in expenses either returned to the men or met by the Society's funds. Men who wanted to emigrate were sent for a time to the London Reformatory for Adult Criminals, and women to Mrs. Meredith.

The Reformatory and Refuge Union came to the aid of the

short-sentence man in London. The Discharged Prisoners' Relief Committee, later known as the Metropolitan Discharged Prisoners' Aid Committee, was formed in 1862 with agents appointed to the different gaols to help the men on release, Mrs. Meredith again dealing with the women. It was the Reformatory and Refuge Union, also, which called the first general conference of discharged prisoners' aid societies in 1871 and which supplied the link between these societies until it was superseded by the Central Discharged Prisoners' Aid Society in 1918, now part of the Central After-Care Committee. Thus a comprehensive and efficient system for the after-care of the prisoner was gradually reached in the later decades of the nineteenth century.

Yet the aid society frequently allowed the ex-prisoner to slip through its hands, either because the agent had to wait for the prison authorities to notify him of the prisoner's release, or, as often happened in London where the prisons were large and numerous, there were too few agents to contact all ex-prisoners. To remedy this, prison gate missions were started, whose workers met the prisoners as they emerged from the prison in the early morning, invited them to breakfast in a nearby room and discussed their future with them, offering what help they could.

Mrs. Meredith set the example at the Tothill Fields Prison in 1866. As George Hatton, the superintendent of the St. Giles Mission, writes:

> It was the sight that met our eyes one cold bleak morning outside Tothill Fields Prison, that first inspired us to go and do likewise for the men daily discharged from the metropolitan gaols.[1]

He started similar work at Holloway, Wandsworth, Pentonville and Millbank. Others quickly sprang up. The result of Moody's visit to Ireland in 1875 were the Dublin and the Belfast prison gate missions; Boston and Toronto started such missions; and the Queen of Sweden sent one of her ladies-in-waiting to look at Mrs. Meredith's mission so that similar work might be started in that country. Prison gate missions were to be found at most of the local gaols as well—F. B. Meyer organised one at the Leicester gaol and the Boys' and Girls' Refuges at the Manchester gaol.

---

[1] M. A. Lloyd, *Susanna Meredith*, 1903, p. 33.

The Church of England Temperance Society entered the field in 1879; the Salvation Army started its first Prison Gate Brigade at the Wandsworth gaol in 1884; and the Church Army missioners began to wait at the gates of different prisons in 1888.

This growth in the number of prison gate missions meant that what had begun as a very useful form of social work in contacting the ex-prisoner before he became associated with less desirable influences, often degenerated into competition between the different missions at the prison gate. Some of the aid societies complained that their work was hindered by this, and that ex-prisoners who might otherwise have come to them were waylaid by the agents of the prison gate missions which were usually unable to perform any lasting services for them. This caused Mrs. Meredith to discontinue her prison gate work and by the end of the century most of these missions had been closed. Nevertheless they had a beneficial effect upon the methods of the aid societies. Most of the aid societies tried to contact the ex-prisoner immediately on release, and when prison regulations became less strict they were able, as they are today, to see the prisoner some time before he leaves the prison.

The police courts did not come within the scope of any of this social work for prisoners. Here, there gathered a motley assortment of persons of all types and ages, usually waiting several hours for their case to be heard. Many of them were charged with drunkenness, and some were still in this state. There was no one to look after the women, no means of refreshment and rarely any facilities for washing. A visitor to the Lambeth police court in the seventies describes what he saw:

Look around you. You feel sick and faint. . . . What is that lying on the floor? It is a woman; she has had a fit, and there she lies with a bag of straw under her head, and not a single woman in the place whose duty it is to attend to her. What is that cowering in the corner? Well, that has been a woman driven years ago by the devil of sensuality into the wilderness of sin, where she took to herself other devils. But only one has her in his grip now. Drink! . . . That in the other corner is reported to be a woman. She has got men's boots on, no hat or bonnet, no jacket or mantle; her arms are bare; her dress, what there is of it, is short; her forehead is low, her broad face cut and bruised, her eyes are inflamed and her hair hangs loosely down. Twenty-four years of age they say, and she has been in that court one hundred and fifty times.[1]

A working painter, Frederick Rainer, had drawn attention to this state of affairs in a letter to the Church of England Temperance Society in 1876. He hoped that it might be possible to do something about it, and enclosed 5/-. The outcome was the appointment that year of the first police court missionary to deal with drunkards at certain of the metropolitan courts. As more were appointed their duties were extended so that in 1889

> the missionaries are at the Courts for some time before the magistrate takes his seat on the Bench, and during this time they make acquaintance, in the cells or in the prisoners' waiting rooms, with those that are about to be charged. Then, as each prisoner attends in the dock, the missionary being in his place in the court, the magistrate will constantly ask what can be done for this or that case. At the suggestion of the missionary many cases are put back till the afternoon, or remanded for a longer period for the purpose of investigation, and the magistrate and missionary often consult together on the various cases . . . the missionaries help all classes of persons, not those only who are charged with ill abuse or intoxicating drink, but any case that may be handed over to their charge by the magistrate. They deal principally with the first offenders, but they have, by the Grace of God, reclaimed many from the depths of sin and evil. . . . One man, for instance, who had been charged five hundred times, at various English Police Courts.[2]
>
> Many of these cases are visited in their homes—others at a distance are handed over to the parochial clergy, with the details of the circumstances. The aim is to offer sympathy at a time when sympathy is most needed—to try and find a pathway for those to whom life offers only despair.[3]

Other societies, as well as the C.E.T.S., began to send missionaries to the police courts, among them the British Women's Temperance Association, the Manchester and Salford Refuges, and the Salvation and Church Armies. But some two thirds of the missionaries were connected with the C.E.T.S., which organised the work on a diocesan basis.

[1] Thomas Holmes, *Pictures and Problems from the London Police Courts*, 1902, p. 18.
[2] *London Police Court Mission*, annual report, 1902.   [3] *Ibid.*, annual report, 1889.

After the passing of the Probation of First Offenders' Act of
1887, magistrates sometimes chose the police court missionary as
a suitable person for guiding, assisting and befriending those
placed under voluntary supervision. Where the home was
inadequate a young person could be placed in some institution,
and several diocesan police court missions ran homes for boys.
Similarly those without employment could be encouraged to
work in the labour yards which the missions opened to test a
man's capacity to work and they often had small inebriates' homes
to help the alcoholic. The Probation of Offenders' Act of 1907
made supervision compulsory in certain cases, and so supervisors
had to be appointed. In almost every case the local police court
missionary was employed in that capacity, and some of them were
made children's probation officers in connection with the new
children's courts. The Departmental Committee which enquired
into the working of the Act reckoned that

> the value of probation must necessarily depend upon the efficiency
> of the probation officer. . . . So far as we can judge, the courts have
> been fortunate in being able to enlist for this duty a large number of
> men and women who are eminently qualified to perform it. That
> this is so is largely due to the circumstances that have placed at their
> disposal the carefully chosen and experienced staff of the Police
> Court Missions.[1]

From then until 1938, when the probation work was transferred from the voluntary societies to the direct care of the Home
Office, these police court missionaries were an essential part of the
public welfare services. Theirs was highly specialised personal
work, requiring an intimate knowledge of persons and their
environment, and a sympathy and capacity to help at a time of
crisis and decision for which the missionary character was well
suited. They were all men and women with strong Evangelical
beliefs and they pursued their work in this spirit. The parochial
organisation of the Church of England, to which most of them
belonged, made it possible for them to pass on cases from one area
to another and to use the services of the local vicar and his workers

[1] *Departmental Committee on the Working of the Probation of Offenders Act*, 1907, report,
Cmd. 5002, 1910, pars. 28 and 29.

14. 'Bos'n Smith', The Rev. George Charles Smith

15. 'The Soldiers' Friend, Mrs Daniell

16. A Missions to Seamen Service

to maintain continuity. Thus they built up a well-defined and devoted service.

Many of the present-day probation officers, though trained by the Home Office, are nominees of the police court missions, and in the case of the London Police Court Mission reside in their students' hostel. This is therefore an outstanding example of Evangelical social work which pioneered in a particular field, organised the service for some sixty years, and still plays an important part in it. The reason for this probably lies in the fact that these police court missionaries were able to combine a lively Christian faith with a sound scientific and practical approach to the problems of the offender and so were frequently successful in the rebuilding of character.

A final group of offenders for whom some special treatment was particularly needed were juveniles. Attention was constantly being drawn during the nineteenth century to the numbers of offenders under the age of sixteen. Quakers and members of the Clapham Sect who investigated the problem in 1816 found that there were some 8,000 boys engaged in crime in the metropolis, and the prison inspectors in 1849 classified some 13,000 prisoners in the gaols of England and Wales as "juveniles". As is the case now, they tended to form themselves into gangs which were noted for their rivalry and violent fights, which were the terror of some parts of London.

Both now and then parental neglect was an important causative factor, but the reasons for such neglect were different, as the following quotation from the Royal Commission on Popular Education of 1861 makes clear:

These children are without education, not because their parents cannot pay the school pence, but because they prefer to spend their money in the gin shops. Abandoned from the earliest infancy, they either die of starvation or pick up a precarious subsistence by petty depredation. . . . Their parents are so dissipated, their homes are so wretched, the influences to which they are exposed are so demoralising that unless taken away from home they must inevitably be ruined.[1]

Until Mary Carpenter put forward her threefold scheme, in the 1850's, of ragged schools for the children of the very poor,

---

[1] *Newcastle Commission on Popular Education,* 1861, *op. cit.,* p. 386.

industrial schools for children likely to become offenders, and reformatories for those who had been convicted, only the last group had received any serious attention. The Philanthropic Society had been started in 1788 for the "reformation of criminal children", the Warwickshire magistrates had opened a reformatory at Stretton-on-Dunsmore in 1818 and the Children's Friend Society had been formed in 1830 to arrange for the emigration of such children. But relatively few juveniles were reached by these societies and when the first prison inspectors made their visits in the mid-thirties they found the gaols full of children committed for trivial offences as well as many awaiting trial. The authorities suggested separate accommodation for juvenile offenders, and opened Parkhurst on the Isle of Wight for the purpose. But it did not prove successful as a means of juvenile reform and was soon put to other uses.

Meanwhile an experiment in the care of delinquent children was being tried out on the continent, at first by the Evangelicals in Germany. Dr. Wichern of the Inner Mission, who had opened the Rauhe Haus in 1833, began to care for such boys, placing them in small families under the charge of a house-father, who had been specially trained for the position. The boys spent most of their time on agricultural work in the fields, and remained as long as was thought necessary for their good. The same methods were followed by the colony at Mettray, near Tours in France, which was started by Monsieur Demetz in 1839. Both these institutions became known in England, the Rauhe Haus through the writings of the American educationalist, Horace Mann, who in 1843 was much impressed by the "combined power of wisdom and love in the reformation of children" which he found there, and the colony at Mettray as the result of a visit from the chaplain of the Philanthropic Society, Sidney Turner. Interest was roused in this country, and several reformatories on similar lines were opened, among them the Bristol reformatory at Kingswood by Mary Carpenter in 1854. The reformatory movement developed along two lines. On the one hand conferences were held to gain publicity and to try to persuade the authorities to recognise the institutions and send delinquents to them. At the same time an increasing number of homes were opened for such children.

The Evangelicals took little part in the first of these, although Lord Shaftesbury and the Hon. Arthur Kinnaird attended some of the conferences. Mary Carpenter and her Unitarian friends were largely responsible for the passing of the Reformatory Schools Act of 1854 and the Industrial Schools Act of 1857 which placed such institutions on a statutory footing with regular inspection and authorised the courts to send juvenile offenders, or children in need of care and protection, to them.

Because of her Unitarian leanings, many Evangelicals were loth to associate themselves with Mary Carpenter, and therefore they concentrated upon starting their own reformatories and industrial schools. Many of these became linked with the Reformatory and Refuge Union which arose from a conference held in connection with the existing reformatories in February 1858. Lord Shaftesbury was the president for some time and the Hon. Arthur Kinnaird, Lord Radstock, Quintin Hogg and John Macgregor were prominent committee members. Most of its officers were leaders in some form of Evangelical social work. Robert Hanbury, the honorary secretary from 1856 to 1867, had been a founder of the Farningham Homes for Boys; the Rev. Sidney Turner of the Philanthropic Society was closely connected with the Union from the beginning and became its first inspector of reformatories; and other interested members were Dr. Barnardo, William Williams, George Holland, William Quarrier, John Middlemore, George Muller, Ellice Hopkins and Mrs. Meredith.

At first the work of the Union was entirely with children, but it included a far wider range than those sent to reformatories:

Among those who are cared for are children who have already fallen into crime, and those who are in danger of falling; children who from destitution or neglect have become vagrants or idle wanderers; children, who, having been left friendless orphans, have become utterly destitute; children, whose parents have themselves broken the law, or have gone they know not where; children whose natural protectors have turned them into the streets or forced them by ill-treatment to leave their homes; children who, having first been led away by bad companions, have in their turn become bad companions themselves; children whose widowed mothers can strive to earn their bread if but some of their numerous families are provided for; children who only need to be rightly trained, and they will become useful members of society.[1]

In order to care for such children the Union was first and foremost a centre of information. It published a classified list of institutions with types of accommodation and ages of admission, so that workers might know where to send children; it advised how best to deal with different types of children; and it issued the *Reformatory and Refuge Journal* to keep those interested in touch with developments in the movement. It also encouraged those already engaged in the work by starting, in 1856, a fund, now known as the Children's Aid Fund, to give grants to new and expanding institutions; it held conferences for governors and matrons at which views and experiences could be exchanged; it organised an employment bureau for staff; and in 1888 inaugurated an annuity and pension fund. To develop the movement, the Union began in 1857 to advise magistrates as to suitable reformatories ready to receive the various types of child offenders, and to send officers to the police courts to look after the children up for trial. John Macgregor had been responsible for instituting the first of these officers, or "child beadle" as he was called, and as more were appointed their duties not only included helping the magistrate to commit a child to a reformatory or an industrial school, but also providing temporary shelter for any homeless or neglected child he might find, making enquiries as to his home background, and if the latter were not suitable, placing him in a refuge or a children's home.

It was this widespread character of the work of the Union which earned the disapproval of Mary Carpenter and her associates. She felt that more could be done for reformatories and industrial schools if all energies were concentrated on them, and for a time the National Association of Certified Reformatories and Industrial Schools (1881) existed in opposition, though in 1898 it was amalgamated with the Union. No doubt such criticism had some justification for the Union inaugurated the Female Mission to the Fallen in 1858, and in 1862 began work for discharged prisoners. But in the nineteenth century, when prostitution, crime and

[1] *Reformatory and Refuge Union*, annual report, 1863.

drunkenness were so closely allied and when children were constantly involved in their consequences, associations of this nature
had many advantages.

A further difficulty which the Union had to meet was in regard
to its educational standards. Many of the institutions affiliated to it
were not certified or approved by the authorities. This meant that
the teachers could not obtain the necessary certificates for teaching
in the recognised schools. Nor had its inspectors any powers to
enforce their standards, since any institution could withdraw at
will. This was gradually overcome by a concerted effort to raise its
standards, and by a greater number of its institutions gaining State
certification. Since 1933 the Home Office has taken over control
of all the reformatories and industrial schools, renaming them
approved schools, and this has left the Union, now called the
Children's Aid Society, to assist those children in need who do not
come before the juvenile courts, most of whom are children without satisfactory homes of their own.

It is not easy to disentangle the relative parts played by the
Evangelicals and by Mary Carpenter and her colleagues in the reformatory movement, for they were very much interwoven. The
methods of treatment used by the German Evangelical, Dr.
Wichern, at his Rauhe Haus had a widespread influence, but it was
Mary Carpenter who defined his principles more precisely. The
Evangelicals provided many of the reformatories and industrial
schools, but Mary Carpenter was successful in gaining State recognition for them, and in persuading the magistrates to commit
young offenders to them. The Reformatory and Refuge Union
undertook the necessary co-ordination, but did not always do so
in a generally approved manner. Nevertheless, with the aid of the
Evangelicals and of Mary Carpenter, the principle of reforming
the young offender rather than punishing him became the general
rule, and in 1891 it was at last made unnecessary for him to spend
any time in prison before being sent to a reformatory.

The contribution which the Evangelicals made to penal reform
as a whole in the nineteenth century was the emphasis they placed
upon influencing the character of the offender. Instead of sternly
punishing him for his wrong-doing, they regarded him as one
whose whole attitude to life needed to be changed and who

required sympathetic and friendly direction in order to do so. John Howard and the Quakers first introduced these ideas at the end of the eighteenth century, and they were continued by Elizabeth Fry and her friends, Mrs. Meredith, William Wheatley and other Evangelicals throughout the century. In the case of the prisoner undergoing sentence, it was possible to give practical expression to these ideas only in the early decades of the century when the prison administration was loose, and again at the end of the century when those in control had begun to realise the advantages of such treatment. They were applied throughout the second half of the century in the after-care of the prisoner, and in the methods of dealing with the juvenile delinquent outside the adult prisons.

This reformatory approach was not entirely confined, however, to the Evangelicals. It is to be seen in the prison reforms of Jeremy Bentham and of Sir Walter Crofton, and in the approach of Mary Carpenter and her colleagues. Nor was it the only factor which led to a movement away from the retributive outlook in the treatment of crime. Improvements in education and a more humane attitude of mind both had their parts to play. But the Evangelicals provided a constant reminder, even when the authorities were determinately against it, that the reformatory principle was preferable to the punitive.

Today it is this principle which dominates, and voluntary societies continue to work with the State in putting it into effect. This is a sphere of social work in which the Evangelical element is still found. It is present in many of the approved schools which have remained under voluntary management; in some of the discharged prisoners' aid societies whose roots lie in the previous century; in the scope for, and great extension of, prison visiting; and in the probation service, many of whose officers have some link with the police court missions.

CHAPTER XI

The Blind and the Deaf

THE BLIND and the deaf have always received a certain amount of pity, but no active steps were taken to help them until comparatively recently. In a rural economy their position was more tolerable, but with the development of an industrialised and urban society there was little room for those who could not earn a living in competition with the fit. The humanitarians of the late eighteenth century first drew attention to this, and the Evangelicals of the nineteenth century put their ideas into practice.

In most cases their problems were similar. Both had lost one of their faculties which made it more difficult to fit into community life. Therefore the most important thing was to train them in their youth to overcome this defect as far as possible. The State realised this when in 1893 the Elementary Education (Blind and Deaf Children) Act was passed. Deafness made little difference to employment once a person was trained, so for the deaf there was usually no employment problem. But this was not so with the blind. Few of them could find a place in the open market and some provision had to be made for sheltered employment. Then there were those who had gone blind or deaf later in life. They needed help to adjust themselves to a new set of conditions, particularly with regard to their relationships with other people. Finally there were the aged deaf and blind who were usually happier if they could associate with their own kind.

The number of blind in Great Britain in the mid-nineteenth century was around 30,000, very many of them in the large towns. In 1860 it was estimated that

in and around London are nearly 5,000 blind persons of which 100 are in affluent circumstances, 400 subsist on the bounty of friends, about 1,000 drag on a poor, but independent existence, by working at a trade, selling a few baskets and matches or by playing on some musical instrument in the streets or at public houses. The remainder are utterly destitute, just saved from starvation by begging from door to door; recipients of the benefits of the several public charities for the blind in London; or inmates of a workhouse.[1]

Mayhew gives us the following description of the blind beggar:

I am sixty years of age; you wouldn't think it, perhaps, but I am. No, I was not born blind; I lost my sight in the smallpox, five and twenty years ago. I have been begging on the streets eighteen years . . . I make about a shilling a day, never—scarcely never—more, sometimes less—a good deal less; but some folks are very kind to me. I live at Poole's Place, Mount Pleasant. There are a good many engineers about there, and their wives are very kind to me; they have always a halfpenny for me when I go that way.[2]

The blind were the first group of handicapped people to receive voluntary help and Henry J. Wagg, in his *Chronological Survey of Work for the Blind*, mentions several societies for this purpose functioning in the late eighteenth century. But the greater number were formed in the second half of the nineteenth century, particularly in the sixties when some twenty were started. The societies which were in London tended to specialise upon some particular age-group, but those at the large provincial centres usually cared for all the needs of the blind in their area.

The primary need was to educate and train the young and experiments were made in this by Valentin Hauy in Paris in the 1780's. This led to the opening of several schools in this country, the first of which was started by Edward Rushton in Liverpool in 1791, to be followed in two years by one in Bristol under Quaker management, which later was called the Royal School of Industry for the Blind, Bristol. The only other school of definite Evangelical foundation was the Yorkshire School for the Blind (1833) which was a memorial to William Wilberforce. It was noted for its advanced outlook, and one of its superintendents, the Rev. William Taylor, was a founder of Worcester College (1866) "for the blind sons of gentlemen", which was the first institution to provide secondary education for the blind.

---

[1] Edmund C. Johnson, *The Blind of London*, 1860, p. 3.
[2] Peter Quennell, ed., *London's Underworld*, 1952, p. 405.

By the mid-nineteenth century there were some twenty of these schools, most of them in the provincial centres. They were usually residential, accepted pupils from the age of five to twenty-one, taught them to read and write and trained them in some suitable trade. But they had two conspicuous deficiencies. A variety of scripts were used so that a blind person had to learn several if he were to read much literature, and there was no system of after-care for those who had graduated from the institutions. Unless they continued to work in close connection with the school, they were likely to be unable to sell their products and so have little incentive to continue their work. Many of those who took to street trading or begging had received some training in their youth.

An Evangelical, Dr. Thomas Rhodes Armitage, made it his aim in life to remedy these two things, and founded for this purpose the British and Foreign Blind Association for Promoting the Education and Employment of the Blind (1868), which is now known as the Royal National Institute for the Blind. He had spent much of his youth in France and Germany and was well acquainted with work for the blind in those countries. When incipient blindness forced him to give up his medical practice in 1866, he and his wife decided to devote their time and money to the welfare of the blind in England. His main preoccupation was with the education and subsequent employment of the young, while his wife was particularly concerned with the welfare of the adult blind. Together they covered most aspects of work for the blind, and formulated much of the policy which was followed in later years.

His first concern was the use of a uniform script. After studying the various forms of embossed script and talking to numerous blind persons, he decided that Braille was the most suitable for teaching the young, and for the first twenty years of its life the British and Foreign Blind Association devoted its resources to the introduction of Braille. Braille literature was printed by the Association in the early seventies and voluntary transcribers employed to prepare the script. The first book to be embossed was the Bible, "that the blind by this means might be led from theological darkness into light", but the Association did not confine itself to religious publications; all forms of literature were produced, in particular books for use in the schools. Writing in 1868 Dr. Armitage noted that there was

> not a single institution for the blind in the United Kingdom in which the Braille system was in use and the number of individuals who could use it did not exceed twenty,

but by 1882 he was able to report that

> there is now probably no institution in the civilised world where Braille is not used, except in some of those in North America.[1]

This did not mean, however, that all learnt Braille in the schools where it was taught. It was some years after Dr. Armitage's death in 1890 before it became usual for all blind children to be taught Braille.

The use of Braille for the embossing of music was of particular importance since it enabled Dr. Armitage to open up an occupation for the blind which could lead to a lucrative livelihood. He managed to persuade Francis Campbell, the head of the music department at Perkins Institution, Massachusetts, who was on a visit to this country, to stay in England and help him start the Royal Normal College for the Blind (1872) where specially chosen pupils could learn music. Most of these were trained as church organists and piano tuners and were in great demand, so that in 1885 the College reported that 170 of its students were at work, almost all of them in self-supporting jobs where they earned the standard wage. The College, which has now moved from Upper Norwood to Shrewsbury, still trains blind boys and girls as musicians, piano tuners and as typists.

Meanwhile the British and Foreign Blind Association developed as a centre for co-ordinating the work for the blind. Other institutions were invited to conferences to discuss their methods, books, magazines, and music, and various appliances for teaching were produced, and support given to a lending library for the blind which had been started in 1882. When, in 1893, the school boards had to make special provision for blind children they frequently used the schools connected with the Association, and in 1902 began to

[1] J. M. Ritchie, *Concerning the Blind*, 1930, p. 66.

introduce Dr. Armitage's methods into their own classes. Thus
his innovations became the basis upon which the authorities built
up their own system of education for blind children. With the
passage of years the Royal National Institute for the Blind has
not only taken over the administration of many of the other
voluntary societies engaged in such work, but has also been the
source for new developments, the most noteworthy being St.
Dunstan's (1915), which grew out of a committee appointed by
the Institute to consider the needs of those blinded during war
service.

The second matter with which Dr. Armitage was greatly concerned was the after-care of those who had been trained in the
school workshops. The Royal Commission on the Blind, Deaf
and Dumb of 1889 had found that 42 per cent of those trained in
the voluntary institutions were unable to practise the trade taught
them, and about 34 per cent of those in employment earned well
below the living wage. He first thought of using the agents of the
Indigent Blind Visiting Society for this purpose. This Society had
been formed in 1834 by Lord Shaftesbury and Lord Ebury to
read the Scriptures to the blind in their homes and covered most
parts of London. When Dr. Armitage joined the committee in
1866 he introduced day classes for teaching Braille and simple
occupations such as knitting. Paid agents visited the people in
their homes, reported on their progress, and in a few cases helped
those who had learnt a trade to refresh their knowledge and set
up in business. But the agents were too few to undertake such
work adequately, and many of the blind remained unvisited. He
therefore recommended the Saxon system which was used by the
Dresden Institution of the Blind and supported by the German
government. Under this system the training institution kept in
close contact with those who were trained by supplying tools
and raw materials for work at home, by employing an agent to
pay regular visits and by arranging for the sale of the goods
produced. But the British authorities refused to grant aid for the
purpose, and the voluntary institutions had insufficient funds to
finance their own schemes, so little could be done.

The alternative was the sheltered workshop where the adult blind
could work together under supervision and where arrangements

could be made for the goods they produced to be sold for them. A few of the training workshops in Scotland employed their pupils under such conditions after they were fully qualified, but this was not the custom in England. The first workshop for adult employment originated with Elizabeth Gilbert, who made provision in 1853 for the employment of seven blind men in her home. The second daughter of the Bishop of Chichester, she had been blind since the age of three, but her parents were determined to bring her up as a normal child. When she grew up she began to realise that the indigent blind were far worse off than she was, and so she decided to devote her life to helping them. Her acquaintance with William Hanks Levy, a teacher at St. John's Wood School for the Blind, led to the formation of the Association for Promoting the General Welfare of the Blind in 1855 and to the renting of a room in Holborn where, under his supervision, men could be trained in types of work suitable for them and employed on the premises. After a period of experiment she found that basket and brush making were the most suitable trades, and that a retail shop of her own was better than trying to sell to wholesalers. Her shop was opened in Berners Street, but was moved after her death in 1885 to its present site in Tottenham Court Road. Here were combined a retail shop, storerooms, workrooms and training school, the workers living in their own homes but coming daily and being provided with their meals. The numbers for which she found employment were never large, but her work is important as being the first attempt to place blind persons on the same occupational footing as the sighted. She had hoped that her workshop would be self-supporting from the first, but this was not so, and for some time help had to be received from other sources.

As her work became known other institutions were started on the same lines and frequently on her advice. The earliest of these were opened at Cheltenham and Leicester in 1858 and were followed by others at provincial towns, some of them organising home teaching societies for those who lived too far away to come to the workshop. The Alexandra Institute was the first to follow her example in London and the Association for Establishing Workshops for the Blind (1866) tried to extend such work in the metropolis. Workshops have now become a common method of employment for the adult blind who are accessible and capable of training, and most of them follow the traditional occupations of basketry, mat and brush-making, machine knitting and boot and shoe repairs. Similarly in many cases the piece rate earned has to be supplemented to enable the blind worker to earn a living wage.

The purpose of the schools and workshops was to meet the needs of those born blind, or blinded early in life, who were capable of benefiting from training, but there were many, possibly as much as 80 per cent of the total blind, who became blind or almost sightless in later life. Some of these were to be found in the workhouses, but many lived on their own in abject poverty. They were too old to learn Braille and yet alert enough to read if they could be taught. It was to help such persons that Dr. William Moon organised the first home teaching societies in 1855. Like Dr. Armitage, he had been led by incipient blindness to devote his life to the welfare of the blind. Having mastered various embossed scripts he began to teach them to the blind of different ages in Brighton. But many, particularly the older ones, found the contractions used by Braille far too difficult to learn. He therefore evolved a form of embossed script which resembled the Roman characters. This Moon script was not intended to compete with Braille, but was taught to those who had once been able to read for themselves and who would find Braille too hard to learn. The urgent need for the Bible in this easy script led Dr. Moon in 1848 to set up printing presses in his own home, and within ten years the whole Bible had been transcribed.

A trip to London in 1853 showed him the importance of having some systematised scheme whereby the blind could be contacted in their own homes, taught to read, or if unable to do so, to have the Scriptures read to them. For many years, Miss Graham, a zealous Evangelical worker, had helped him and together they visited the poorer parts of London to try and start some home teaching. Wherever they could raise interest, a committee was formed, a teacher appointed, who was usually blind, to search out and instruct all who were willing to learn, and afterwards to lend them books. By 1855 it was possible to form the London

Home Teaching Society with Lord Shaftesbury as president. The work quickly spread over the metropolis and by the end of the century there were seventeen itinerant teachers, each with his own library, who visited the blind in their own homes or in the work-house, and who read the Scriptures to them if they were unable to learn for themselves.

In subsequent years Dr. Moon travelled extensively throughout the British Isles and home teaching societies were formed in most large towns. They were particularly important because of the welfare work which they undertook, and were frequently the first society in an area to care for the blind. In the rural areas of Scotland the same type of work was performed by the missions to the outdoor blind of which the earliest was the Glasgow and West of Scotland Mission (1859). Since few other societies existed, these missions frequently taught trades to the younger men and employed the able-bodied.

Though these societies have been criticised for the standard of their teaching, it is doubtful if Dr. Moon would have regarded this as their primary purpose. They reached a very large number of blind people, who, except where the guardians interpreted their duty broadly, would have received no other form of help. They offered to such people friendship in their loneliness and the comfort of the Scriptures, and so made life easier and more bearable for them. It was for personal rather than educational reasons that these societies had been formed.

There were also a certain number of blind pension societies, a few of which were old foundations, dating back to the fifteenth century, for the elderly blind who were no longer able to work. Such societies were greatly needed in the nineteenth century when industrialism had loosened home ties and when the provision of out-relief was meagre, and during the century several new pension societies were formed. Most of these granted pensions at the usual age of 65 or 70, but the Evangelicals were aware that blind persons needed some financial help at an earlier age than the sighted. Thus, the Christian Blind Relief Society of 1843 was the first society to grant pensions to blind persons of all ages, and it was copied by the Society for Granting Pensions to the Adult Blind (1858) and the Protestant Blind Pension Society (1863).

The pensions paid by these Evangelical societies—usually £6 to £20 per annum according to need—were too small to render any great material aid, but they set the precedent for granting blind pensions at an early age, which the State followed in 1920 when it began to give the old age pension to blind people at the age of fifty.

If the elderly blind had no one to look after them and were unable to care for themselves, they usually had to end their days in the workhouse. The Rev. Henry Bright, sometimes known as the "Blind Evangelist" who had worked for some years with the Indigent Blind Visiting Society, was well aware of this. The Society had run a home for the elderly for some years, but it was closed in 1876, and so Henry Bright and his wife decided to take a few blind women into their own home. Lord Shaftesbury, Dr. Armitage and other leading Evangelicals, among them T. A. Denny, R. Cory and R. C. Morgan, supported the work and the North London Homes for the Blind were opened in Holloway in 1880. The qualifications for entry were "old age, blindness amounting to entire incapacity, poverty and a credible evidence of piety". Over a hundred men and women were cared for, and at the end of the century they claimed to be the only home of the kind in the United Kingdom. The need for such homes was gradually recognised in the early years of the present century and emphasised in the Blind Persons Acts of 1920 and 1938. The North London Homes were included in the official list of approved agencies for this purpose and they still continue to fulfil it.

Another form of care for the blind, which was initiated by Evangelicals, was that of blind babies. Most people today are familiar with the Sunshine Homes for Blind Babies but it is not usually known that homes for such children were started by the Evangelicals in the 1870's. The recognised age for admission to the blind schools was five, so that before this age the child was unlikely to receive any particular attention. Its lack of sight would probably grow worse, and it would suffer from its inability to behave as other children of the same age. Miss E. F. Bready seems to have been the first to do something for them, opening the Kilburn Home for Blind Children in 1870. She accepted them from birth and sent them to suitable institutions when they were old enough, and some of her children eventually graduated from the Royal Normal College. Miss S. Rye followed her example in 1874 by starting the Home for Blind Children in College Avenue, Hackney. She took them from the age of two until they could be sent to a blind school, and any who were unacceptable at the schools were kept at her home in Wood Green. Little is known as to how these homes were run, but they preceded by several years the separate houses which were set apart for blind children by the large orphanages, and by several decades the Kindergarten School for Blind Children at Birmingham (1905).

The result of this awakened interest in the blind in the second half of the nineteenth century, brought about almost entirely by the Evangelicals, was the formation of numerous small and local groups to help the blind. This raised the reprobation of the Charity Organisation Society which in 1876 reported adversely upon their work. No doubt some of the societies were inefficiently run, but the real trouble was the lack of co-ordination between them. Gardner's Trust of 1882, which distributed its proceeds between all the different forms of voluntary work, did not improve the situation. Some form of independent control was needed and this could only be supplied when the numbers and distribution of blind persons in Great Britain was known. This came about in 1920 when the registration of all blind persons was required and the local authorities assumed some degree of responsibility for their welfare.

Thus there has developed a partnership between the statutory and voluntary agencies in the care of the blind. Many of the voluntary agencies still continue with their work, and the influence of the nineteenth century Evangelicals is still to be found in the predominating part which the home teaching societies play in carrying out the social policy of general blind welfare. Braille and Moon, both of which owe their popularity to Evangelicals, are the most usual forms of blind script; the Royal National Institute for the Blind, which was the child of Dr. Armitage, has become the centre today from which new methods of learning and teaching are disseminated and more varied services developed;

and the aim of Elizabeth Gilbert for the employment of the blind
on a parity with the sighted is now the policy of all concerned
with blind welfare. Although today there is a greater attention to
a psychological understanding of the problems of the blind, the
basic methods for helping them remain very much the same, and
it is these which were first suggested and put into practice by
some of the outstanding Evangelical social workers.

While the blind occupy a privileged place in the social services
for the handicapped because they are unable to earn their living
without special training and employment, the difficulties of the
deaf are mainly social and spiritual. Those who are born deaf are
unable to speak and so the first essential is to teach them the use
of words. Once they have learnt this they can usually take their
place among the hearing. Those who are deafened later in life
need help to adjust themselves to the life of the community of
which they still form part but in which they are now unable to
participate fully because of their infirmity. In both cases psychological attitudes are of outstanding importance, though they differ
between those born deaf and those deafened later in life. As one
writer points out:

> At the beginning of their lives the deaf are abnormals shut off from
> that stream of verbally conveyed ideas which moulds the individual
> mind to general sameness with the mental pattern of society, and
> throughout their lives the deaf are struggling towards full normalcy.
> The deafened, on the other hand, are normals threatened with the
> horror of abnormalcy. To the change in their state, and particularly
> to the change in the behaviour of other people towards them, they
> are peculiarly sensitive—the least tendency on the part of the public
> to treat them as "different" from normals fills them with acute dis-
> tress, in some cases, indeed, amounting to torment.[1]

One of the main difficulties in making any provision for the
deaf is to find out where they are and how many there are of
them. This is not so hard in the case of deaf children, for parents
are usually willing for a deaf-mute to be taught, and since the
passing of the Elementary Education (Blind and Deaf Children)
Act of 1893 the schools will notify to the authorities those children

[1] J. D. Evans, "Voluntary Organisations for the Welfare of the Deaf" in A. F. C.
Bourdillon, ed. *The Voluntary Social Services in the Modern State*, 1945, pp. 73-4.

who are obviously unable to hear. But adults are rarely willing
to confess that they are deaf unless their deafness is acute and they
try to follow their normal manner of living far beyond the time
that they can do so adequately. Thus the State made no provision
for the adult deaf until the National Assistance Act of 1948 and
left voluntary charity to do its best for them.

The lack of speech of the deaf-mute usually has no physiological
cause, but is entirely the result of deafness. Therefore the first
essential is to bring about some means of communication. Two
methods of teaching the deaf had been tried on the continent in
the eighteenth century. The French, following the lead of Abbé
Charles Michel de L'Epée, used the miming or manual method,
by which signs were made with the hands; and the Germans, on
the lines of Samuel Heinicke, adopted the oral method of teaching
the deaf how to speak in the normal manner with the mouth,
and how to lip read when others spoke to them. Obviously the
first of these methods could be acquired more easily and quickly,
but it had the serious disadvantage of only enabling the deaf to
communicate with those people who had also learnt this method
of communication, and it did not enable them to take part in
ordinary conversation. Both methods required special teachers
and teaching in separate schools or classes, and so deaf children
could not mingle with hearing children at their lessons.

The first schools for the deaf in Great Britain were for those
who could pay, and their methods were closely guarded by the
Braidwood family which supplied most of the early teachers,
among them Joseph Watson. It was two members of the Clapham
Sect, Henry Thornton and William Wilberforce, who awoke
the nation's conscience to the fact that the deaf were a group in
the community in need of help, and that nothing was being done
to teach the deaf children of the poor. In 1792 Henry Thornton,
John Townsend, the minister of the Congregational Church at
Bermondsey, and the Rev. Henry Cox Mason helped to form a
society to undertake the education of the "indigent deaf" in the
parish of Bermondsey, renting a house in which six deaf-mutes
were installed and engaging Joseph Watson to teach them. Since
the numbers applying were always greater than could be admitted, an institution known as the Asylum for the Deaf and

Dumb Poor was built in the Old Kent Road in 1807, and it became the leading school for the deaf children of the poor. In 1862 it moved to Margate and is now called the Royal School for Deaf and Dumb Children. Children were admitted to this Asylum at an early age to "protect them from a cruel and competitive world". This school introduced two new features for teaching the deaf children of the poor—residential accommodation so that regular and continuous tuition might be given, and free teaching of the highest quality then available. Instruction was given in both the oral and manual methods, ordinary elementary subjects were also learnt, and on the advice of William Wilberforce, tailoring and shoemaking were taught to the boys, needlework, knitting and housework to the girls, and employment was found for them when they left. Institutions, modelled on this school were to be found at Birmingham, Manchester, Liverpool and several of the other large provincial centres in the early decades of the century.

But this high standard of education was not maintained, and in 1856 when a deputation from Ireland visited these schools they found that the number of free places was greatly reduced, that the pupils only stayed for five or six years which was too short to give them a good grounding, that in almost every institution the manual rather than the oral method was taught, and that only the Edinburgh Institution provided any occupational training. Most of the teachers were men, even in the girls' classes, and they showed little sympathy with or understanding of the psychological needs of the children. Nor did they exercise any after-care. The pupils were discharged at the age of fourteen or fifteen with no attempt to help them find a place in a hearing world. Thus they fell far short of the standards set by the Old Kent Road Asylum.

Two Evangelicals, Thomas Arnold and Dr. William Stainer, were largely responsible for rectifying this. Thomas Arnold, a zealous Moravian, who later became a Congregational minister in charge of Doddridge Chapel, Northampton, was the chief exponent of the oral method in England, and he did his utmost to introduce its use into the schools. In 1868 he had opened a secondary school for the deaf, and by using the oral method enabled the first deaf-mute boy to matriculate. His books, *The Method of Teaching the Deaf and Dumb Speech, Lip-reading and Language* (1881) and the *Education of Deaf Mutes; a Manual for Teachers* (1888) became standard textbooks for those teaching the deaf. He urged the use of this method in the two training colleges for teachers at Fitzroy Square and Ealing, and was firmly supported by the first international conference for the deaf at Milan in 1880, and by subsequent conferences. His major opposition came from the British Deaf and Dumb Association (1890) which adopted the rather short-sighted policy that the rising generation of deaf children would be cut off from social intercourse with other deaf people if they did not learn the manual method. Nevertheless he persuaded many of the institutions to teach the oral method, was supported by the Royal Commission on the Blind, Deaf and Dumb of 1889, and was successful in getting it used in the classes of the London School Board when in 1893 it began to provide its own classes for the education of deaf children. The result of this insistence on the oral method was that by the early twentieth century there were few schools in which this method was not taught.

But in the 1870's only a very small proportion of deaf children —about one tenth—received any education and these were mostly the children of parents who could pay. By the Poor Law Act of 1862 and subsequent acts the guardians were allowed to send deaf children of the poor to one of the voluntary institutions and to contribute up to £25 per annum for their keep, but very few did so and a large number of the indigent deaf children received no instruction whatsoever. After the passing of the Education Act of 1870 it was found that many deaf children had to be excluded from the schools on the grounds that they could not benefit from the education. It was at this stage that Dr. William Stainer made the suggestion that they could quite well be educated in the same schools as hearing children, but in separate classes with special teachers.

Dr. Stainer had been a teacher at the Old Kent Road Asylum and was the co-editor of the *Quarterly Review on Deaf-Mute Education*. He was asked by the London School Board in 1874 to try out his suggestion and began that year to teach five deaf children in connection with one of the schools. His example was copied by the school boards in Leicester, Nottingham and Oldham, and as a result day classes for deaf children became a duty of the education authorities in 1893. Many parents, however, found it difficult to send their children to these schools because of the distance from their homes and because the school boards were not authorised to pay for food or lodging for such children. Stainer, therefore, opened residential homes for them where they could board by the week or term when classes were being held. The first of the Stainer Homes was opened in 1875 in the Pentonville Road and housed twenty children, and by 1887 there were six of these homes in different parts of London. Though recognised by the London School Board, they were financed from voluntary sources, and only the education of the children was provided by the authorities. After the Act of 1893, when the school boards were permitted to set up their own residential homes, they followed closely the pattern of those of Dr. Stainer, and became the means by which all deaf children were enabled to obtain some education. The day classes which Dr. Stainer introduced are still the means of educating deaf children in the great centres of population, though it is more usual for children from the rural areas to be sent to the residential schools.

The after-care of those who had passed through the schools and day classes became the responsibility of the missions for the deaf which had been established partly with this in view and partly to help those deafened later in life. Most of them started with the purpose of enabling the deaf to take part in religious services though they nearly all developed a widespread scheme of welfare activities. Scotland took the lead in this when, in 1822, John Anderson conducted worship in his own house in Glasgow for the deaf "in a way in which they could understand". In typical Victorian style they stated that

> our design is to carry the Gospel to the Deaf and Dumb of this great city, and throughout the towns of the West of Scotland; to help them to bear patiently their daily burden, and to resist firmly all evil and intemperate habits; to raise the standard of right among them; and with Divine blessing, to lead them to a knowledge of Him who

"hath done all things well, who maketh both the deaf to hear and the dumb to speak".[1]

The first deaf congregation in Edinburgh was established in 1830 in a small room in Lady Stair's Close, Lawnmarket, and within five years there had developed from it the Edinburgh Deaf and Dumb Benevolent Society which assisted those in distress and helped to maintain the poor and aged not only in the capital city but through its branches in other parts of Scotland.

In England the first and largest of these missions was the Royal Association in Aid of the Deaf and Dumb, still known as the R.A.A.D.D. Its initial purpose, when opened as the Refuge for the Destitute Deaf and Dumb in Holborn in 1840, had been to provide welfare services, and in particular to train boys and girls from the educational institutions in some trade or in domestic subjects. For a time it had a shop in Theobalds Road to sell the goods which were made in its workshops, but eventually it concentrated upon finding ordinary employment for those whom it trained. Although religious services were held in 1842 at the Chapel of the Scottish Corporation in Fetter Lane and later in Red Lion Square, Bloomsbury, this did not become an important part of their work until Samuel Smith of the Doncaster Institution for the Deaf was appointed as missioner in 1855. Under his superintendence the work of the R.A.A.D.D. moved rapidly forward. Taking Holy Orders in 1861, he became the vicar of the first church for the deaf, St. Saviour's in Oxford Street (1873). London was divided into districts, each with its missionary and eventually its church. William Stainer was in charge of the western district for a time and John Macgregor took a close interest in the work of the Association. The R.A.A.D.D. became the pattern for the many missions for the deaf which were formed in Great Britain in the second half of the nineteenth century.

Some twenty of these missions were started between 1850 and 1880, seventeen in the decade 1880–1890 when the evidence of the Royal Commission drew public attention to the needs of the deaf, and eighteen in the first thirty years of the present

[1] *Mission to the Deaf and Dumb in Glasgow and the West of Scotland, a brief account of its history, development and activities,* 1937.

century. Some were started by the Church of England, either as diocesan work, as was the case with the Carlisle Diocesan Association for the Deaf and Dumb (1854); or linked with several churches in an area, like the Church Mission to the Deaf and Dumb in South Staffordshire and Shropshire (1886). But the majority were undenominational, and were frequently started to supplement the work of the schools. The Liverpool Mission (1864), which arose from services held in the local deaf and dumb school, and the North Staffordshire Mission which was an ancillary of the Manchester Institution for the Deaf, were examples of these. Four of the missions were in Scotland and three in Ireland and, according to the Royal Commission of 1889, of the 12,000 deaf in Great Britain some 4,000 were visited regularly by them.

Social and welfare activities always formed an important part of their work. Jobs were found for those who had just left the deaf schools or who were capable of normal employment. Social and recreational evenings were held for all age groups and classes organised for teaching the sign alphabet. There were usually sick and provident clubs to which all were encouraged to contribute, and many missions, as was usual at that time, had their own branch of the National Deaf and Dumb Teetotal Society (1877). The Liverpool Mission (1864), which was a particularly large and thriving one, had a branch of the Girls' Friendly Society, a needle-women's guild and a young men's auxiliary. But the most important aspect of this work of the mission was the personal contact which each member had with the missionary. He was the friend of all, acted as the link between the hearing and the deaf, sorting out many a difficulty and interpreting the actions of the deaf to those unable to understand their point of view.

The missions had one important drawback in that they all used the sign alphabet, which tended to emphasise the isolation of the deaf person from the community and to force him to rely entirely upon the company of other deaf people. Recently they have tried to overcome this by encouraging the study and practice of lip-reading. Most of these missions still function and are usually very popular with the deaf and deafened. Their work is now co-ordinated by the Royal National Institute for the Deaf (1911) which acts as a centre for promoting their interests and improving their welfare. Though, under the National Assistance Act, 1948, the local authorities have the ultimate responsibility for the welfare of the deaf, these missions still undertake a very large amount of the welfare activities.

Little was done for the aged deaf because their infirmity did not often debar them from participating in the pension and almshouse charities which were available for the aged poor in general. A few of the missions had pension schemes financed from their provident funds, but only one society existed solely for the purpose, the Charitable and Provident Society for Granting Pensions to the Aged and Infirm Deaf and Dumb (1836), of which William Stainer was treasurer, thus linking it closely with the R.A.A.D.D. It granted pensions of £6 to £10 per annum to deaf persons over sixty who had been deaf since the age of ten and who were unable to follow any occupation. But the Society had only some thirty pensioners, which were negligible in relation to the numbers of the aged indigent deaf, who were mostly to be found in the workhouses.

Nor were there many homes exclusively for the aged deaf. Two of the larger ones were Evangelical homes, one for men and the other for women. The men's home was opened at Dorking in 1887, was called the Lawrence Home after Lady Lawrence, one of its benefactors, moved first to Wennington and then to Woolwich where it was taken over by the R.A.A.D.D. and is now the Tower House Home. The home for women had been started in 1851 as the British Asylum for Deaf and Dumb Females by Mr. and Mrs. Sutton at Homerton. It was both a training home for women and girls, to enable them to earn their own living, and a refuge for destitute deaf women. It, too, has now become closely connected with the R.A.A.D.D. Thus the R.A.A.D.D. has assumed an increasingly important part in the welfare of the adult deaf in the Home Counties, and now has some thirty centres where their spiritual, social and general welfare is cared for.

The welfare services for both the blind and the deaf followed a very similar pattern in the nineteenth century. At first there was a growing consciousness that their needs were dissimilar from those of the ordinary poor, and therefore not met by the existing services of the Poor Law. This was followed by the provision of special education and training for the young; then by care for those blinded or deafened in later life; and finally by some small but significant efforts to deal with the particular problems of the aged. Criticism of the methods adopted was rife, particularly on the part of the Charity Organisation Society. Nevertheless, as we have seen, when the authorities began to take some interest in these services at the end of the century they followed very closely the basic principles which had been used by the voluntary societies.

The noticeable point in the development of these services is the predominant part played by Evangelicals both in initiating them and in introducing methods which are still used today. It was the Clapham Sect which first managed to draw sustained attention to the need for training both the blind and deaf children of the poor, and which encouraged the early institutions for this purpose. Outstanding educationalists, such as Thomas Armitage, William Moon, Elizabeth Gilbert, Thomas Arnold and Dr. Stainer were all Evangelicals; the home visiting societies for the adult blind and the missions for the deaf were Evangelical organisations; and most of the work for the aged was done by Evangelical societies. At the present time, when the welfare services for the blind and the deaf are performed partly by statutory and partly by voluntary groups, it is still these nineteenth century societies which undertake the greater part of the work, on lines which were first suggested by these Evangelicals.

CHAPTER XII

The Unsound in Mind and Body

APART FROM the deaf and the blind, the other main groups of handicapped people were the insane and the cripples, as they were called in nineteenth century terminology—people whose minds or bodies did not function normally, so making them unable to play their full part in the life of the community. But whereas the cripple could be left to fend for himself without causing any harm to others, this was not the case with the insane. Their activities were therefore controlled by legislation from the early eighteenth century, but it is only since the National Assistance Act of 1948 that the authorities have had any obligation for the welfare of the adult cripple.

In the early years of the nineteenth century the insane were in a very poor state. As the report of the Committee on Madhouses in England in 1815 found:

> There are not in the country a set of Beings more immediately requiring the protection of the legislature than the persons in this state; a very large proportion of whom are entirely neglected by their relatives and friends. If the treatment of those in the middling or in the lower classes of life, shut up in hospitals, private madhouses, or parish workhouses, is looked at, your committee are persuaded that a case cannot be found where the necessity of a remedy is more urgent.[1]

Three important things were needed. One was more strictly drawn legislation with regard to certification; the second was a differentiation between the different types of insanity and so the provision of separate methods of treatment; and the third was an increase in the number of institutions taking care of the insane that

[1] *Committee on Madhouses in England*, report, 1815, H.L.70 of 1819, p. 3.

they need no longer occupy space in the workhouses, hospitals and prisons.

The various Acts passed in the first half of the nineteenth century made some improvement in all of these, and they culminated in the Lunatics Act of 1845, often known as "the magna carta of the liberation of the insane" which was the beginning of modern legislation. It established a board of commissioners in lunacy which controlled admission to, and conditions within, all institutions in Great Britain which housed the insane. It was followed in 1886 by the Idiots Act which was the first to make a distinction between the different types of insanity.

Of the many reformers who were responsible for this legislation the most outstanding was Lord Shaftesbury. He was only twenty-six when, after a few months in Parliament, he had become one of the metropolitan lunacy commissioners and was assiduously visiting most of the asylums, while at the age of eighty-four he was still defending the operation of the existing laws in the House of Lords. In the intervening period he had taken a strong stand against Edwin Chadwick's proposals to bring the county asylums within the scope of the Poor Law; as chairman of the Lunacy Commissioners he constantly defended their work in Parliament, moving an address to the Crown in 1852 which resulted in the opening of Broadmoor (1860) as the first asylum for criminal lunatics; and in 1841 he helped to found the Medico-Psychological Association to study the mental processes of the insane. His personal vigilance over the administration of the law, and his care for the patient in the asylum stamped his personality upon most of what was done for the insane in the nineteenth century. In Scotland, Evangelical influence was exerted over legislation in a similar manner by Lord Kinnaird, the Member for Perth, who, with the Member for St. Andrews, succeeded in securing the passage of the Act of 1857 which provided for a board of commissioners in lunacy for Scotland with functions similar to those of the board already existing in England.

Evangelical influence was also to be found in the methods of treatment used in the asylums for the insane. The old physical methods of treatment—bleeding and purging, the frequent use of intimidation to cow the patient, and leg-locks and strait-jackets to restrain him—were gradually replaced, largely due to the new methods introduced by William Tuke and his successors at the Retreat at York. William Tuke had been appalled at the conditions which he found in the York asylum when visiting a Quaker colleague, and determined to start an institution where sympathy and consideration would be shown, and the patient treated as normally as possible. Tuke's wife was not impressed with the idea. "Thou hast many children of thy brain, William, but this last one will be an idiot," she told him. Yet in 1792 the Retreat was opened and became the model for most future asylums. Samuel Tuke, his grandson, says of it in 1813:

> In describing the particular benefits of this undertaking it seems proper to mention that of occasionally using the patients to such employment as may be suitable and proper for them, in order to relieve the languors of idleness, and to prevent the indulgence of gloomy sensations. . . . The Superintendent has also endeavoured to furnish a source of amusement to these patients whose walks are necessarily circumscribed, by supplying each of the courts with a number of animals, such as rabbits, seagulls, hawks and poultry. These creatures are generally very familiar with the patients and it is believed that they are not only the means of innocent pleasure, but that the intercourse with them sometimes tends to awaken the social and benevolent feelings.[1]

As a result of evidence given at various select committees in the early decades of the century, the methods at the Retreat became widely known and the ideal towards which every type of institution strove. By the middle of the century its methods had become the accepted ones in the county asylums and the more enlightened private madhouses. The work of the Retreat continues on the same basis, remaining a small institution, financed largely by the Quakers, but making its main purpose the advancement of new methods of treatment in which the spiritual and moral aspects of mental health play as important a part as the medical.

An important problem with regard to these county asylums was the difficulty which patients found in adapting themselves on release to normal life. Most of the paupers migrated almost at once to the workhouse where they either remained or were returned

[1] Garrod and Knight, "The Retreat", in *Friends' Quarterly Examiner*, April 1946.

again to the asylum. Lord Shaftesbury helped to solve this when in 1879 he became one of the founders and the first president of the Mental After-Care Association. This Association boarded out patients from the asylums with suitable people until work could be found for them. It had an uphill task, for there was a strong prejudice against employing persons from the asylums and also a lack of co-operation from many of the asylums themselves. Only gradually did the authorities awaken to the real value of the work and it was not until the end of the first world war that full co-operation was shown. Since 1928 the London general hospitals have used its facilities for caring for those in the early stages of mental and nervous disorder and it still continues to deal with both types of case, sending them when necessary for a brief change of scene and air, and assisting them to find suitable employment.

Until the middle of the nineteenth century the term "insane" covered both those who were mentally ill and those who were retarded in their mental development. Many of the latter, mental defectives as they were called, were to be found mingled with the lunatics in the asylums, hospitals and workhouses, and they also formed an appreciable proportion of those who lived in the refuges and common lodging houses or passed in and out of the prisons. It was not until the Idiots Act of 1886 that the State recognised this distinction, and this was largely as a result of the provision that the Rev. Andrew Reed, a Congregational minister, had made for this type of child. In the thirties he had observed the difficulties of mentally defective children in his orphan asylums, and had gone over to the continent to study experimental work which was being done there in relation to such children. This led him to consider opening a separate institution for mentally defective children who were capable of some training. Public support was forthcoming, the patronage of the Queen and Prince Consort gained, and an experimental home for twenty-seven idiot children was opened at Park House, Highgate, in 1848. It proved successful and a prominent M.P., Sir Morton Peto, offered the lease of Essex Hall, Colchester, as a permanent institution.

Reed favoured a regional scheme to cover the whole of England, with the result that Earlswood, near Redhill, was opened in 1855, the Western Counties Asylum, Exeter, and the Royal Albert

Asylum at Lancaster in 1864, and the Midland Counties Asylum at Knowle, Birmingham, in 1868. The trust deeds of Earlswood give an idea of their purpose. They state

> that the design of this charity be, not merely to take the idiot and the imbecile under its care, but especially, by the skilful and earnest application of the best means in his education, to improve his bodily powers, to prepare him, as far as possible, for the duties and enjoyments of life.[1]

The method followed was to give the children the care and love of the ordinary family and at the same time to teach them some simple trade such as shoe-making, tailoring, mat-making, carpentry, gardening, farm work or printing which they could follow under supervision when they grew up. At first it was hoped to make the pupils self-supporting, but this proved impossible and after a probationary period the pupils were allowed to remain for life. Some of them were paid for by their relatives, but most were supported by the charity and only the Royal Albert and Starcross took pauper pupils for whom the guardians contributed the same amount as they did to the lunatic asylums.

Until the Idiots Act of 1886 Andrew Reed's asylums were the only institutions outside London where mental defectives could be educated and trained. The Metropolitan Asylums Board, however, copied his methods in 1870 when they opened asylums at Leavesden and Caterham for adult defectives and at Darenth for children. Though the Idiots Act empowered local authorities to build similar institutions, few did so because they depended to a large extent upon mental defectives for the domestic work in their institutions. It was not until the present century that they recognised their responsibility for the pauper defectives and began to build institutions for them, and when they did so they followed closely the methods of Andrew Reed in providing simple tasks which would both occupy and interest the defective.

Andrew Reed's asylums also became renowned as pioneer establishments in the study of mental deficiency. It was Dr. D. F. Duncan, of the Eastern Counties Asylum, who first suggested that defectives should be graded into idiots, imbeciles and simpletons,

---

[1] *Royal Commission on the Care of the Feebleminded*, report, Cmd. 4202, 1908, p. 479.

and each given appropriate forms of treatment, and this was the classification which was recommended by the special committee of the Charity Organisation Society on the Education and Care of Idiots, Imbeciles, and Harmless Lunatics in 1877, and was later adopted by the Idiots Act of 1886. This special committee also drew attention to the feebleminded, or those whose defect was only slight. The Y.W.C.A., the M.A.B.Y.S. and other societies for the adolescent frequently came into contact with girls of this type, since most of them were incapable of keeping a job for any length of time, and many were easily led into immorality or crime. Mrs. Meredith had for some time set aside a cottage in her Village Homes at Addlestone for girls of low intellect who were criminally inclined, the M.A.B.Y.S. had a home for girls of low intellect in Whitechapel, and Miss Stacey at Birmingham trained so-called "improvable" girls and either employed them on laundry work at the home or sent them out to daily domestic jobs. But there was need for some more co-ordinated action. This was forthcoming when the National Association for the Care of the Feebleminded was formed in 1895. It was at the home of an Evangelical, Isabella Head, who was a leader in the Factory Workers' Union of the Y.W.C.A., that the Association was first mooted and she took a prominent part in its formation. The Association was successful in gaining the affiliation of the many homes which were springing up in the large towns to help feebleminded girls and also in pressing for a Royal Commission to consider the needs of the feebleminded. This Commission reported in 1908 and as a result the Mental Deficiency Act of 1913 was passed which was the first act to deal comprehensively with defectives. The National Association for the Care of the Feebleminded was re-organised as the Central Association for the Care of Mental Defectives and now forms part of the National Association for Mental Health.

The epileptics form a category of their own since the sufferer has lucid periods in which he can take part in normal activities and be treated as an ordinary rational human being, and in the early stages of the disease a cure is often possible. Neither of these things was widely recognised in England until the last decade of the nineteenth century. Epileptic children frequently languished at home without medical care or education, and the adolescent and adult epileptic would be found doing the domestic jobs in the workhouse until the severity of the disease made it necessary for them to be moved to the lunatic asylum.

Attention was drawn to this situation in England in the 1890's largely as the result of two foreign experiments in the care of epileptics in France and Germany, both conducted by groups of Evangelicals. The first was that of Pastor John Bost at La Force, near Dordogne in South West France. Finding that little was done by existing charities for incurables and imbeciles, he opened an institution for them in 1848, calling it the "Famille Evangelique". In 1855 separate homes were started for epileptics, run on the family system, where open-air treatment rather than the usual bromides and hydropathy was followed and where each patient was encouraged to engage in outdoor activities so far as possible. News of this reached Germany, and a meeting was held at Bielefeld, a small town on the Rhine, by the provincial committee of the Lutheran Inner Mission, following which it was decided to start a similar type of institution in Germany. In 1872 "Bethel" was opened by Pastor Friedrich Von Bodelschwingh to house twenty-six epileptics. This developed on a much larger scale than in France. It became possible to group different age groups and degrees of illness together and to provide appropriate treatment for them. A village was gradually built with homes for each class of epileptic, a hospital, a school for the children, industrial and agricultural employment for those who were able to undertake it, and an asylum for imbecile epileptics. Deacons and deaconesses were trained to care for them and to start home mission work of the same sort in other parts of the country.

The nearest approach to this in England was the epileptic colony at Lingfield in Surrey, started by the Christian Union for Social Service soon after it was established in 1896. At first there were two separate homes for epileptic boys and girls. Another for those over school age was opened at Starnthwaite in Westmorland, and a farm at Browhead was adapted for those who were capable of work. For several years they were cared for by "brothers" and "sisters" trained by the Union. This turned out to be the most successful of the experiments of the Christian Service Union, as it is now called, and this part of their work is still carried on at Lingfield.

Bielefeld also influenced other forms of work for epileptics in England. The Maghull Home, near Liverpool, was started in 1888 by a merchant, Henry Cox, who, at the instigation of his parish doctor, had visited Bielefeld. An old manor house was taken, male epileptics with a prospect of cure were accepted, and they were given "a well ordered home life, plain diet and careful supervision and employment". The Meath Home of Comfort was opened near Godalming in 1892 to provide the same facilities for women and girls, especially those connected with the Girls' Friendly Society in which Lady Meath was interested. Since neither of these followed the colony method, which was an important feature of Bielefeld, the National Society of Epileptics was formed in 1893 which opened the Chalfont Colony in Buckinghamshire for sane epileptics. It had a farm of 200 acres and nine residential homes with room for nearly two hundred colonists. Farm work and gardening were the chief occupations for men and needlework, housework and laundry work for women.

The constructive work of these institutions led directly to Government action. It was realised by the school board officers and by interested members of the public that there were numbers of epileptic children who could benefit from such treatment and many other less bad cases who needed some special care. A committee investigated the subject in 1898 and the Education (Defective and Epileptic) Children Act was passed in 1899 which made provision for special classes at the schools for epileptic children and encouraged voluntary societies to open more homes for severe cases. In some instances the guardians opened their own homes, as for example the Lanho colony in Lancashire started by the Chorlton and Manchester guardians. But quite often they paid for pauper children to be sent to the existing voluntary institutions, in particular to the Lingfield colony which expanded greatly at this time. All the voluntary institutions which have been mentioned here are still functioning. They are the chief means of residential care for epileptics today and they continue to follow the methods put into practice by Pastor Bodelschwingh. But with modern drugs it is possible for many more to remain in their homes, and to take part in the ordinary life of the community, and this is encouraged so far as possible.

Thus the Evangelicals did the pioneer work, not only for the institutional care of the epileptic, but for most of the other groups of the insane. The only group in which their influence was not predominant was that of the feebleminded, and here the Charity Organisation Society supplied the initiative and helped to organise many of the homes. In the legislative sphere, the Benthamites played an important part in helping to gain the passage of early legislation, and therefore in defining the ways in which the services should be administered. But Lord Shaftesbury was largely responsible for the ways in which such legislation was interpreted, and in particular for isolating the care of the insane and preventing it from passing into the control of the Poor Law authorities.

The outstanding contribution of the Evangelicals in this form of welfare work was their kindness and consideration, derived no doubt from their religious beliefs, which made it possible, within a quarter of a century, to substitute methods of comparative freedom and of simple occupational activities for the close confinement and physical restraint which had been characteristic forms of treatment for so long. The fundamental desire to make the life of the patient as normal as possible and, where suitable conditions prevailed, to restore him to the life of the community can be traced to the work of the Evangelicals in the nineteenth century. This has become the prevalent attitude today, and the one which makes the positive approach of mental health the goal of the social services of this type, rather than the cure of mental sickness once it has occurred.

The cripple was in a very different category from the insane. His deformity might cause a certain amount of interest and sympathy, but there was no vital need for anything to be done for him and he could usually earn some sort of living even if it were only by begging in the streets. Mayhew describes for us the crippled street-seller of nutmeg-graters:

> His struggles to earn his own living (notwithstanding his physical incapacity even to put the victuals to his mouth after he has earned them) are instances of nobility of pride that are I believe without parallel. The poor creature's legs and arms are completely withered;

indeed he is scarcely more than head and trunk . . . he is unable even
to stand, and cannot move from place to place but on his knees,
which are shod with leather caps, like the heels of a clog, strapped
round the joint; the soles of his boots are on the upper leathers, that
being the part always turned towards the ground while he is crawling
along . . .

"I sell nutmeg-graters and funnels" said the cripple to me. . . .
"On a wet day when I can't get out, I often go without food. I may
have a bit of bread and butter given me, but that's all—then I lie
a-bed. I was in the workhouse with a fever all the summer. I was
destitute afterwards, and obliged to begin selling in the streets. The
Guardians gave me 5/- to get stock. I had always dealt in tin ware, so
I knew where to go to buy my things."[1]

Here was an adult managing to keep himself; it was therefore pre-
sumption on the part of the Victorians to think of doing anything
for him. But the crippled child was different. He needed protection
and help to train him for some future employment, and the Victorians recognised this.

It is difficult to say how many of these children there were. A
school board enquiry at the end of the century found that five out
of every 1,000 school-children were crippled, maimed, or deformed, but it took no account of those unable to attend school
because of their disability. These had to stay at home and

> the slums became dotted with little cripples on improvised beds,
> generally soap-boxes tied to the rails of their filthy tenements;
> when it rained they were carried in and placed in the lobbies for
> shelter.[2]

The less helpless were to be met at the street corners, selling or
begging for alms, and in some instances they were hired out to a
master who employed them to trade on the pity of the passer-by.
Two things were needed; medical attention to help them to overcome the restrictions of their deformity and make it easier for
them to find work; and some education and recreation which
would give them something to do and so make life happier for
them. Humanitarian motives were behind the majority of the
developments in medical aid, as, for example, the work of Sir

[1] Peter Quennell, ed., *Mayhew's London*, 1952, p. 155.
[2] Sir Robert Jones, *The Cripple*, pamphlet, n.d.

Robert Jones and Dame Agnes Hunt at Baschurch in Shropshire, which culminated in the opening of the well-known orthopaedic hospital at Oswestry. But most of the educational and social work for crippled children was performed by the Evangelicals.

Since many of these crippled children were confined to their homes the most urgent need was to seek them out and see what could be done for them. As we have already seen, the ragged schools were the first to do this. John Pounds had set the example at his ragged school in Portsmouth, where he had cared for several crippled children, the shoeblack brigades had employed some of the less disabled and in 1860 some ragged school teachers had temporarily started a club for young cripples. But it was only when Charles Boyer had drawn attention to the numbers of crippled children in the East End of London in 1888 that the Shaftesbury Society decided to concentrate upon such children. Miss Cole, a friend of Annie Macpherson, was chosen to direct the work and it became one of the principal functions of the Society. The aim was to find, for each crippled child, a wise and sympathetic Christian friend, who would visit the child and do what she could to bring some brightness into its life. London was divided into four districts, each under a local superintendent who was assisted by voluntary visitors. Those confined to their homes were visited regularly and according to their degree of incapacity provided with some sort of occupation. "Cripples' Parlours" were opened for those who could be brought from their homes and on certain days of the week handicraft classes, games and other amusements were organised for them. Cripples' choirs were started to sing in the local churches, holiday homes opened and visits to the seaside arranged; and, to encourage children who were better off to help those who were less fortunate, the Crutch and Kindness League was started in connection with the Shaftesbury Society by the Rev. J. Reid Howatt, the editor of the children's newspaper *The New Age*. Each member of the League was put into touch with a seriously crippled child and expected to write regularly and send magazines and toys. Though the form of these activities has somewhat changed, they closely resemble what is done for crippled children today.

It was intended that while the Shaftesbury Society concentrated upon the social needs of such children, the Invalid Children's Aid Society should attend to their medical needs. This Society had been formed in 1888 by Mr. Allen Graham and Mrs. Warrington Howard and had no close connection with the Evangelicals. Its purpose was to advise the parents of crippled children, who were out-patients at the hospitals, on the use of splints and other appliances and how to follow the directions of the doctor. The Society worked in close connection with the Charity Organisation Society which was greatly concerned with the lack of suitable medical care for crippled children, and it used the settlements as centres for its work.

The need for a combination of such social and medical care was gradually realised by Dame Grace Kimmins. When working as a "sister" at the Wesleyan West London Mission she had read Mrs. Ewing's popular book, *The Story of a Short Life*, which describes the unhappiness of a little crippled boy until he adopted the family motto, *"laetus sorte mea"*, decided to make the best of his lot and to help others in the same predicament. This drew her attention to the importance of the right attitude of mind of the cripple to his infirmity and the extent to which this could help him to improve physically and to take a more active part in the life of the community.

In 1894 she gathered together the cripples in her mission district in the West End and formed them into a "Guild of Brave Poor Things". Meetings and social entertainments were arranged for them, her aim being not so much to relieve want and suffering as to create a new spirit and a new discipline of life among them and to encourage them to help one another to make the best of their disabilities. After a time she decided to separate the children from the adults, forming "Guilds of Play" for the children. Her example was copied by other Wesleyan Missions and by some of the settlements, and many notable people, among them Mrs. Henry Fawcett, the wife of the blind postmaster-general, Adeline Duchess of Bedford and Lady Henry Somerset came to help her.

Guilds on similar lines were started in different parts of London and at some provincial towns, a well-known one being the Guild of the Handicapped at Bristol, organised by Ada Vachell to help both the crippled and the blind to find a more hopeful approach to life. These guilds were the forerunners of the cripples' aid associations which were started in the main industrial centres in the early twentieth century to organise local work among young and adult physically handicapped persons, and they became the pivots around which Sir Robert Jones and Mr. Girdlestone built up their national scheme for cripples' welfare, which in 1920 became known as the Central Council for the Care of Cripples. Many of these voluntary organisations are still used by the local authorities, which since 1948 have become responsible for the welfare of cripples in their neighbourhood.

The psychological effect of the companionship and encouragement which these guilds provided did much to improve the physical condition of their members. But Dame Grace realised that more specific attention was needed in the medical treatment of the young, since at an early age it was often possible to make some radical improvement. With the help of her husband, who was a noted educationalist, she started the Heritage Craft School and Hospital at Chailey in 1903, which was the first residential school which also provided medical treatment for cripples. It began with seven boys drawn from her Guild of Brave Poor Things, who were housed in part of an old workhouse and industrial school which had already been condemned as unfit for habitation. The buildings were renovated, and the boys given the best medical treatment available and at the same time educated and taught a craft so that they could do some useful work and also lead a happy social life. In forty years the numbers had increased to more than five hundred boys and girls who now live in modern buildings and are trained in the arts and crafts to become intelligent, independent and self-supporting citizens.

This was by no means the earliest attempt to educate cripples. The starting of several small orthopaedic hospitals in the forties, combined with the experience of ragged school teachers, drew the attention of a group of Evangelicals to the fact that no provision was made for the education of crippled children. With the help of Lord Shaftesbury and Lord Kinnaird several homes for this purpose were opened in the 1850's. The Winchmore Home in the Marylebone Road, started by Miss Caroline Blunt for two crippled girls in 1851, was the first of these homes, and it is now under the control of the Church of England Children's Society. In the later decades of the nineteenth century it took about a hundred girls, aged between twelve and fifteen, and gave them an elementary education with some training in hat-making, embroidery, needlework, and dressmaking. A similar home for crippled boys was started in Wright's Lane, Kensington, in 1866, where some hundred boys of thirteen to eighteen were trained in harness-making, relief stamping, copper-plate writing, tailoring and carpentry; and in the following year the Moore Street Home, off the Edgware Road, was opened for younger boys of eight to thirteen to give them a general education before passing on to the training at Wright's Lane. Similarly there were cripples' nurseries at Old Quebec Street, off Oxford Street, and near Regent's Park for children of from two upwards. Thus it was possible for the crippled child to receive a continuous education and training from a very early age.

This group of homes could benefit only a very small number of those who were crippled, but they were important because they drew attention to the need for some special provision for the care and education of crippled children. Thus some of the orphanages began to make special arrangements for their crippled children. Mrs. Giniver's orphanage was the first to do so in 1877 when she opened a special house for "crippled and afflicted children", teaching them dressmaking and other occupations with which their deformities did not interfere. The Waifs and Strays took similar action in 1880 and were followed by Dr. Barnardo's, the Manchester and Salford Refuges and the National Children's Homes. An increasing interest in the education of cripples developed, which led to their inclusion in the Education (Defective and Epileptic Children) Act of 1899 which empowered local authorities to provide special schools for all children suffering from physical defects who could not be taught in the ordinary schools. The first of such schools in the London area was started by Mrs. Humphrey Ward at the Passmore Edwards Settlement.

The biggest problem which faced the adolescent cripple was that of finding suitable employment. In most cases those who were trained at the homes were placed in employment, but there were many whose infirmity made it impossible for them to compete with the able-bodied. This was brought home to John Groom, the superintendent of the Watercress and Flower Girls' Christian Mission (1866) when he found that in organising his Flower Girls' Brigade the crippled girls could not earn as much as the others. He therefore persuaded his council, which included Lord Shaftesbury, Samuel Morley, Baroness Burdett-Coutts and F. A. Bevan, to start a special department to train crippled girls to make artificial flowers and to provide sheltered employment for them. A workshop was opened nearby his mission in Clerkenwell, an instructor found, and a floral exhibition held to advertise the work. Hotels and ballrooms in London and the large provincial towns were his chief customers and a thriving trade developed which tended to replace the import of artificial flowers from the continent. Houses were rented near the workroom where the girls could live and no destitute crippled girl who was capable of learning the trade was refused admittance. As street trading gradually declined, the Mission came to concentrate increasingly upon the work of the "crippleage" until by the end of the century it had virtually become a mission for cripples. In 1932 a move was made to Edgware where the present factory was built surrounded by gardens in which were cottages where the workers lived, a recreation centre and a home for those too old to work. The only other parts of his older mission which still survive are homes for girls at Westerham and for young children at Cudham.

This was the first instance of sheltered employment for cripples and it provided a model for other institutions. The Liverpool Workshop and Home for Cripples was started on similar lines in 1902 and more recently the Cripplecraft Home at Herne Bay. Dame Agnes Hunt went a step further in 1929 when she combined the workshop with hospital treatment at the Durwen Cripples Training Home, some three miles from Oswestry, where hospital patients could receive some industrial training and be employed in a sheltered workshop. It is now the duty of the local authorities to see that such sheltered workshops are provided for the disabled, whether crippled in ordinary life or as the result of war, and they frequently use those of the voluntary societies.

Except on the medical side, the Evangelicals were the pioneers in all these different forms of social work for cripples. Concerned with the numbers of crippled children which they discovered in the course of their mission work, they were the first to provide for the educational and vocational needs of crippled children, to open sheltered workshops for those unable to compete in the labour market, to organise recreational activities for those cut off from normal social contacts, and to show, at the end of the century, that the adult disabled needed similar attention. Upon these beginnings the structure of the present-day welfare work for the physically handicapped has been built up.

Dame Grace Kimmins and Dame Agnes Hunt stand side by side as representatives of what the Evangelicals and the medicals could do for the cripple. To Dame Grace we owe the modern forms of therapy, devised to combine social, medical and spiritual care so that the morale of the physically handicapped person can be maintained; and to Dame Agnes can be traced the nicely balanced arrangement of medical treatment with occupational training. Together they have formed the basis of the modern services for the disabled. As Dame Agnes said in 1928:

> More than a quarter of a century ago Mrs. Kimmins and I started on the same cripple problem from widely different standpoints. Mrs. Kimmins, if she will forgive me for saying so, did not mind much whether the disability of the cripple were relieved as much as possible. I did not mind much whether they were educated to take their place in the world, or not. Had we forgathered then we should possibly have fought tooth and nail. Many years, however, passed before our lines crossed, and those two parts of the whole became intermingled, and both of us realised that treatment and education must go hand in hand.[1]

Thus the same pattern of development is to be found in the welfare work for both the unsound of mind and of body. Evangelical concern played an important part in rousing the public conscience to an awareness of their needs. The Evangelicals provided most of the early social services, and upon their methods much of the modern forms of treatment is based. They introduced an attitude of care, love and compassion for the individual, which was greatly lacking at that time. This arose directly from their beliefs and was

---

[1] Agnes Hunt, "Chailey and Papworth", in *The Cripples Journal*, July 1928.

particularly important in the case of the insane. Today the claims of rehabilitation are strong, and the chief emphasis is upon restoring the person to the life of the community, as fast and as far as possible. Much of this, as well, can be traced to the pioneering work of the Evangelicals who were the chief group in the nineteenth century to recognise a responsibility towards the handicapped.

CHAPTER XIII

The Care of the Sick and the Aged

THE CARE of the sick and the aged has been regarded as a social obligation by most communal groups from early times. It became the duty of the Poor Law authorities in England in 1601 to care for the sick and the aged pauper, which they did both by indoor and outdoor relief. But by the nineteenth century, within the workhouse "the sick were housed with prostitutes, ex-gaolbirds, tramps, and other characters of the worst description, and their sufferings were not infrequently aggravated by the incessant ravings of some neglected lunatic", and the arrangements for those who were sick at home were "almost infinitely various". In the case of the aged, the choice between indoor and outdoor relief was left entirely to the discretion of the guardians, the central board issuing no general instructions.

By the mid-nineteenth century a certain number of voluntary hospitals had been opened. There were some sixteen general hospitals in London dealing with all types of sickness, and about fifty-four special hospitals taking those suffering from some particular disease, and one or two hospitals in most large provincial centres. They were supported by contributions from the public, usually in the form of donations or regular subscriptions, and patients were admitted on the presentation of a "letter" from one or other of these benefactors. Such "letters" could usually be obtained from the clergy or social workers, and they made free medical attention available for the patient. Adequate finances to maintain these hospitals were always a difficulty, and to raise money from as wide a public as possible the Sunday and Saturday Hospital Funds were started. The idea was that of an Evangelical clergyman, Canon Miller, who in 1850 persuaded some of the churches in Birmingham to donate their collections on a particular Sunday to the local hospitals. This became a national effort in 1873, and the next year the Hospital Saturday Fund was started to raise contributions in the factories, offices, at football matches and other sports and by street collections, ostensibly to reach those who did not attend the churches. These Funds were an important source of finance until the hospitals came under State control.

The sick poor who were not ill enough to go to hospital found things more difficult. They could call in the Poor Law doctor, but this meant contacting the relieving officer and so caused loss of time and often of wages. Some of them were members of the provident dispensaries which the Charity Organisation Society sponsored in the 1870's. But in order to be treated by them it was necessary to have paid in a regular weekly contribution, and many of the poor could not manage this. There were always the out-patient departments of the hospitals where free treatment was provided, but these were very overcrowded and scant attention was given. In view of all this, Dr. William Fairlie Clarke, a member of the Charity Organisation Society and a leading Evangelical, suggested the setting up of medical missions in the poorer districts where the people could obtain free advice and medicine.

A few medical missions had already been established in some of the provincial centres. The idea had first arisen when some American missionaries visited Edinburgh in 1841 and encouraged the formation of the Edinburgh Medical Missionary Society. But the intention was to train medical missionaries for service abroad. It was only when one of the students, Dr. William Burns Thomson, was visiting in the slums of Cowgate that he realised the great need for medical missionary work at home. In 1859 he rented an old dram shop at 39 Cowgate, opened it as a free dispensary, and began to train medical students for medical missionary work in the slums of Great Britain. He had the support of some of the leading medical men in Edinburgh University and this made it possible for him to adapt the medical training to suit these particular circumstances and to extend the work throughout the country.

The Edinburgh Medical Mission became the pattern for the others which were subsequently formed. The dispensary was opened daily with a doctor and nurse in attendance, and those who were too ill to come were visited in their homes. If hospital treatment was required, arrangements were made with the local hospital, and there was a convalescent home for those who were recovering. There were, as well, the usual mission activities of regular home visiting, social evenings, and sick and benefit clubs. This enabled the mission staff to know personally the families in the district and so to be able to combine medical with social help. The following is a contemporary description of the Edinburgh Medical Mission when Dr. Burns Thomson was in charge:

> It is the hour for the patients' gathering. They come dropping in one by one. . . . Gradually the room fills with sufferers of every age, and under well-nigh every sort of ill. As the patients gather a lady comes in, and sitting down among them, begins reading the Bible. . . . To many of these poor patients, the word of God is absolutely a new sound. . . . It is now two o'clock. A thin, worn man enters the room with an active springy step, and his forefinger between the leaves of the Bible. It is Dr. Burns Thomson, the superintendent of the Institution. A short prayer follows the sermon, and then the doctor retires to a separate room, where he sees the patient himself, with the students, several of whom are being trained for the work of medical missions. . . . A correct register is kept of the name, address, ailment and treatment of every patient. All cases that require it are visited at the patient's home. The necessary medicines are given at the dispensary, and medicines, like the advice, are all free. The number of patients verges on seven thousand for the year.[1]

Much of his time was spent travelling round the country to advocate the formation of such missions. That in Liverpool was the first to be formed in 1866 and was followed by another in Aberdeen in 1868 with a nephew of Dr. Burns Thomson in charge. The Birmingham Medical Mission was formed in 1875 with four local dispensaries and the Glasgow Medical Mission in 1868. Manchester followed in 1870, and Bristol and Brighton in 1871. The first medical mission in Ireland was connected with the Irish Church Missions, and it consisted of a travelling dispensary with a nurse in attendance, a method which was later to be copied in the less populated areas of Scotland.

Medical missions were slow in coming to London, but when they did come they were established on a widespread scale. Dr.

---

[1] W. Burns Thomson, *Reminiscences of Medical Missionary Work*, 1895, pp. 42–3.

Burns Thomson had left Edinburgh in 1870 and come to live at the Mildmay Institution. From here he was able to advise on the development of medical missionary work both in connection with the Institution and throughout the metropolis as a whole. The large-scale organisation of scattered missions and trained workers made the introduction of medical missionary work by the Mildmay Institution comparatively easy, and this was the only place in Britain where it assumed its complete form of medical missions with a central mission hospital so that both home care and institutional treatment could be undertaken.

Medical work was started in connection with the Mildmay mission centres at Bethnal Green, Walworth and Old Ford, and also with the Mildmay Mission to the Jews in Whitechapel. Full-time medical staff were employed and they were helped by deaconesses who had taken the course in nursing started by the Institution in 1866. The Mildmay Mission Hospital was opened in Turville Street, Bethnal Green, in 1877 with wards for men, women and children and a small maternity wing. Preference was given to patients from the medical missions and all were accepted without any other recommendation or subscriber's letters. When the hospital was rebuilt in 1892 it could accommodate 400 patients and connected with it were several convalescent homes and a home for the aged. Thus it represented home medical missionary work at its best, and continued to meet the needs of the poor in this way until well into the present century. Its hospital and maternity home now form part of the National Health Service.

Meanwhile, a friendship had sprung up between Dr. Burns Thomson and Dr. Fairlie Clarke, which led the latter to consider introducing medical missionary work in London in a plan similar to that followed in Edinburgh. Dr. Thomson had already encouraged Dr. George Saunders to open a medical mission in Endell Street, St. Giles, in 1869 and it was Dr. Saunders and Dr. Fairlie Clarke who in 1878 formed the Medical Missionary Society which was both a training centre for students and which also started medical missions at Canning Town, St. Pancras, Deptford, Islington, Kentish Town, Lambeth and Forest Gate. The journal, *Medical Missions at Home and Abroad*, under the editorship of Dr. Fairlie Clarke did much to publicise the work of these missions and recommend the starting of similar medical work by other voluntary organisations.

By the last two decades of the century medical missionary work had become a usual part of church and chapel social work, particularly in connection with the Church and Salvation Armies and the central missions of the Wesleyans and Baptists, where the sisters and deaconesses were used to nurse the poor in their homes. Most of the larger Christian missions opened free dispensaries and there were several independent medical missions. Thus these missions made it possible for many more of the poor to receive free clinical treatment.

They were not without their critics, the Charity Organisation Society in particular deploring the fact that no payment was asked, and others suggesting that the medical services were inferior and that the students were allowed far too much freedom in treating the patients. Be this as it may, there is no doubt that they filled an important gap in the provision of medical services for the poor in the latter part of the nineteenth century and only as these other services improved were they gradually closed. The Medical Missionary Association still exists, though it now concentrates on helping students to qualify for the foreign field, and a few of the medical missions remain, among them the Islington Medical Centre.

An important offshoot of medical missionary work was an increased interest in the care of the mother and her infant. The maternity hospitals and a few of the general hospitals accepted difficult cases, but most working class mothers had to depend upon the help of a neighbour or midwife at the birth of a child. Only about half of such women were attended by midwives, and the midwives showed "not merely a want of any special education, but gross ignorance and incompetence, and a complete inability to contend with any difficulty that may occur".[1] An infant welfare institution had been opened for a short time in London at the end of the eighteenth century, but the only means that mothers had to learn about the care of their children 100 years later was through some of the more enlightened mothers' meetings of the

[1] Kerr, Johnstone and Phillipps, *Historical Review of British Obstetrics and Gynaecology, 1800–1950*, 1954, p. 334.

few Ladies' Sanitary Associations which existed in some of the larger towns and which gave lectures to women on hygiene and family care.

The first organisation to concentrate upon the welfare of mothers and young children was the Zenana Bible and Medical Mission, an Evangelical institution started by Lady Kinnaird in 1852 for the care of the secluded women of India. Knowledge of the type of work performed here encouraged the formation of several institutions for the care of women in England, among them the North Eastern Dispensary for Women in Bethnal Green (1867) and the East London Dispensary for Women (1868). Some of the early women doctors, who trained at the London School of Medicine (1874) showed interest in such work, in particular Annie McCall.

After graduating from the London School of Medicine she had taken an extensive training in midwifery and obstetrics at Berne, and on her return was invited by Mrs. Meredith to superintend the medical mission which she had opened at Battersea in 1885 for women and children. Her eighteen months' experience there revealed to her the desperate need of the average woman of the lower classes for skilled care at the birth of a child and for some understanding of the early upbringing of children. In 1887 she opened her own clinic in Clapham Road for the ante-natal and post-natal care of mothers, and two years later started the Clapham Maternity Hospital for those attending the clinic who needed in-patient care. The mothers were visited in their homes before and after the birth of the child, and meetings were held to teach them the elements of child care. Her example was copied by several of the settlements which worked among women, and set the pattern for much of the voluntary and, later, state welfare services for mothers and young children.

She also played some part in securing more adequate training for midwives. A school of midwifery was attached to the Clapham Maternity Hospital, students doing their practical training there and at the Lambeth Infirmary and taking the examination of the London Obstetrical Society. At the Select Committee in 1893, which considered the desirability of registering midwives, she described her methods at the Clapham School of Midwifery and when the Central Midwives' Board was set up in 1902 she was one of its members and examined for them for the next twenty years. Thus she helped to raise the standards of the trained midwife and to secure their services in the homes of the poor.

Though on the whole a high standard of medical attention was provided by the hospitals, there was always the tendency for the patient to be "a case" rather than a human being. The Evangelicals tried to overcome this by their Flower and Letter missions which always involved some personal contact with each patient. The idea of taking a nosegay of flowers to persons in hospital or the workhouse was not new, but the Bible Flower Mission (1875), which is still in existence, organised this on a widespread scale, making it possible for all in the larger hospitals to be individually visited in this way. To do this five distribution centres were opened in London, at the Mildmay Institution, the Home of Industry, the Bedford Institute, Park Chapel Christian Institute and the Clapham Conference Hall. Flowers from the country would be sent to these centres and hospital visitors would meet daily to make them up into posies and take them to the hospitals where they would give them personally to the patients and usually stop for a short chat. The visitor was able to learn something of the domestic difficulties of the patient and was expected to help wherever possible. Thus she anticipated some of the duties of the modern almoner.

Letter missions were first started in 1871 in the Brighton hospitals by the Rev. E. B. Elliott of St. Mark's, Kemp Town, who asked his parishioners to write letters to the patients to be placed on their pillows on Christmas morning. This Hospital Pillow and Letter Mission, later known as the Christmas Letter Mission, was extended by his daughter, who used the Mildmay Institution as the centre, to cover the whole of Great Britain and many military and naval hospitals abroad. A similar mission was the Invalid Letter Mission (1877) which was started by a group of Evangelical ladies to bring incurable, lonely or aged invalids into touch with some Christian friend who would write regularly and send things which might be needed. Churches and missions were asked to send the names of persons whom they knew would be helped in this way.

Missions such as these received stern criticism from certain groups, among them Canon Barnett and his friends, on the grounds that they were confusing religion with friendship, and forcing texts and Evangelical propaganda on those who were not in a position to refuse them. In a few cases such criticism may have been justified, but it was more than outbalanced by the therapeutic value of such work, which offered mutual sympathy and interest at a time when this was greatly needed, and which often helped to restore a sense of confidence in those who were otherwise isolated, in this way setting a precedent for some of the modern forms of therapy.

Patients were frequently discharged from the hospitals before they were by any means well, and except for Samaritan societies and one or two convalescent homes connected with a few of the large hospitals, nothing was done for their after-care. To deal with this problem, a large number of convalescent homes, independent of the hospitals, were started during the second half of the nineteenth century. Some of these were connected with benevolent and friendly societies or with the trade unions, but a large number of them were run by Evangelicals, and they became a favourite form of charity. Practically all the Christian missions, the Y.M.C.A., the Y.W.C.A., the Girls Friendly Society, the societies for the handicapped and the orphanages had small convalescent homes for their members who had been ill or were overworked, and it was quite usual for such a home to be used for convalescents out of season and as a holiday home for mothers and children during the summer. Their standards were very variable, and this roused some comment at the time, but the stay of most convalescents was so short that this had few harmful effects unless special nursing or feeding were required.

An interesting convalescent home was that started for social workers by Miss Charlotte Mason. It is noteworthy, not only because it is still in existence, but because it recognised social workers as a professional group subject to the usual occupational hazards and needs. She had first rented a cottage in Wellington, Shropshire, in 1866 where she took biblewomen, deaconesses and nurses for short periods of rest, but with the support of Mrs. Wightman, Mrs. Pennefather and Miss Agnes Weston, she was enabled to purchase premises in Cambridge Gardens, Kilburn, to which she moved her Christian workers in 1870, adding a small home for aged workers in 1890 and a seaside holiday home at Eastbourne. As many as 900 were said to pass through her homes in a year, and they became a refuge for those who had been in hospital, were overworked or in need of a short holiday.

Other forms of after-care provided by the Evangelicals were the invalid kitchens attached to most of the Christian and medical missions which supplied broth, arrowroot and other invalid food to those who had been seriously ill; and the societies, such as the Surgical Aid Society (1862), which supplied free surgical appliances. These were viewed with concern by the Charity Organisation Society which opposed the free distribution, on the grounds that some small payment should be demanded to prevent misappropriation.

These improvements in medical care, both within the hospital and outside, were of limited use unless accompanied by better nursing. In the early decades of the nineteenth century the quality of nursing was at a very low ebb. Most of the dressings were done by medical students and the nurses attended to the work of cleaning and caring for the needs of the medical staff. Most of them were elderly and decrepit and had had no specialised training, and though there were some kindly souls, many were of the type described by Dickens as "habitually drunk, with an easy-going, selfish indifference to their patients, and no knowledge or skill of nursing". They were almost all of the working class and were regarded on a level with beadles, porters and other superior servants. Few could read or write and so they were incapable of carrying out written orders or understanding the directions upon prescriptions.

An improvement can be traced to the work of two German Evangelicals, Pastor Theodore Fliedner and his wife, who started the training of deaconesses for the care of the sick in connection with their other forms of social work at Kaiserswerth in the mid-1830's. A hospital was opened in 1836 and the deaconesses taught not only methods of nursing tuition and practice but kitchen work, laundry and gardening. The notes of lectures given by Frederike Fliedner became the standard textbook for nurses at that time, and Nutting and Dock, the well-known authorities on nursing history, considered that "it cannot but be recognised that the early motherhouse, following the lead of Kaiserswerth, laid down every fundamental principle of good training". Florence Nightingale, somewhat more cautiously, felt that nursing proper had not been taught there, but recalled with admiration the high tone, pure devotion and attentiveness to the patients' needs which she had witnessed there.

Both religious and secular nursing in England owed much to the example of Kaiserswerth. Some of the newly formed High Church sisterhoods began to undertake nursing as one of their duties and two Evangelical deaconess institutions, Mildmay and Tottenham, followed the methods of Kaiserswerth more closely, particularly Tottenham whose founder, Dr. Laseron, had come from Germany. They both opened hospitals, trained nurses, and sent them out for private work and to nurse the poor. Mildmay started its nursing training in 1866 and used both the Mission Hospital at Bethnal Green and the Memorial Hospital at Mildmay for the purpose, and the Tottenham Deaconess Institution and Hospital was opened in 1867, and continued to train nurses until the end of the century, when the hospital passed to other control and is now the Prince of Wales General Hospital. The number of religious nurses was never large, but they helped to fill the gap between the passing of the old, uneducated and unreliable type of nurse and the new order of trained secular nurses. The lasting influence of Kaiserswerth, however, is to be found in the gradual growth of lay nursing orders.

Elizabeth Fry and Florence Nightingale adapted the ideals of Kaiserswerth to the organisation of lay nursing. Elizabeth Fry had visited Kaiserswerth in 1840, and Florence Nightingale in 1849 and 1851, on the latter occasion staying for three months to work with the deaconesses. Elizabeth Fry's Institute of Nursing, which was started in 1841, with the help of Bishop Bromfield in Whitechapel, and later moved to Devonshire Square, Bishopsgate, is important in that it was the first group of lay nurses organised on modern lines. But although the Institute survived until the Second World War, it did not exert any dynamic influence upon the development of nursing. This came from Florence Nightingale.

Though she was an Evangelical by upbringing, her maternal grandfather, William Smith, being associated with the Clapham Sect, and though her early contact with Lord Shaftesbury had brought her into touch with ragged school work with "her little thieves" at Westminster, and had encouraged her to study blue books and hospital reports with a view to taking up nursing, it is doubtful if, in later life, she would have acknowledged any particular religious denomination. According to her biographer, Sir Edward Cook, she had

> a profound sense of personal religion. She felt as all saints must feel, that a religious life means a state of soul . . . if she was resolved to dedicate her life to the service of man, she was no less convinced that such service should only be rendered, at the best and highest in the light and with the sanction of service to God.[1]

Her aim was to give her nurses something of the devotion possessed by the deaconess orders, combined with the advantages of scientific knowledge and of the practical experience which she had gained in the Crimea. She retained the strong discipline of the "mother-house" in the person of the trained matron who controlled every aspect of the non-medical work of the hospital, but instead of the all-round social work of the Kaiserswerth deaconess, her nurses confined their activities to nursing, and, instead of being maintained by the religious community, they were paid professional workers. Yet nursing was to be a vocation rather than a career, and its motive a divine call to help the sick and suffering. Since the Nightingale nurses were taught to train rather than to undertake private nursing or the nursing of the sick poor, they went out in small groups to most of the large hospitals in Britain and the Commonwealth and many of the American and other foreign hospitals. The Nightingale spirit spread and has become the basis of modern nursing.

Evangelicals were also to the forefront in the nursing of the sick poor outside the hospitals, either in their own homes or in the sick ward of the workhouse. It was a Unitarian, William Rathbone, a business executive of Liverpool, who took the initiative in relation to both these groups and, with the help of Florence

[1] Sir E. Cook, *Life of Florence Nightingale*, 1913, vol. i, pp. 53 and 58.

Nightingale, introduced improved district and workhouse nursing into Liverpool in the early sixties. But it was frequently Evangelical organisations which put his ideas into action.

In London, after the mid-century, two Evangelical organisations were formed to undertake domiciliary nursing in the homes of the poor—the East London Nursing Association and the Ranyard Nurses, both started in 1868. Both used nurses of the same social class as those among whom they worked and placed them under the superintendence of a "lady" who would keep a general watch over their work and supply them with medical needs and "letters" for hospitals and convalescent homes. The East London Nursing Association had been started by the Hon. Mrs. James Stuart-Wortley to nurse cholera patients and was the smaller of the two, though it worked in close association with the East End Mothers' Home, another Evangelical organisation, to which were sent difficult maternity cases. The Ranyard Nurses were the nursing branch of the London Bible and Domestic Female Mission, and they showed a fairly close resemblance to the Kaiserswerth deaconesses in being both biblewomen and nurses, though they had no affiliation to any order nor took part in the communal life of a motherhouse. The importance of Mrs. Ranyard's nurses lies in the emphasis which she placed upon principles which later became fundamental in district nursing. She saw the need for combining theoretical instruction, hospital experience, and practical work in training and insisted that the right type of woman should be selected.

> She should be not much of a talker, but a quiet, kindly, gentle, and yet capable and handy woman, willing to receive instruction in her duties which can be practically given in a large hospital, including a sufficient variety of the different forms of sickness; and then she will further need the mother-wit to apply the knowledge thus gained amongst the London poor amid surrounding difficulties. She must still follow out the original principle of the Bible and Domestic Mission in the nursing department "to help the poor to help themselves" and she will need to have a winning way of doing it.[1]

She also stressed the positive need for the nurses to teach the patients the way to maintain their health. "It is with dirt that we

[1] *Missing Link Magazine*, July 1, 1868.

want our good women to grapple, and with disease born of dirt."
Many areas copied her methods, the local clergyman or some
other person forming a nursing association, which, like the
Brough Nurses at Paisley (1884), often nursed both in the home
and the workhouse, and in the country districts would undertake
housework as well if the mother was ill.

It was this combination of nursing with other aspects of social
work which Florence Nightingale frowned upon, and when a
Nightingale nurse was asked to report upon district nursing in
London and found that "nursing the sick was still looked upon in
great measure as a religious rather than a professional occupation", she fully supported her. Thus, when Queen Victoria on the
occasion of her Jubilee in 1887 gave £70,000 to further district
nursing, the nursing associations which became affiliated with
Queen Victoria's Jubilee Institute had to concentrate entirely upon
their professional duties. For this reason several associations did
not join, among them the Ranyard Mission which still keeps its
religious emphasis.

The only qualification laid down for the nurse in the workhouse
infirmary was that she should be able "to read written instructions
upon medicines", and in the majority of cases the sick pauper was
nursed by other inmates of the workhouse who were less decrepit,
but who were often drunken and altogether unsuited to the purpose. When William Rathbone asked Florence Nightingale to
help him improve the nursing in the Liverpool infirmary, she sent
him Agnes Jones. She was a staunch Evangelical whose friends
"thought she received a silent baptism of fire in the time of the
Irish Revival, which sent her forth from the quiet retirement she
best loved" to train at Kaiserswerth. She then nursed for a time
with the North London Deaconesses and took charge temporarily
of Mrs. Ranyard's Mission while she was absent in 1862. She went
to Liverpool in 1865 and within the three years before her death in
1868 had completely transformed conditions in their Poor Law
infirmary.

In the Infirmary there were some 1,300 patients, two or three
times more than the number of beds, and the foul language, drunkenness, vicious habits and bodily and mental degradation were
indescribable. She took with her twelve nurses and eighteen

probationers from St. Thomas's, and used the services of fifty-four of the more reputable pauper nurses. But she had little support from the board of guardians, most of whom were sceptical of her ideas and were merely waiting to see the failure of her period of trial. She had, however, the constant encouragement and sympathy of William Rathbone and the mature advice of Florence Nightingale and within a year her success had converted the board of guardians who agreed to make the experiment permanent in the Liverpool Infirmary and to recommend its use in other workhouses around Liverpool. Her death from typhus in 1868 left her work well established in Liverpool, and gave to it a publicity which it might not otherwise have had, so that other boards of guardians proved willing to adopt similar methods.

It was on these lines that a scheme for training workhouse nurses was drawn up and the Metropolitan Poor Act of 1867 made its adoption permissible in the newly established Poor Law infirmaries in London. The Workhouse Infirmary Nursing Association was formed to introduce it into as many infirmaries as possible and by 1884 some twenty in London and several in the provinces were following these methods. By 1892 the Select Committee on Metropolitan Hospitals was able to report that trained matrons were always elected to the poor law infirmaries, and unskilled pauper nurses were only employed in a few of the sick wards of the workhouses. Thus what had been started as a pioneer work by Agnes Jones had become a standard practice in London and was rapidly spreading throughout the country.

It can, therefore, be seen how the influence of Kaiserswerth spread throughout the whole of the development of nursing. It supplied two qualities which have become characteristic of British nursing—an emphasis upon both theoretical and practical nursing, and a devotion to duty. A definite period of training was encouraged for all. The hospitals were gradually staffed with trained nurses; district nurses' associations were to be found in most areas with members who had received the appropriate instruction and experience; and the Poor Law infirmaries slowly acquired qualified nurses. The nurses were expected to regard their work as a vocation, giving to it a singleness of mind and purpose. The close touch which Florence Nightingale kept with these developments, coupled with her dominating personality, enabled her to bring together these two aspects and form them into a more precise system. The effect was to make it possible for British nursing to steer a middle course between the devoutly religious and the entirely scientific, and so to offer human sympathy and encouragement, combined with a high technical skill.

Lastly there was the problem as to what to do about those who were nearing the end of their life. Some of these were suffering from some incurable disease; others were merely old and unable to look after themselves. But whichever group they fell into, they were unacceptable at the general hospitals, which existed essentially for the cure of the sick, and they usually drifted to the workhouse where they ended their days in the infirmary ward. Charles Booth reckoned that nearly 30 per cent of the aged sought parish assistance in the course of a year, and it was estimated in 1860 that of the 80,000 persons who died annually from the three main forms of incurable disease, 50,000 of them were entirely destitute.

The Congregational minister, Andrew Reed, in the course of his work for idiots, had come across innumerable cases of needy incurables and this prompted him to write in 1845 that "it would be a blessed thing if we had provision in this land to give shelter to despairing incurables". The support of some members of the medical profession enabled him to put this desire into action, and both the Royal Hospital and Home for Incurables at Putney, and the British Home and Hospital for Incurables at Streatham were the result of his efforts. In July 1854 he announced

> for those who require it, a final home will be found where every comfort may be enjoyed to mitigate affliction, and where the best medical skill and care may be had, with the hope of making disease something less than incurable.[1]

A small house at Carshalton was leased for four patients, and pensions granted to several out-patients. Reed had wished his home for incurables to be built alongside his Orphanage for Fatherless Children at Coulsdon, but disagreement among the sponsors arose with the result that two homes were eventually opened, one at Melrose Hall, Putney, which became in 1865 the Royal Hospital

[1] L. French, *The Hospital and Home for Incurables, Putney*, 1936, pp. 19–20.

and Home for Incurables, and the other the British Home for Incurables which was first housed in the disused premises of the British Orphan Asylum at Clapham Rise, and which moved to its present quarters in Streatham in 1894.

In many ways these institutions were alike. Both took their patients on the election of governors and subscribers, both offered a pension or home according to whether or not the patient could be cared for by relatives or friends, and both asked for some payment from those who could afford it. About three-quarters of the patients in each institution were women, many of them having pensions at first but later being taken into the home when their relatives or friends could no longer care for them. Their chief differences seems to have been in the type of patient admitted, the British Home preferring those who had previously been in reasonably comfortable circumstances and steady employment.

Several other small homes were started on similar lines, both by the Evangelicals and the High Church sisterhoods, among the former being the Mildmay Home for Incurable Consumptives at Torquay, the Broomhill Home at Glasgow for "the relief of incurables in Glasgow and the West of Scotland", and a home for Protestant Incurables at Cork. But even after taking account of all these homes, it is unlikely that more than 1,000 destitute incurables were receiving help in this way.

Unless they were already residents, the dying were refused admission to the homes for incurables. The High Church and the Catholics were the first to provide homes for this purpose, the earliest recorded being that of the Sisters of All Saints in 1851, followed by the Roman Catholic Hospital of St. John and St. Elizabeth, which opened a ward for the purpose in 1856, and the Hostel of God, Clapham Common, which was started by the Sisters of St. Margaret, East Grinstead, in 1891. Except for a small home opened for a short time in connection with the North London Deaconesses by Elizabeth Ferard, the first Evangelical home for the dying was Friedenheim, started by Miss Davidson in close connection with the Mildmay Institution. It later moved to Swiss Cottage and is now St. Colomba's Hospital. A second home was St. Luke's Hospital, Regent's Park (1893), which was run by the Wesleyan West London Mission for "some twenty of the very poor who would otherwise have been sent to the workhouse to die".

These homes could only care for a very small number of destitute incurables and dying, and the rest were to be found in the workhouses where they were usually treated in the same way as the ordinary pauper. It was to improve their conditions that Louisa Twining began, in 1860, to draw public attention to the need for Poor Law reform in the treatment of destitute incurables in the workhouses. Though not an Evangelical herself, she received strong support from Lord Shaftesbury, and together they recommended a separate ward for incurables in the workhouse, permission for friends to visit them, and the provision of extra comforts, such as air and water beds, soft pillows, screens, flowers and some extra butter and tea. A few of the London workhouses were prepared to adopt these suggestions, and when they did so, it was usually put into effect by the Workhouse Visiting Society which Louisa Twining had formed for this purpose.

Some provision had been made for a very long time for old people who could no longer live with their relatives. At first it took the form of charitable bequests which either gave pensions or built almshouses for certain aged persons. No less than forty six of such charitable trusts had been founded before 1485 and 740 existed in 1795. But the age of these trusts, the peculiar whim of the founder, and the changes in social life and conditions often made the original intention inapplicable or ineffective.

By the nineteenth century the problem of the aged had assumed much greater proportions. The great growth in population and its concentration in the towns meant that their numbers were increasing and their families less able to care for them. Very many of them had to seek Poor Law relief, either in the form of assistance to enable them to live on their own or by entering the workhouse, and only a very small number could be accommodated in the almshouses. Nineteenth century social reformers approached the problem in two ways. They did their best to increase the number of charitable institutions for the aged; and they suggested the payment of pensions to the old to help them to remain independent as long as possible. The Evangelicals took part in both these ventures.

A certain number of the old type of almshouse were built by them; for example the Metropolitan Almshouses in connection with Spurgeon's Tabernacle which were rebuilt and greatly extended in 1867, and Vaughan's Almshouses (1866) which were erected at Ashford, Middlesex, by the congregation of the Surrey Chapel. They also sponsored two homes for "gentlewomen in reduced circumstances"—a group which was becoming increasingly numerous with the increased number of single ladies who had to earn their own living. Miss Sheppard's Annuitants' Home (1855) in Bayswater was for lady pensioners of different societies whose income was insufficient for them to live on their own, and Miss Smallwood's Society for the Assistance of Ladies in Reduced Circumstances (1886) granted pensions to those who, through ill-health or age, were unable to support themselves.

The innovation which the Evangelicals introduced into the care of the old was to start organisations which combined the provision of pensions with homes for those who could no longer live on their own and nursing homes for those needing constant attention. Thus as age crept on, the old person could be transferred from one to the other. The Aged Pilgrims' Friend Society (1807) was the first example of this. Started in connection with Whitefield's Tabernacle for the care of "the Lord's aged poor" it gained the support of Wilberforce, Admiral Lord Gampier and, later, Lord Shaftesbury. On the recommendation of lady visitors, pensions were granted to suitable persons and a home opened at Camberwell for them when they could no longer live on their own. When a second home was opened at Hornsey Rise in 1871 a small hospital was added to which pensioners could be sent when ill and could stay if necessary until they died. A third home at Stamford Hill was opened in 1886, and these three homes as well as the pension fund still exist for elderly folk of any Evangelical denomination.

Other similar homes included the Homes for the Aged Poor (1869), now known as the Harrison Homes, which provided rooms for aged couples in suburban villas in several of the London suburbs with one or two villas for the sick and infirm; and the South London Homes for the Aged Poor (1885) which gave pensions and residential care in the Kennington area. The Christian missions often opened small homes for old people where a few of the aged poor in their area were cared for by one of the mission workers. Examples of this were the Twig Folly Mission, Spitalfields, where in 1867 the premises of the Elizabeth Fry Refuge were taken over as a Home for Aged Christians, and the Mildmay Institution which had a home for aged destitute men and women above their workmen's hall.

Though these Evangelical institutions formed only a very small part of the charitable provision for the aged poor, their importance lies in the way in which they helped the old to maintain their independence, and when this was no longer possible provided residential care for them until the end of their lives. This was an entirely new approach in the method of charitable care for the old, for though in theory it had been the policy of the Poor Law, in practice the old were usually sent indiscriminately to the workhouse. Thus they introduced the modern methods of care for old people which consist in keeping them in their homes as long as possible and then providing residential accommodation for them.

Mention has already been made in Chapter IV of the part which the Evangelicals played in the demand for State pensions for the old. Like other groups in the community they realised that the increasing numbers of elderly people could remain independent for much longer if they received some regular monetary help. This could not be achieved satisfactorily by charitable means, and therefore it was the duty of the State to make some provision. Various schemes were suggested, but one by one they were turned down.

It was at this stage that groups of Evangelicals united to take up this cause, and as with the other nineteenth century campaigns, gave it the nature of a religious crusade and worked up an infectious enthusiasm throughout the country. The Browning Settlement became their centre, and the Fellowship of Followers at the Settlement the nucleus for the work. The campaign started as a result of a P.S.A. meeting when the agent-general for New Zealand had described the old age pension scheme there. Members of the Christian labour movement were present and took up the cause with enthusiasm. Charles Booth was invited to a conference at the Settlement, a series of meetings were arranged for him in different towns, and the National Committee of Organised Labour formed to press for legislation. The support of the trade unions, the co-operative societies and the friendly societies was gained, the P.S.A.'s and the adult schools held lectures and meetings to further the cause, the Methodists offered strong support and the Congregational Union recorded a vote in its favour. Meanwhile daily prayer meetings were held at the settlement and volunteer speakers sent to men's meetings throughout the country. As the passage of the bill was continuously delayed so the religious enthusiasm mounted, and groups of working men began to gather for prayer at the local P.S.A.'s and Brotherhood meetings. Eventually in 1908 the Campbell-Bannerman ministry made the necessary financial arrangements and at the beginning of 1909 old age pensions of 5/- per week became payable to all old people at the age of seventy whose income was less than a given amount.

Thus the Evangelicals gave the much needed impetus to public opinion which was already beginning to favour old age pensions, and thereby caused the government to initiate legislation. It is interesting to notice that while this campaign was in progress the Browning Settlement opened old people's homes at Dulwich and Whyteleafe, Surrey, showing in this way the two-fold need of pensions for old people living in their own homes, and residential institutions for them when they can no longer live alone, a principle which is recognised by the granting of contributory pensions to the retired, and the provision of old people's homes under the National Assistance Act of 1948.

Though the contribution of the Evangelicals to the care of the sick and the aged in the nineteenth century was somewhat fragmentary, largely because these were forms of social work which had already advanced some distance, they did succeed in finding the gaps in the existing services, and in filling them to the best of their ability. Thus medical missions were provided for those too poor to contribute to the provident dispensaries but unable to get help easily from the Poor Law authorities, better midwifery and clinical services were made available for working class mothers, the homes for incurables helped a group whose needs were barely understood, and the residential homes for the old, since they stipulated no special entry qualifications, took those who were ineligible for any of the charitable foundations. Perhaps their most important contribution, however, was in relation to the reform of nursing. Had it not been for the influence of Kaiserswerth, Florence Nightingale might have followed other lines, and so deprived British nursing of some of its unique characteristics.

Once again the Evangelicals supplied a quality absent in the older institutions, namely a more humane understanding and desire to help those whom they befriended to become as happy as possible in spite of their circumstances. Homes replaced almshouses and asylums, flower and letter missions brought a personal interest and care to the sick and housebound, and various attempts were made to improve the circumstances of the old. Thus they introduced the human element into the existing services, and prepared the way for the more personal care which is provided today.

CHAPTER XIV

The Sailor and the Soldier

EVANGELICAL PHILANTHROPY also showed concern for men and women engaged in certain occupations. They realised that there were frequently hardships arising from the nature of some employments, and that workers were often placed in positions of temptation because of the work which they were doing. The employers rarely took any account of this, and left the workers to cope with the situation as best they might. Sailors and soldiers were an outstanding case because they spent the greater part of their lives away from home and family under living conditions which were highly artificial and which placed them in positions of temptation and need. The Elizabethan Poor Law had given preferential treatment for "the maimed, hurt or grievously sick soldier", but the local administrators paid little attention and treated the soldier and sailor in the same way as the ordinary pauper. The authorities were concerned with the efficiency of servicemen while on duty, but made little provision for their leisure time, or for the welfare of their families. The Merchant Shipping Act of 1894 was the first piece of legislation to exercise any control over pay and conditions of merchant seamen and fishermen. There was, therefore, much scope for voluntary charity in the nineteenth century.

Most of the nineteenth century seamen's charities can trace their origin to the remarkable revival of religion among soldiers and sailors which took place in the first two decades of the century. The *Sailors' Magazine and Naval Miscellany* records:

> In the year 1800 the moral and religious condition of the marine population of Great Britain was most deplorable. . . . When in 1802 war terminated there was a considerable revival of religion, and when war broke out again in 1803 and raged until 1815 it was from this

newly enlightened and revived population that our Navy received its supply of seamen and marines.[1]

Attention to the spiritual state of soldiers and sailors had been an aspect of the work of the Clapham Sect, Henry Thornton, William Wilberforce and their friends starting the Naval and Military Bible Society in 1780 which distributed some 100,000 bibles in the following thirty-five years. At the same time several Evangelical clergy were advocating the cause of seamen in the pulpits, among them William Romaine, the Rev. Rowland Hill, and Dr. Rippon; and Admiral Lord Gampier and a group of naval officers were spreading evangelicalism in the Royal Navy. But the most outstanding was the Rev. George Charles Smith, who concentrated particularly upon the men of the merchant service, and from whose efforts most of the subsequent social work for sailors sprang. Among the societies with whose formation he was connected were the British Sailors' Society, the Shipwrecked Fishermen and Mariners' Society, the Red Ensign Club, the Seamen's Christian Friend Society, and several of the sailors' orphan homes. The Rev. James Sherman, the successor of Rowland Hill at the Surrey Chapel, said of him:

> I connect with the name of G. C. Smith the commencement of one of the greatest moral revolutions England ever saw; he was the morning star of the sailors' reformation. God stirred up this man to do things at which others trembled.[2]

Born in London in 1782, he had spent the years 1796 to 1802 at sea until deciding to enter the Baptist ministry. While training at Plymouth, he heard about the growing interest in religion in the Navy and started a correspondence service with some of the men. Then from 1814 to 1816 he served as a voluntary chaplain with the British Army in Spain and returned with the intention of devoting his time exclusively to the needs of seamen and soldiers. Like David Nasmith, the originator of the city missions, he had unbounded energy and numerous projects are attributed to his initiative, but he possessed little perseverence and many failed to continue or passed into the hands of others. He entered

[1] *Sailors' Magazine*, December 1820.
[2] Theophilus Smith, *The Great Moral Reformation of Sailors*, pamphlet, 1874.

the sailors' revival at a point when organisation was much needed and successfully provided this, but then left others to carry on.

His first step was the formation of the Bethel Seamen's Union in 1819, to co-ordinate the prayer meetings for sailors which had been started on board the colliers in the Lower Pool of the Thames in 1814 by a boy, Zebulon Rogers, who was a member of the Wesleyan Church at Rotherhithe. The purpose of the Union was

> to unite and extend the prayer meetings; to ascertain the state of British seamen in every port throughout Great Britain, in the navy and the merchant service, and to adopt such measures in connection with friends in maritime towns as may best conduce to their moral and religious interests; to establish a Foreign correspondence, and solicit information and direction as to the best means of doing good to Foreign sailors, so that the limits of this society shall be the circumference of the globe; to publish a sailors' magazine (monthly) for the improvement of seamen, and the communication of general information concerning this interesting portion of the human race.[1]

This was encouraged by G. C. Smith who

> would visit the port, go to the docks, see the ministers and leading men, and create under God a perfect tempest of enthusiasm. He would point to what had been done in London. Hence you would soon find a floating chapel and a society usually called the "seamen's friend society".[2]

An immediate result was the opening of chapels for seamen. The Port of London Society was formed in 1819 for this purpose, and purchased and reconditioned the sloop *Speedy* as a floating chapel for seamen on the Thames, and in 1824 the Danish Church in Wellclose Square, London Docks, was used as the first chapel on land for seamen. America copied the idea with the Mariners' Church in New York, and a seamen's church in Philadelphia. At the smaller ports "seamen's friend societies" were formed to hold "bethel" services, and this spiritual work was followed in almost every case by some form of social work. The Port of London Society rented 52 Hermitage Street, Wapping, as a lodging house for sailors in 1821, and portable libraries were sent by the "seamen's friend societies" to many of the ships so that their crews

[1] *Sailors' Magazine*, January 1820.   [2] *Chart and Compass*, vol. i, December 1879.

might have something to read. These activities were extended by
the Rev. William Henry Angas, who was appointed in 1822 by
the Bethel Seamen's Union as the first missionary to seamen to
travel round the British and continental ports, supervising the
existing societies and starting new ones. Until his death in 1832
the Bethel Seamen's Union remained independent, but was
amalgamated in 1833 with the Port of London Society to form
the British Sailor's Society.

The effect of these varied activities sponsored by G. C. Smith,
and the publication of the *Sailors' Magazine* which recorded them,
gave a wide publicity to the needs of seamen. Many seamen's
institutes or "bethels" were opened where the men were given
a comfortable room for reading and writing, some recreational
facilities and possibly light refreshments. Meanwhile at the ports
"Seamen's Friend Societies" were being started by captains and
other officers who were members of the Bethel Union. These
were formally organised as the Seamen's Christian Friend Society
in 1846. According to its first minute book

> the Society shall be engaged in missions to ships etc. in the port of
> London and in the sea coasts, to barracks, prisons and the poor in
> general as heretofore, having purely for its objects the moral and
> spiritual welfare of our sailors and soldiers and the poor, and be con-
> sidered as having grown out of the operations of a society established
> in the year 1819, and now constituted under the management of a
> new committee whose business shall be to govern and direct the
> financial department and see that the missionary operations are effec-
> tively carried out proportionately to its pecuniary support.[1]

This Society expanded it work under the secretaryship of the
Rev. George Teil Hill and his son the Rev. George John Hill,
and by the end of the century had institutes in nineteen ports
which supplied ships with books and provided refreshments and
leisure occupations for the men when on land. It still has several
institutes and sailors' homes and maintains the King George V
Merchant Seamen's Memorial Hospital in Malta.

An important service rendered by most of these sailors' organisations was the banking of sailors' money and itsr emittance to
their families. This was made necessary by the hoards of "crimps"

[1] *Hill of the Ratcliffe Highway*, a Memoir, 1932, pp. 23-4.

and loose women at the docks who would use every device to make the sailor patronise their lodging houses and then obtain any money he might have on him. As Mayhew remarked in 1851:

> When a sailor comes on shore, he will probably go to the nearest sailors' home, and place his money in a bank. Drawing out a pound or so with which he may enjoy himself for a day or two, he will then have the rest of the money transmitted to his friends in the country, to whom he will go as soon as he has had his fling in town.[1]

Hostels for seamen were rare in England until the last decade of the century, though they had been an early form of social work for sailors in America. Except for one small home opened by Mr. Green, an eminent ship-owner, for the men from his own ships, the only other one was the still-existing Sailors' Home and Red Ensign Club, built on the site of the Brunswick theatre in 1829. G. C. Smith is said to have been the instigator of this home, and Admiral Lord Gampier with several naval officers collected the funds for it. Originally intended for unemployed seamen, it was used as a hostel for sailors who had returned from long voyages and, with the help of Queen Adelaide, was enlarged in 1848. The first of the homes to be opened by the larger sailors' societies was the Seamen's Rest in Jeremiah Street which the Wesleyan Seamen's Mission started in 1887, and this was followed by the British Sailors' Society Home at Millwall in 1892 and, that of the Mission to Seamen in Poplar in 1894. By this time hostel accommodation was usually provided by the sailors' institutes.

The sailors' revival was also the source of Anglican work among seamen. An article, "Have Churchmen no obligation to do good among British Seamen afloat?", appeared in the *Sailors' Magazine* of 1820, and attention was again drawn to the need in 1823, with the result that the London Episcopal Floating Church Society was formed in 1825 which used a floating chapel until St. Paul's Church in Dock Street was consecrated in 1847 as a seamen's church. Several other local Anglican missions were formed at the time, including the Bristol Channel Mission (1837), the Thames Mission (1844), the Mersey Mission to Seamen (1857)

---

[1] *London's Underworld, op. cit.*, p. 59.

and the St. Andrew's Waterside Mission at Gravesend (1864). To introduce some co-ordination, William H. G. Kingston and the Rev. Theodore A. Walrond formed the Missions to Seamen in 1856, in which most of the existing missions were gradually absorbed.

The work of the Missions to Seamen followed the usual pattern of religious services leading to various forms of social work. During the first year chaplains and scripture readers were appointed for the Mersey area, the Bristol Channel and several other places, making themselves known to the men through the emblem of the "flying angel", but at the second annual meeting it was decided "to use such means as might better his temporal position" in their work for the sailor. On Lord Shaftesbury's suggestion institutes were opened at Deal (1861), Swansea, Margate, and Southampton, where canteens and some sleeping accommodation were provided and in several instances a seamen's church opened. Similar provision is still made by the Mission at its many stations at home and abroad.

The Wesleyan Seamen's Mission, though formed in 1843, was local in character until the 1880's, largely because all Wesleyan work had to be confined within the surveillance of a circuit. Like other local sailors' societies, its workers visited in the lodging houses and other resorts frequented by sailors, but with the formation of the seamen's chapel circuit in 1885 it was able not only to build the Seamen's Rest, which is still used as a hostel by seafaring men in the Port of London, but to open branches throughout the London Docks and start homes in ports such as Chatham, Devonport and Pembroke Docks, as well as at some of the more important naval stations abroad.

The Presbyterians employed, for a time, a seamen's missionary in connection with their East India Road Chapel, Poplar, but they did little other organised work for sailors. It is also probable that some of the High Church parishes worked among sailors, since Charles Lowder is said to have opened a mission house and restaurant for them at 42a Dock Street in connection with his church at St. George's-in-the-East. Such work, however, was usually temporary and confined to the ministry of some particular pastor or priest. The two large denominational societies, the

Missions to Seamen and the Wesleyan Seamen's Mission, thus shared with the British Sailors' Society and the Seamen's Christian Friend, the greater part of the provision of institutes and homes for sailors in the nineteenth century, the work of the last two, since it was undenominational, predominating at the smaller ports where there would be only a few sailors of any one religious sect.

Besides these larger societies for seamen, there were many other small undenominational missions, usually at ports where these societies had not established branches. A typical example was that of Henry Cook at Gosport. A house painter and decorator, he had, in his spare time, opened an industrial school for destitute boys and to this had added a seamen's bethel. In the sixties he decided to expand his work for seamen, and built a seamen's mission at Gosport with three bethels at Gosport, Portsmouth and Rudmore, each with sleeping quarters. Two gospel ships, manned by the boys from the industrial school visited the ships in Portsmouth harbour, Spithead, and the fishing fleets of the nearby coastal districts. When he died the work was handed over to the British Sailors' Society. Other similar work was that of the Hon. Elizabeth Waldegrave and Mary Hunt at Southsea, Charlotte Hunter at King's Lynn, and Miss Robinson at Portsea.

Miss Child's work for seamen in the Ratcliffe Highway was distinctive in that her purpose was to help the sailor who had succumbed to drink or immorality and so was not acceptable at the other institutes and homes. At the suggestion of Annie Macpherson she had first visited sailors in the public and lodging houses in the district and had then decided in 1877 to open a home for these types. She offered food and clothing and, if necessary, a bed to the destitute sailor, who had often been picked up on one of her periodical visits to the neighbouring dance halls, gin palaces, and brothels. She used the method, which was commonly found among scattered groups of workers, of keeping in touch with them through a "Christian Lifeboat Crew" of trustworthy sailors who acted as friends to others and found them suitable lodgings at the different ports.

The proportion of foreign sailors was particularly large in the big ports since not only did British ships employ them, but foreign ships were frequently registered under the British flag.

The foreign sailor was a ready prey for the "crimps" and other undesirable characters in the dock areas since he could rarely speak or understand the language, knew little of the customs of the country, and did not often make use of the existing sailors' institutes and bethels. The first attempt to do anything for them was made by the Maharajah Djulep Singh in 1854, when he sent a donation of £500 towards a home for Asiatic sailors. The oversight of the home was given to the London City Mission since several of their missionaries could speak an oriental language. They visited the sailors on board, invited them to the home, helped them with financial and other problems, and found alternative employment for them if they did not rejoin their ship.

It was probably this home which inspired Reginald Radcliffe to open his "strangers' rests" in London and other large ports. He had been one of the leading speakers in the 1859 revival, and took an important part in the campaign of Moody in East London in 1875. This had revealed to him the plight of the foreign sailor, particularly from the European countries, and he had started a small "rest" for them in his home town, Liverpool. Its success led him to repeat the experiment and in 1877 the Strangers' Rest was opened in the Ratcliffe Highway, and this became the headquarters for similar "rests" at other British and continental ports. His method was first to rent a house or shop in a thoroughfare frequented by sailors and to display invitations in different languages in the windows. Then he would visit the ships and lodging houses and invite foreign sailors whom he met to come to the "rest", where he would have a group of voluntary workers who were able to speak various foreign languages. The usual refreshments and games were available and the sailors were either recommended to suitable lodgings or arrangements made for them to sleep on the premises.

Miss Agnes Hedenstrom's Home for Scandinavian seamen was an offshoot of the London Strangers' Rest. For some years she had been helping with the Swedish sailors at the Rest, her chief difficulty being to obtain lodgings for them. Therefore, with the support of T. A. Denny, she opened a hostel in Leman Street in 1889 where they could stay. Like the English institutes, she banked their money, and made special arrangements to remit part of it to their families in their home country. The need for these "strangers' rests" lessened by the end of the century, for by then the larger sailors' societies were beginning to provide facilities for foreign sailors. So some of the "rests" were closed, a few were taken over by the Seamen's Christian Friend Society to become sailors' institutes, and the Strangers' Rest in London turned to general welfare work in the neighbourhood, which it still performs.

Though the naval rating could share the benefits of the various seamen's societies with the sailors of the merchant navy, it was not until the seventies that Agnes Weston managed to persuade the authorities that more definite interest should be taken in his welfare. The chaplain was responsible for both the social and the spiritual welfare of the sailors of the Royal Navy. But many of the smaller vessels had no chaplain, and it was only after 1860, when the Royal Naval Scripture Readers' Society was formed, that licensed lay-readers were allowed on board. Even then the emphasis was on the spiritual side and little was done for the welfare of the rating when on land.

Agnes Weston had spent her early days in Bath where she had been fascinated by the books of Catharine Marsh and for a time had helped Miss Fyffe, the superintendent of the Carus Wilson work among soldiers. Her particular job was to correspond with soldiers when they were moved abroad. She then discovered that the naval rating at sea was just as lonely as the soldier abroad, and so included them in her correspondence. While on a visit to Devonport in 1873 she noticed that the boys of the four training ships spent their free time wandering round the streets with nothing particular to do. She therefore invited them to tea, and this led to more organised activities for them. Visits on board the men-of-war to speak to the naval ratings followed and eventually she gained the permission from the authorities to start social work for them at the naval ports.

A Sailors' Rest was opened for them at Devonport in 1876, to be followed by others at Portsmouth, Sheerness, and Portland. She was careful to make her Rests suitable for all types. The religious and social work were kept distinct, no sailor being asked to attend a meeting or accept a tract, nor were any refused admittance, even when drunk. Each Rest had a booking office for the receipt and safe-keeping of the sailors' pay, a restaurant where meals were available for all servicemen, a petty-officers' coffee room, reading, writing and smoking rooms, and rooms and dormitories with bathing facilities for those who wanted to stay. They were encouraged to make their rooms or cubicles as much like home as possible, and allowed to hang up their own pictures and keep their treasured possessions around. She took great pains to get to know each sailor personally and to keep in continuous contact with him through her publication *Ashore and Afloat* which always contained a personal letter from her and which was distributed to the ships-of-war and gunboats all over the world, as well as to reformatory and industrial ships, to coast-guard stations, to deep sea fishermen and even to the ships of the American navy. As she herself said:

> thus the seed was sown that has resulted in thousands of written and printed letters exchanged with men all over the navy; and this correspondence, this golden cord of friendship, binds myself and my work to every ship in the navy.[1]

Her success gained for her the respect of the high-ranking officers of the Navy, Queen Victoria granted her patronage to the "Rests", and she was one of the few women asked to give evidence before the Select Committee on the Royal Patriotic Fund in 1896. Her work represented an important step forward in drawing attention to the need for better welfare conditions among the men of the Navy, and though her "Rests" were badly damaged in the last war, they still offer a varied range of facilities for servicemen.

Another group for whom help was required were the deep-sea fishermen trawling along the Dogger Bank of the North Sea. Until the end of the century steamships were little used, the sailing trawlers setting out in fleets of twenty or thirty ships, each with its "carrier" to which the boxes of fish were rowed every day from the trawlers and rushed back to port. Not only was the work highly dangerous, but conditions of life aboard the trawlers were very bad. The cabins were minute and often flooded, there

[1] Agnes Weston, *My Life among the Bluejackets*, 1911, p. 73.

was no means of drying wet clothes, little cooked food was provided and few sanitary arrangements existed. Only very elementary aid was available for accidents and no provision made for sickness. It is therefore not surprising that many took to "drink", especially since this could be obtained in large quantities and at cheap rates from the German and Dutch "coopers" or "bumboats". Their permissible and ostensible purpose was the sale of duty-free tobacco, but once the fishermen went abroad they were "tempted to barter their owners' warps, nets, ropes, sails and fish for drink, and the boys and apprentices are demoralised by the obscene pictures and cards so frequently disposed of".

It is said that the "bethel" flag had been hoisted among the fishing vessels of the North Sea at the time of the sailors' revival and that the fleets were visited by the Moravian mission ship *Harmony* in 1832 and again in 1861. But nothing was done for their social welfare until, in the late sixties, Miss Peacock of the Mildmay Institution began to make muffattees and warm clothing for the men sailing from Lowestoft. Then, in 1881, public attention was drawn to their conditions by the shocking murder of an apprentice by the skipper of one of the smacks. This incident prompted E. J. Mather and his friend, the Rev. R. B. Thompson, the vicar of a Yorkshire parish, to visit one of the fleets, "The Short Blue". As a result they were both convinced that the primary need of the men was medical help, and the Mission to Deep-Sea Fishermen was formed in 1881 in order to provide this. For the first eight years it was under the personal supervision of E. J. Mather who, with the help of Messrs. Hewett and Company, one of the largest trawler owners, was allowed to use first one fishing smack and then another as a first aid centre and small hospital for those ill or injured at sea, as well as a chapel and store for books, bibles and tracts. The Mission also had to support itself in its early years by trawling, but competition from the other fishing smacks and lack of time made this increasingly difficult, and as the Mission became better known, unnecessary. Dr. W. T. Grenfell, later to become the well-known missionary to Labrador, introduced two larger vessels with room for a well-equipped hospital and the services of a surgeon, when he became superintendent in 1889. This meant immediate attention to the sick and injured and quicker transport to a shore-based hospital. The mission ships also contained a shop where warm clothing and other necessities could be bought at low prices, a lending library, a club room and recreational centre to which the men could go in their spare time.

All this helped to keep the men away from the "bumboats", but it was strengthened by the co-operation of the Board of Trade which allowed the mission ships to sell tobacco at duty-free prices, and by W. D. and H. O. Wills who offered them the tobacco at cost price. This was the first stage in the abolition of the liquor traffic in the North Sea, and led eventually to the international treaty of 1894 which made the sale of cheap liquor in the North Sea illegal. Thus, through its influence on legislation and its welfare services, this Mission helped to bring about a change in the conditions of life of the deep-sea fisherman. The use of refrigeration and the introduction of steam trawlers in the early twentieth century lessened the hazards of their employment, so that the Royal National Mission to Deep-Sea Fishermen has now withdrawn its ships and provides instead hostels and institutes at the chief fishing ports, with welfare service for the wives and families of the fishermen.

This great growth in seamen's charities of one form or another in the nineteenth century helped to keep pace with the enormous development of shipping. Except for a few organisations such as the Dreadnought's Seaman's Hospital (1921), the Royal National Lifeboat Society (1824), and the Merchant Seamen's Orphan Asylum (1824), which owed their support largely to the interest of the "Sailor King", William IV, and his wife, Queen Adelaide, they were almost all evangelical societies and closely connected with the remarkable work of G. C. Smith. Many of them eventually became linked with the British Sailor's Society the Missions to Seamen, and the Seaman's Christian Friend, which are now the three main societies which deal with the welfare of sailors.

The operations of these voluntary societies in the nineteenth century had a great effect on the morale and comfort of the sailors. The Foreign Office report of 1899, which stated that as many as 14,000 men deserted yearly from British ships largely as a result of the influence of crimps, undesirable women and drunkenness, found that this was much more 'prevalent where sailor's institutes were not available. In consequence the authorities paid far greater attention to the welfare of seamen while afloat, and encouraged the voluntary societies to provide for their welfare while on land. Such work is now sustained to a large extent by King George's Fund for Sailors (1917), with the larger societies of the nineteenth century still performing the greater part of the work.

Soldiers, much more than seamen, formed a distinct group in the community. They were on the whole a more rough and turbulent group and did not command the romantic interest which the sailor was able to arouse. Major-General Sir J. Macdonald, speaking in 1836, noted that

> the soldier's life is wholly unsuited to what are termed the better class of society in this country. Moreover the result of my observation is, and I had the superintendence of the recruiting of the Army since 1817, that few of the better classes of young men enlist in this country, except for some quarrels with relatives; that few enlist for the mere sake of being soldiers, and considering that a better profession than any other.[1]

The first attempts to help soldiers, like those for seamen, were chiefly spiritual and turned out to be largely sporadic and of short duration. John Wesley had preached to soldiers and many joined his societies, some becoming local preachers, while as early as 1744 there were little groups of "methodists" in the army, meeting together for spiritual fellowship. Walker of Truro, one of the early Evangelicals, is reputed to have had much influence upon soldiers, and the aim of the sailors' revival of the early nineteenth century had been to include soldiers in their work, so that seamen's and soldiers' friend societies were started at Chatham, Woolwich, Plymouth and Stonehouse.

G. C. Smith's interest in soldiers had been raised as a result of his two years' service as a voluntary chaplain with Wellington's forces in Spain, and there is an account of a remarkable meeting held by him for men of the Lifeguards stationed at the Royal Barracks, Knightsbridge, which led to services at the Trevor

[1] *H.M. Commissioners for enquiring into Military Punishments in the Army*, report, 59 of 1836, evidence p. 71.

Chapel, Brompton, and meetings for soldiers and their wives held twice a week within the barracks.

> As this business now assumed an importance that was not suspected in its earliest appearance, it was deemed necessary to lay the particulars before the committee of the British and Foreign Seamen's Friend Society and Bethel Union, which had incorporated soldiers in its exertions wherever there was a military depot.[1]

Plans were made for some society to perpetuate and extend this work, but they do not appear to have come to the same fruition as those made for sailors, nor to have had the same permanent effect. The only sign of any continuity of work among soldiers is the opening, in 1830, of a soldiers' chapel by G. C. Smith near Tothill Street, Westminster, which probably encouraged the London City Mission to regard soldiers as a group needing special attention, and so prompting the formation of the Soldiers' Friend Society and the Army Scripture Readers' Society, both of which sent lay-readers to work among the troops.

The Crimean War and the Indian Mutiny of the late fifties focused public attention upon the conditions of soldiers, and both the authorities and private individuals began to show some concern for their social welfare. These wars awakened the Victorians to the need for a standing army which was well-trained and equipped. Training grounds were introduced, the chief ones being at Aldershot and the Curragh in Ireland, and more attention was paid to the recruiting and instruction of the troops. At the same time, with the expansion of our overseas territories, more troops were needed at foreign stations and this involved the added problems of transport and family relationships. These changes happened to coincide with the mid-century revival which provided the driving force for much of the Evangelical social work for soldiers. A small book by Catharine Marsh, *The Memorials of Hedley Vicars*, appeared in 1856 and had a very wide circulation in Evangelical circles. It was the biography of a Christian officer who was killed at the Crimea, and described in detail the difficulties and temptations of the ordinary soldier. This helped to attract both money and workers to the needs of the soldier.

[1] *Sailors' Magazine*, December 1821.

Two soldiers' institutes were opened in 1858, one by an Evangelical lady, Miss Lucy Papillon, at the Shorncliffe Camp, Sandgate, and the other at Portsmouth by the Rev. W. Carus Wilson. Both followed the usual institutional method of providing rooms where the soldiers could spend their leisure time, read or write, or play table games. There was a great need for this, because up to this time soldiers' day rooms were the only place in the barracks where they could go when off duty, and one of these was the canteen where great quantities of liquor were sold, which according to the Army historian, John Fortescue, were "rank poison and a fertile source of crime". The Army authorities were well aware of this, and one of the recommendations of the Committee of 1862, which enquired into the living conditions of soldiers, was the establishment of soldiers' institutes outside the barracks. As a result some, like those at Chatham and Gibraltar, were entirely secular in character, and closely linked with the military authorities; others were started by Evangelicals and usually had some connection with the work of Mrs. Daniell and her daughter, Miss Robinson and Miss Sandes.

The suggestion by the Rev. Pennefather at the Barnet Conference of 1862 that a mission for soldiers should be started at Aldershot led to the commencement of Evangelical work both there and elsewhere. Between 1855 when the camp was established at Aldershot and 1862 when Mrs. Daniell opened her institute there the population of the town had increased from 600 to over 7,000 inhabitants and the camp numbered some 15,000 men, most of them housed in wooden huts within the camp precincts. Captain Pilkington-Jackson reported to the Secretary of War in 1862 that

> there are twenty-five public houses, several of which have large halls attached, fitted up with great splendour. As an inducement to the men to visit their places and spend their money in drink the attendance of prostitutes, gaily dressed, is encouraged. The proprietors or tenants of these music halls compete with each other in attempts to make them attractive; first in their appearance and comfort; secondly in the varied character of their entertainment; and thirdly by an excitement of a highly demoralising and injurious tendency. A small entrance fee is usually charged, but the great remuneration for the large outlay is derived from the sale of intoxicating drink . . .

There are forty-seven beer houses, which are, I understand, almost without exception public brothels of the worst description. The women generally live in these houses and have the free use of certain rooms in consideration for drawing men to drink in the houses, and in some cases the women pay for this privilege, making what they can from the men; they usually treat men well on first arrival, to induce them to return, and rob them when opportunities occur . . .

It must be borne in mind that the men of Aldershot are cut off from all respectable society, and are necessarily exposed to the temptations referred to; even the good conduct men . . . have no resort but bad houses, and no company but prostitutes.[1]

Mrs. Daniell was the widow of an Army officer, and had already established five successful village missions in connection with the Country Towns Mission. She had the support of leading Evangelicals, the goodwill of the Army Chaplains and local clergy and the help of many officers in the camp in opening her institute at Aldershot. Using Mrs. Bayly's Working Men's Hall at Notting Hill as her prototype, she adapted it to the needs of soldiers, and her institute, like many of those who copied her, was built in an attractive Elizabethan style, had a bar for refreshments, a dining room from which cooked food could be taken away, recreation and class rooms and some sleeping accommodation for those on leave. The particular concern of her assistant, Miss Robinson, was with the women of the area. She visited them in their lodgings, did what she could to persuade them to leave the soldiers alone, and for a time had a small rescue home for them. Miss Daniell took over control when her mother died in 1871, and it was during her period of superintendence that branches were opened at Weedon, Manchester, Colchester, Plymouth, Chatham and 170 Buckingham Palace Road, London, a few of which, as well as the Home at Aldershot, are still functioning.

Miss Robinson did not stay long at Aldershot. She felt that the more usual methods of the institute were not entirely suited to soldiers. Loneliness and isolation were the chief cause of their troubles, and what they needed most was someone with whom they could talk and confide their difficulties. She, therefore,

[1] *The Report of Charles Pilkington-Jackson, R.A., to the Secretary of State for War on Soldiers' Institutes at Aldershot and at Portsmouth*, 126 of 1862, pp. 2 and 4.

started to visit the different military stations, gained permission to talk with the men in the barracks, in the married quarters and the hospital, and held informal discussions with them in the regimental school room. She would arrange for money orders to be sent home to wives, correspond with the men when she left, and found employment for those whose period of service was over, and in so doing discharged many of the duties of the modern social worker. Her work was recognised by the Naval and Military Bible Society which used her as one of their agents, and by the military authorities who nominated her as a lecturer to the troops.

When she eventually opened her institute at Portsmouth (1874), her purpose was to deal with the problems associated with a port of embarkation. The "unofficial" wives and children of men going abroad would travel there in the vain hope that they might manage to get aboard at the last moment, widows and orphans of men dying abroad would arrive there, the sick and wounded would wait there for further transport, and the ordinary troops would frequently experience much delay. At her institute she had a few beds, at 6d. per night, for those in transit, women and children were housed temporarily until arrangements could be made for their future, a trade training school was conducted where carpentry, joinery and cabinet making were taught to those who wanted to set up in civilian employment, facilities were provided on the wharves for the sale of coffee and cakes and for last-minute letter writing, and workers were available to give information as to existing military charities and other sources of maintenance for widows and orphans. These services were continued until the authorities made better arrangements for their troops in transit and some of them still form part of the work of the Soldiers', Sailors' and Airmen's Families Association. Her home at Portsmouth is now run by the Y.M.C.A.

The needs of the soldiers stationed in Ireland were the concern of Miss Elise Sandes. She was a convert of the mid-century revival who began to take an interest in the welfare of soldiers, inviting some to her house that she might teach them to read. This led to the opening of a home for soldiers in Cork in 1877 and later through the help of several Evangelical friends, among them

William Palmer, Samuel Morley and T. A. Denny, to the extension of her work to Northern Ireland, the Curragh and other camps, and to the ports of embarkation for England. Miss Sandes combined Miss Robinson's personal approach with an endeavour to keep in continuous touch with the men wherever they were. She therefore believed in a large number of small homes, frequently ordinary dwelling houses which she adapted to suit her needs, and tried "to make them true substitutes for the homes the men had left, and to have those in them who can really take the place of their mothers and sisters". The evacuation of British troops from Ireland in 1922 and from India in 1947 caused the closing of some of her homes, but several of the Sandes Homes still remain.

The smaller homes and institutes for soldiers in the different towns in Britain also owed much to Mrs. Daniell, Miss Robinson and Miss Sandes. Mrs. Daniell's close link with Mildmay enabled the Institution to send deaconesses to her for special training before they became superintendents of some of the smaller homes. Several of Miss Robinson's workers left to start homes of their own, notably Mrs. Digby Dent who opened the Woolwich Garrison Home in 1876; and many small homes were formed on the suggestion and advice of Miss Sandes.

In most cases these Evangelical homes were encouraged by the authorities who placed them "within bounds" and permitted their agents to visit the barracks, and often some high ranking officer would serve on the board of management or as one of the trustees. These homes were mostly undenominational, though by the end of the century both the Wesleyans and the Church of England had opened homes of their own on similar lines, the latter under the auspices of the Church of England Soldiers' and Sailors' Institutes (1891).

In comparison with the soldiers' institutes opened by groups of officers at some of the barracks, these Evangelical homes were usually less spacious, but they offered a more homely atmosphere, and the presence of lady workers made it possible for many family difficulties or personal complications to be sorted out. Their effect upon the newly enlisted was far greater than upon the older soldier, and it was chiefly the former who frequented them, the latter preferring the canteens and regimental institutes where alcoholic liquor was available and where there was no chance of any religious intrusion. It is therefore likely that the Evangelical homes exercised a strong preventive pressure, by helping to counteract the drunkenness and prostitution which tended to demoralise the recruits.

Nineteenth century soldiers and sailors had two important problems in common—how to cope with the needs of their wives and children during their long periods of absence; and how to avoid intemperence when the drinking of large quantities of alcohol was regarded as essential for their health and when it was made available for them by the authorities. Both these problems became the concern of those who managed the institutes and homes.

The sailor's wife and family rarely followed him from port to port, nor did the employers arrange for part of the sailor's wages to be sent to her. As we have seen, most of the sailors' societies made arrangements for this and some of them sent their agents on board the merchant ships to collect a portion of the wage before it could be spent. In the Royal Navy it had been possible since 1758 to allot a certain proportion of the wage to the wife, but this was not widely known and was rarely practised. Miss Weston was largely responsible for seeing that this was carried out. At first her agents were allowed on board to bank the pay of ratings and transmit a portion to their wives. She then persuaded the authorities to encourage seamen to conform to the Act of 1758, though this still involved a personal application at the pay office of the nearest dockyard. Eventually she protested to the authorities with the result that permission was given in 1894 for payment to be made through the post office, and this paved the way for the payment of separation allowances to be made to sailors' wives in 1914.

Soldiers' wives were in a somewhat different position, since only those married "on the strength" were provided with quarters and allowed to draw rations for themselves and their families, and these constituted only some twelve of every hundred married soldiers. Many of the others accompanied their husbands in England but the soldier had to meet the cost of food and lodging from his own pay which at a maximum was around 10/– per week. Mrs. Daniell had formed the Aldershot Soldiers' Wives Aid Association in 1863 to provide sewing for wives "off the strength" and Miss Robinson started the Soldiers' and Sailors' Wives Aid Association (1876) for a similar purpose at Portsmouth. Though the authorities would not recognise these societies, they frequently gave them orders for soldiers' shirts and other articles of clothing.

These efforts led directly to the Soldiers' and Sailors' Family Association started by Major Gildea in 1885. At first it worked in co-operation with Miss Robinson, supplying areas which she was unable to reach, but it was gradually possible to extend the Association over the whole of Britain, each area being placed under the control of a local committee whose function was to help the wives and families in their district. Since soldiers' wives, married "off the strength", received no medical attention, the Association started a district nursing service at Aldershot, the Curragh, York, Devonport, Gosport and several foreign stations. From its beginnings the Association received full support from the Military and it became usual when troops were ordered abroad for the commanding officer to report to the local committee the names of wives who were left behind. The Navy did not show similar enthusiasm, though Miss Weston worked in close co-operation with the Association. Thus the early example of Evangelical societies has led to the widespread work for wives and families of servicemen which S.S.A.F.A. carries on today. It supplies those welfare services of a personal nature which the authorities are unable to provide and is recognised by them as a necessary part of the welfare organisations for the families of service and ex-service men.

The problem of intemperance in the services was dealt with in a similar manner to that in the country as a whole. The excessive drunkenness at the Crimea drew attention to the matter in the Army and led to the formation of two local Evangelical societies, the Soldiers' Total Abstinence Society (1862) in India, and Mrs. Daniell's Total Abstinence Society (1863) at Aldershot, the Chaplain-General giving his support in both cases. Miss Robinson approached the problem in a different manner, by including "temperance" as a subject in her courses of lectures to soldiers, and by personally taking a mobile coffee stall to Dartmoor, Cannock

Chase and Aldershot when the men were on manoeuvres. A determined effort to reduce intemperance throughout the Army dates from this period, the National Temperance League approaching every garrison, barracks and depot, and the Church of England Temperance Society forming regimental branches and adopting Miss Robinson's method of mobile coffee stalls on field days. The outcome was the formation of the Army Temperance Association in 1894 with the sanction of the War Office and the help of a government grant.

The Royal Naval Temperance Society (1873) owed its beginning to Miss Weston who had become convinced of the need for temperance both among the boys in training at Portsmouth and among the men on board ship. As the work expanded the National Temperance League came to her help, and in 1879 the Society which by then had branches aboard some 230 ships, was recognised by the authorities. Meanwhile the Naval Church Society was formed for members of the Church of England, though in effect it concentrated upon ships and marine barracks which were not reached by the Royal Naval Temperance Society.

By the early twentieth century there had been a marked improvement in the drinking habits in both the services. This, to some extent, reflected a similar tendency in England at that time. It was also helped by the authorities who were less lavish in their provision of "drink", and by the short service arrangements which induced servicemen to save for the future. But a strong incentive was supplied by these Evangelical temperance societies and strengthened by the counter-attractions of the soldiers' and sailors' institutes and mobile coffee stalls. It should be noted that the authorities supported these Evangelical efforts, and in some instances set up similar organisations.

Two noteworthy factors led to these various social services for seamen and soldiers, the stimulus of war, which in both groups happened to coincide with the second factor—a period of religious revival. In the case of the seamen it was the Napoleonic Wars and the sailors' revival of the second and third decades of the nineteenth century; in that of the soldiers, the Crimean War and the mid-century revival. There is little documentation of G. C. Smith and the remarkable revival among sailors, and the facts we have

are somewhat confused and "written up" by his supporters. But
there is no doubt that most of our large sailors' charities have their
origins there. The effect of the mid-century revival upon the
welfare of soldiers was less conspicuous, but social work for
soldiers was one of the important forms of philanthropy which
this time of revival initiated.

On the whole, these societies followed very closely the pattern
of other forms of social work of the period. They used the institute
as their centre and developed various services around it, and they
kept in constant touch with the men, wherever they were,
through personal correspondence. On the other hand, much of the
work was carried out by middle-class women who were exclusively in charge of societies dealing with the needs of men—an
arrangement which was rarely found in other fields of social work
in the nineteenth century. The reason for this was that "these
ladies" were remarkably successful in providing comfortable and
homelike surroundings which were otherwise lacking in the
garrison towns and ports, and yet were able to keep a certain
degree of discipline. Similarly they dealt with the many family and
personal problems which today fall within the province of the
social case-worker. Not only did they encourage the authorities
to pay far greater attention to the welfare of sailors and soldiers,
but the names of Miss Weston, Mrs. Daniell, Miss Robinson and
Miss Sandes are still known to a generation of servicemen who
live some half century after their deaths.

CHAPTER XV

Some Other Groups of Working People

SOLDIERS AND sailors were not the only group of workers whose work placed them in conditions of particular hardship or temptation. The London City Mission had, from its early days, recognised that certain other types were in particular need of help, and had allocated special missionaries to these groups, which included policemen, cabmen, railwaymen, navvies, postmen and gipsies. But their function was evangelical rather than social work, though they did, through their reports and their contacts with social workers, make the needs of these people more widely known. This led others to concentrate upon their social welfare, and to provide various services for them.

Navvies were a group who received particular attention. The growth of population and the development of transport led to the employment of as many as 200,000 of them on the laying of railways, the building of bridges, the construction of reservoirs and the erection of docks and sea walls.

> They are generally men who have been in the habit of receiving but very precarious employment, and very low wages in towns; and they are drawn suddenly into an employment which is lucrative to them, and brings them a considerable sum; but notwithstanding that, it is all spent in dissipation, and they are in a state of continual poverty and always in debt. . . . Facility of getting employment induces them on the slightest pretext to leave their present employment and get another, and leave their lodgings unpaid.[1]

> They are brought hastily together in large bodies; no time is given for the gradual growth of accommodation . . . they are crowded into unwholesome dwellings, with scarcely any provision made for their comfort or decency of living; they are released from the useful influence of domestic things, and the habits of their former routine

[1] *Select Committee on Railway Labourers*, report, 530 of 1846, evidence 1656.

268

of life . . . they are hard-worked; they are exposed to great risk of life and limb; they are too often hardly treated; and many inducements are presented to them to be thoughtless, thriftless and improvident.[1]

Though these conditions were brought to the public notice in 1846 when the Select Committee on Railway Labourers published their report, little notice was taken of them, either by the authorities or the employers, and it was left to voluntary organisations to do what they could. Two Evangelical societies, the Church Pastoral Aid Society and the London City Mission, sent chaplains and scripture readers to the areas and the employers usually granted them facilities to conduct religious worship and organise education. In some cases, such as that of the Rev. Dr. Fremantle who worked among the navvies of the Leicester to Newark line, the work was entirely spiritual, but it was more usual for Sunday and day schools to be started for the children and classes for adults. Such education could rarely be continuous and there was often difficulty in getting the children to attend. As one chaplain remarked: "they are living in that state of wildness, that I doubt whether their parents could coerce them sufficiently to attend".[2] Reading rooms were usually provided for the adults and at Bristol "a few gentlemen set up a wooden hut from which cocoa and cheap meals were sold and which was moved down the line as the work progressed".[3]

The views of the contractors were, on the whole, favourable, one saying that

> he was thoroughly satisfied with the religious instruction given the men which had profound practical results . . . the men returned to their work on Monday (a rare thing in those days) and there was less time spent in the public house.[4]

Another preferred the scripture reader to the clergy since his background was more closely linked with that of the men, and it was quite common for city and town missions to be requested by the director of a company to let him have the services of one or more of their missionaries.

[1] *530 of 1846, op. cit.,* p. iii.   [2] *Ibid.,* evidence 304.
[3] *Revival,* November 19, 1863.   [4] *Quarterly Letter to Navvies,* June 1895.

Often, local people did their best to help navvies temporarily employed in their district. Catharine Marsh's work is the most well known through her book, *English Hearts and English Hands*. She began in 1853 to visit navvies who were erecting the Crystal Palace on Sydenham Hill, and writes:

> The building of the Crystal Palace, and the arrangements of the grounds had drawn upwards of three thousand workmen of various trades, but the majority railway labourers, to the neighbourhood. Every cottage in Beckenham and its hamlets which could receive lodgers was filled to overflowing. A dread prevailed among the more thoughtful of the parishioners, that this invasion of their quiet village would be fraught with danger to the tranquility and moral welfare, and this apprehension was not without reason. The men called themselves truly "a rough lot" and at that time the navvy was looked upon as an Ishmaelite, "his hand against every man, and every man's hand against his".[1]

A soup kitchen was opened, and cheap meals provided for the men in the cold weather, and Catharine and her workers would visit the men during their dinner break, find out if any were ill or had met with an accident, and arrange for their nursing or removal to hospital.

When the navvies left a particular district contact with them was frequently lost, and so in 1877 the Navvy Mission was formed, under the superintendence of Mrs. Elizabeth Garnett, to co-ordinate the work of the different local missions and to make it possible for the navvy to be passed on from one mission to another as he changed his place of work. Like Agnes Weston, Elizabeth Garnett used a periodical, *The Quarterly Letter to Navvies*, to keep in touch with them wherever they were. It contained announcements of a personal nature, such as births, marriages and deaths, enquiries by relatives for men with whom contact had been lost, and advertised the starting of work at new places of construction. These letters were free to all navvies, and their circulation in 1889 was around 135,000 copies.

The Navvy Mission kept itself informed of all changes in places of construction and opened missions itself whenever this was not done by the local people. It saw that every mission had proper re-

[1] Catharine Marsh, *A Tale of Old Beckenham*, 1876, pp. 4–5.

ligious and educational facilities and if possible a coffee refreshment room. Several evangelists, such as William Taylor and John Harris, were lent by the Evangelisation Society to visit the different missions, and an orphanage was opened in 1890 for the children of navvies killed on duty. To introduce navvies to these missions, a Christian Excavators' Union was formed of Christian navvies throughout the country, and their job was to see that every new navvy who arrived at a place of construction was at once directed to the mission centre.

Quite often an employer invited the Navvy Mission to open a branch at their works, and missions were to be found in Scotland, Canada and many other countries where construction work was being carried on. When, at the end of the century, the amount of heavy construction had declined, the basis of membership was broadened and other "men on public works" were included in the ministrations of the Navvy Mission, until in 1920 it was decided to affiliate with the Christian Social Union as the Industrial Christian Fellowship which continues to offer personal friendship and advice to all persons in industrial employment.

Railwaymen were subject to conditions similar to those of the navvies. Many of them were absent for periods from their homes, most worked long and variable hours, their only place for rest and refreshment was the public house, and injury when engaged upon their work was common. But their conditions of work did not cause the same degree of isolation and of primitive accommodation, nor the same tendency to form a distinctive group in the community. The London City Mission, in the 1850's, began to care for the spiritual needs of these men in the metropolitan area, appointing special missionaries to minister to them, and, as in the case of the navvies, missions were to be found at some of the railway junctions. But there was no attempt to make any general provision for these men until the Railway Mission was formed in 1881, by which time there were some 400,000 men and boys employed on the railways of England.

This Mission developed from H. Eliot Walton's work among boys employed as junior clerks, messengers, and signal, telegraph, booking and call boys on the railways in the Nine Elms district of South London. Many were country lads, living in lodgings near the station, most of them without any suitable friends. Mr. Walton, in a letter to E. M. Denny in 1876, describes the motives for his work:

> When the work first commenced I was drawn out towards them in noticing that they walked the streets very late at night with unsuitable companions such as the boys and girls of vile principles. . . . By the help of a kind friend I was able to procure the address of one of the boys whom I visited, and by that way I was enabled to have him up to my house with some of his companions. A few weeks afterwards I started an evening class so as to help them with their reading, writing and arithmetic etc., and by that means they are brought under the influence of the Gospel.[1]

The next step was the renting of a room at 11 High Street, Vauxhall, as an institute for the boys and the awakening of an interest by others engaged in youth work, in particular the Hon. Arthur Kinnaird and T. H. Pelham. Waterloo and Clapham Junction were included in their sphere of activities, C. H. Spurgeon allowed them the use of one of his lecture rooms for their half-yearly meetings and Mrs. Meredith gave them a room on her premises at Nine Elms for their senior branch.

Mr. Walton then turned his attention to the adult railway worker, and it was decided to try and co-ordinate the activities of the many isolated missions which local people had started at the different railway stations. The Mildmay Institution, since it already undertook work for railwaymen at some of its branches, was chosen as the centre, and on November 14, 1881, the Railway Mission was inaugurated, with H. Eliot Walton as its superintendent and George Williams of the Y.M.C.A. as a member of its committee.

During the first six years of the Railway Mission, 190 branches were formed in the United Kingdom, some of them newly established, others affiliated with the Mission. Many of them were organised by ladies, a typical example being the railway mission at Brighton which was run by Mrs. Gates. She had been invited by some of the porters and other railwaymen to take meetings for them. A room in the railway works was made available by the general manager of the line, and here she formed her club for

[1] *MS. letter from H. E. Walton to E. M. Denny, June 2, 1876.*

railwaymen which eventually consisted of a refreshment room where they could buy hot drinks and light meals at all times, reading and recreation rooms, and some sleeping quarters.

Like the Navvy Mission, the Railway Mission sought "to advocate the cause of temperance and the care of the injured".[1] Most missions provided refreshment rooms, some on an elaborate scale, and since neither the Common Law nor the Employers' Liability Act of 1880 was much use in practice in the case of injuries, the Mission made its own arrangements. It had a special department to secure letters of admission to the hospitals, the free provision of artificial limbs and the giving of monetary aid to men, who, through an accident, were in financial difficulties. Convalescent homes were opened at Hastings and Southport, and the Railway Benevolent Institution, which worked in close contact with the Mission, helped the completely incapacitated and the families of those killed. The periodical *The Railway Signal* was used to maintain contact between the men at the different branches, and the members of the Railway Mission Christian Association were on the look-out for men newly employed or transferred to their stations. To include stations which were too small for a branch of the Railway Mission, Lady Hope started the Letter and Packet Mission which sent personal letters and periodicals to those employed; and for railway gate-keepers and their families at the level crossings, Annie Macpherson arranged the despatch of a monthly packet of literature.

Both the Navvy and the Railway Missions did much to bring about a sense of solidarity among the workers, and to raise their self-esteem. They tended to draw the men closer together in a common bond of fellowship and to make them realise that their individual needs were frequently those of the group. In many cases, as we have seen, the employers approved of this, and did their best to help, and in some cases began themselves to provide similar services. Canteens, or "shants" as they were called, were opened by the employers at some places of construction, and the larger railway stations began to supply hot meals and refreshments to their employees. Indirectly this improved the facilities for the public as well, since where such refreshments were provided they

[1] *Railway Signal*, May 1882.

were usually available for both the public and for railway servants. Gradually the railway authorities have improved the welfare arrangements for their employees, so that the Railway Mission, now, does largely spiritual work at its mission halls.

A third group of workers whose long hours of outdoor employment attracted the attention of philanthropists were the cab-drivers. According to Mayhew, there were some 5,000 of them in London in the mid-nineteenth century, and many more in the provincial centres. About 2,000 of them were small masters who were among the more respectable men on the ranks, but there were also a certain number of "night-men" of dubious character, who were often involved in the furtherance of prostitution and crime. Heavy drinking was common because of their exposure to all weathers when plying for their trade, and they had few opportunities of getting any refreshments or meals except at the public houses.

Welfare work for them stemmed almost entirely from the mid-century revival. The Cabmen's Club Aid Society (1859) was a direct offshoot of this. Its purpose was to start cabmen's clubs in different parts of London which should be open from 8 a.m. to 11 p.m. The London City Mission played an important part in establishing these clubs which supplied refreshments such as tea, coffee, chops and steaks at all hours and had rest rooms where the men could go between fares. Lord Shaftesbury was most interested in the work, and to extend it started the Cabmen's Shelter Fund in 1875 which made it possible to provide as many as forty shelters in different parts of London to accommodate some 3,000 cab-drivers.

The Mission to Night Cabmen, started in 1861, was also connected with the revival and run in close connection with the London City Mission. The intention of its founder, Mr. Herbert, was to raise the moral standards of cab-drivers, particularly the "night men". The men were contacted at their stands, shelters and public houses by Mr. Herbert with the help of city missionaries and exhorted to take no part in malpractices, and the women with whom they were in league were visited by Miss Herbert. The Christian Cabdrivers' Association, formed in 1889, had a similar purpose. Its members were pledged to report any malpractices and to make

every effort to restore girls who had been abducted to their rela-
tives. Meanwhile a vigorous attack on intemperance was made by
George McCree, the missionary at the Bloomsbury Baptist
Chapel, who established branches of the Cabmen's Temperance
Society at most of the shelters.

Unlike the missions for navvies and railwaymen, there seems to
have been little attempt to co-ordinate the work of the different
societies. The London Cabmen's Mission (1871), started by John
Duprée, did try to keep in touch with all cabmen and their families
through *The Cabman* which was distributed free to all cab-drivers,
but the Mission never assumed a central position in welfare work
for cabmen. This may have been due to the fact that the Church
of England Temperance Society began to take an active interest in
cabmen in 1886, placing Thomas Ryan in charge of the work.
Their large resources and widespread organisation made it possible to combine the different aspects of the work throughout the
metropolis, and eventually it was divided between the Church
Army and the Police Court Mission, Thomas Ryan being
appointed a missionary of the latter society to deal with cabmen
brought before the courts.

Since, in the provinces, the cabstands were usually at the stations
and the men had little to do between the times of the trains, welfare work for them was frequently combined with that for railwaymen. The Cabmen's Mission at Bristol, started by George
Darling in 1855, was an example of this. Having gained the sympathy of the local superintendent of the Great Western Railway,
he was allowed to use the arches under the arrival platform as a
clubroom for cabmen and railwaymen. Here they could rest or
read, and do some simple cooking. Similarly, at Manchester, the
railway company provided a site where a cabmen's and railwaymen's club was built, while in other towns the city missionaries
often organised such work on a small scale. As was usual with
successful voluntary work of this kind, the authorities eventually
followed their example, and some of the local councils began to
provide their own shelters for the cabmen. Shelters can still be
seen on the streets of London and other large towns, which today
provide hot snacks for our taxi-cab drivers.

A final group of workers who received some help in the later

nineteenth century were policemen. The Metropolitan Police
Force had been formed in 1829 and county police forces appeared
in the following decades. To some extent the police shared the
same occupational hazards as the navvies, railwaymen and cabmen. They were out-of-doors at all hours and in all weathers and
worked in comparative isolation from their fellow men. The
authorities paid little attention to their personal welfare at this
time and, except for the visits of London City Missionaries, little
interest was taken in them until Catharine Gurney became
concerned.

She was related both to the Gurneys of Earlham and to the
Tritton family, and when she moved to Kensington in 1870 became interested in a small mission for policemen which had been
started there in 1866 as a result of the revival. With the help of
Mrs. Carlile, the wife of Wilson Carlile of the Church Army, the
meeting was extended, others started in different parts of London,
and the Christian Police Association formed in 1883 by their
union. Several small missions which had already been formed in
the provinces joined, others were started, and within a year there
were nineteen branches with over 700 members. Each branch had
a club where the men could meet and where meals were continuously served. They were supplied with mufflers and tea bottles
to use on duty and for many years a coffee barrow was sent out in
London for their benefit whenever there was an event of importance which involved long hours of work.

Though Catharine Gurney, at the headquarters in Adelphi
Terrace, was the pivot of the Association, the men were allowed a
remarkable amount of self-government and were represented on
all the committees. Like her contemporaries, she kept in personal
touch with them through the periodical, *On and Off Duty*, which
she edited, and sponsored holiday and convalescent homes for
them and their families, and two orphanages for their children.
The Association quickly grew, opened branches in Scotland and
Ireland and eventually abroad. It is now known as the International Christian Police Association, and continues to care for
both the temporal and spiritual welfare of all policemen and their
families.

In a similar manner, the Evangelicals tried to help certain

groups of working women. They did so, either because the nature of their occupation placed them in exceptional moral danger—this was particularly the case with theatrical workers, barmaids, city workgirls and needlewomen—or because through lack of training they were forced to take unsuitable employment. Like the men, each group was dealt with independently, without any obvious co-ordination in policy.

The Theatrical Mission, started by the Rev. and Mrs. Courthope Todd in 1873, was at first a letter mission to keep in touch with girls who had been acting in the Crystal Palace pantomime and were later on tour. Girls such as these, who were employed in travelling companies, always stood the chance of instant dismissal in a strange town if they were ill or if the show were not a success. The intention of the letter mission was to send them a personal letter each month, asking for a reply if any assistance was needed. By 1884 some 1,000 letters were being sent every month. Macready House, in Henrietta Street, was then opened in 1885 as a club for those working in the London theatres. Such girls usually lived in the suburbs and were at a loose end between rehearsals and before the evening show. Cheap lunches and teas were provided at Macready House and arrangements were made to look after any children employed on the stage. Any girl who was expecting a baby was encouraged to seek the help of the Theatre Ladies Guild which would arrange for the confinement and find other work for her after the baby was born.

Barmaids, whether they were employed in hotels, public houses, restaurants or railway stations, were in an exceptionally vulnerable position. Their wages were low because they were reckoned to augment them by "treating" or tips, they were expected to make themselves generally pleasing to their customers, and since their hours were long they frequently had to go home, unaccompanied, very late at night. It is therefore not surprising that Mrs. Bramwell Booth considered that about a quarter of the prostitutes in the West End followed this occupation. The London City Mission from 1853 had regularly visited the public houses and bars in the City, drawing attention to these unsatisfactory conditions, but social work among these girls was first undertaken by the Y.W.C.A. in 1879 when Mrs. Menzies began to send a monthly letter to all young women employed in the station refreshment bars and to follow it up with a personal visit. Others were called upon in the hotels, restaurants, theatre bars and public houses and workers both of the Church of England Temperance Society and of the Girls' Friendly Society helped with this. The interest of Samuel Morley was aroused, and with his help a club was opened at the Morley Rooms, John Street, where the girls could spend their free time and where a certain number could live. The Y.W.C.A. and the National Union of Women Workers then took up the cause, and were reasonably successful in persuading employers to provide lunch and rest rooms for the barmaids so that they might stand less chance of forming undesirable acquaintances.

The social services which the Evangelicals introduced for city workgirls were also to some extent preventive. There were about 40,000 of these girls engaged in various forms of small industry such as envelope-making, book-binding, cigar-making and the manufacture of artificial flowers. Most of them lived at a distance and were obliged to spend the mid-day hour when the workrooms were closed, eating what they had brought with them in the streets. Mrs. Eleanor Fisher, with the help of George Williams of the Y.M.C.A., began to open small restaurants for them in the 1870's where cheap meals could be bought, where they could heat up their own food, and rest in warmth and comfort. The Y.M.C.A. at first lent them a room on their premises at Aldersgate and this was followed by the opening of other "Welcomes", as they were called, in Cross Keys Street and Jewin Street. Employers gradually became interested and some sixty firms eventually asked her to arrange meals for the girls they employed. Her "Welcomes" were probably one of the earliest examples of canteen arrangements for factory and workshop girls, and it was not until 1916 that such arrangements were recommended by legislation.

The Evangelicals did not try to deal with the problem of "sweated labour" as a whole. They seem to have taken more interest in the needs of particular groups of girls rather than in trying to improve the general conditions of their work. There is no indication that they took any part in the women's trade union activities of the 1870's and 1880's nor in the demands for minimum wages in the first decade of the twentieth century. Yet they were not entirely impervious to the long hours and low wages of needlewomen. There are instances such as the Needlewoman's Institute (1860) in Manchester Square, supported by Lord Shaftesbury and Baroness Burdett-Coutts, where women were employed for fairly short hours and at a reasonable wage. Sarah Heckford, at her workshop in Shadwell in the 1880's managed to employ her women at the usual day wage and only work them eight hours. But these are isolated examples and, so far as women industrial workers are concerned, the Evangelicals were content to leave an improvement in their economic conditions to others and to concentrate upon their personal welfare. This was, perhaps, fortunate, for it drew attention to certain services which might otherwise have remained overlooked, and so prepared the way for the great improvement in welfare services which came about as a result of the First World War.

Domestic servants formed a large proportion of the female population in the nineteenth century. Clara Collett estimated at the end of the century that as much as one-third of those in employment were engaged in domestic service. Their greatest need was training, for once a servant was trained she was fairly sure of getting a job, while if she was untrained she was at the mercy of her employer and could be thrown out on the streets for some trivial offence.

The Evangelicals were the first to open training homes for servants. One of the earliest was St. John's Training Home, started by Lady Kinnaird in Milman Street in 1841. The girls were taught cooking and domestic work, suitable employment was found for them when they were trained, and they were provided with a trunk and a change of clothes. The training home attached to the Bedford Institute is noteworthy in that the girls were given pocket money during their three-months' course. A training home at Clapham took the girls straight from school, gave them nine months' training, sent them to daily places for the first two years and only then found them residential jobs. These are only examples from the many Evangelical training homes for servants. Some, of course, did not come up to these standards, but they did at least realise that the trained servant was in a far better position than her untrained counterpart to lead a safe and happy life.

Another urgent need was the provision of authentic registry offices to which the servant could go when out of a job. Many of the so-called registry offices were "bogus", and placed the unwary in the hands of the owners of brothels. Lieutenant Blackmore of the Midnight Meeting Movement was well aware of this and in 1849 opened the Christian Female Servants' Registry at Camden Town. This led many of the Christian Missions to add a servants' registry to their other activities, some of the other voluntary societies did the same and all the training homes had one as a matter of course and usually encouraged the girls to return to the home for a while until a new job was found. This reduced rather than solved the problem, and at the end of the century it was taken up by the National Vigilance Society with the result that the London County Council, followed by other local councils, passed by-laws in 1905 making it necessary for servants' agencies to be registered.

The Evangelicals were also concerned with the welfare of the well-trained, superior servants, most of whom were employed in the large houses and had worked their way up from the lowest ranks. They were on the whole well fed and comfortably housed in comparison with what they would have been in their own homes. Thus their problems were chiefly those of sickness and unemployment. Those receiving relatively high wages would usually join one of the servants' benevolent or provident societies, of which there were several. But Elizabeth Fry, as early as 1813, had realised that there were many who could not afford to do so, and had started a servants' society for them, out of which grew the Female Servants' Home Society (1836) which had a hostel for those out of work and a registry office for experienced servants. When C. H. Spurgeon was its president in the sixties, it had four hostels which could take some hundred servants. Similar in function was the Servants' Mission, started in 1867 by Mr. Goodchild with the help of Miss Anne Malpas. This Mission had hostels for both men and women servants, and kept in touch with all who used them through the Christian Servants' Association.

But while the Evangelicals can claim the distinction of setting the example for both training homes and registry offices for the inexperienced servant and of hostels for the experienced, other groups were concerned with the special problems of the workhouse girls, all of whom, with barely an exception, were sent out to service. Louisa Twining and her Workhouse Visiting Society in the 1860's began to provide special residential training for such girls, and the Metropolitan Association for Befriending Young Servants arranged for the care of those at work in London. The Evangelicals, as a group, played no part in this, though as individuals they often helped.

Certain so-called "gentlewomen" were also in need of some outside guidance, if not help. The increasing numbers of impoverished governesses had drawn attention both to their individual needs and to the fact that middle-class women were in no way educated to earn their living if need be. There had thus developed in the middle decades of the century a growing demand for the improved education of women and the acceptance of such women in a wider range of employments. The inspiration for this was largely derived from the Christian Socialists who played a leading part in the organisation of the Governesses' Benevolent Institution (1843) and the founding of Queen's College. It led on the one hand to the provision of secondary and university education for girls, and on the other to the women's movement which fought to secure the employment of women in the professions and eventually their enfranchisement. Few Evangelicals took part in these developments, largely because the changes they advocated appeared too advanced, or because they were frequently sponsored by persons with more liberal views.

Mrs. Meredith was the exception and she did her best to combine the demands for the better education and employment of gentlewomen with an adherence to the Evangelical outlook. Her problem was to make such education acceptable to strict Evangelical parents so that the girls from such families should not be at a disadvantage with other well-educated girls and should be able if they wished to enter any of the newly opened employments. As part of her work at Clapham, she had formed the Christian Educational Union (1880) as a branch of the Women's Educational Union which had been started six years earlier to promote the cause of a more thorough education for girls. It made the same demands as the Women's Educational Union, namely university and secondary education for girls, but insisted upon an Evangelical basis. Caroline Cavendish, one of her friends who had studied the progress of women's education in America, was made secretary and was responsible for developing the objectives of the Union.

The College by Post was instituted to meet the needs of the older girl who wished to continue her studies but was unable to leave home. It followed the lines of the Society for the Encouragement of Home Study, which had been started by some university professors in 1869, but made a course in Scripture compulsory. Mary L. G. Petrie, a London graduate, was placed in charge and other graduates offered their unpaid services. Two scholastic institutions were also opened, a secondary school at the Poplars, Addlestone, moved to Byfleet in 1881, and the women's college at Westfield, Hampstead, in 1882. The latter was the conception of Constance Maynard. A graduate of Girton, she had wished to start a women's college which should combine high scholastic learning with Evangelical training. For this she had the support of the Girton Prayer Meeting and the influence of such friends as Lord Shaftesbury, Josephine Butler, Charlotte Mason and Lucy M. Moor. Mary Petrie introduced her to Miss Dudin Brown who offered to meet the initial cost, with the result that the college was opened in Hampstead in October 1882 with an endowment of £10,000 for "founding and perpetuating a college for the higher education of women on Christian principles". This college was the only one of the different objectives of the Christian Educational Union which has lasted, chiefly because it was able to gain the support and teaching help of well-qualified women and so to reach a high academic standard.

Nevertheless the Christian Educational Union had its uses during the later years of the nineteenth century when higher education for girls was regarded with a certain amount of suspicion by Evangelical parents who feared their daughters would be contaminated by worldly knowledge and pursuits. It made more advanced learning available to many sheltered middle-class girls and offered a college education to those whose parents were prepared to send their daughters to an institution which appeared to offer an environment similar to that of their homes. Thus it trained for the professions and other occupations many who would otherwise have been unable to benefit from advanced education.

The Evangelicals, however, took little part in helping to open more occupations for gentlewomen, in spite of the fact that Lord Shaftesbury was the president and a firm supporter of the Society for Promoting the Employment of Women. In general they confined their efforts to the welfare of governesses, particularly foreign governesses in this country and English governesses abroad, for whom the Governesses' Benevolent Institution for the care and better education of English governesses in this country, made little provision. The foreign governess in England was frequently dismissed during the summer with no alternative employment or anywhere to stay. The Mildmay Institution sponsored the Christian Home for Foreign Governesses in Onslow Square (1872) and cared for those who were sick or in need of a holiday; and the pastor of the French Reformed Church at Bayswater opened a home and employment registry for those in his area. English governesses in Paris were in need of somewhere to spend their free time or to stay when out of employment. Ada Leigh opened a residential club for them in 1872 in the Avenue Wagram and within six years more than a thousand governesses had sought her help. Her friend, Miss Pryde, had a similar club on the Rue de Tilsit. Clubs such as these were particularly valuable from the preventive aspect, for they made it possible for the governesses to meet other English friends and always took in any who were destitute.

Governesses often took advantage of the other Evangelical charities. They were accepted at Miss Bramwell's home for girls, and the Y.W.C.A. had, for a time, a special home for them at Kilburn. They were sometimes admitted to homes for gentlewomen in straitened circumstances; retired governesses could benefit from some of the annuity schemes for the aged; and they were acceptable at the Royal Home for Ladies. But the help given in these ways was very small in comparison with the very generous help which was supplied by the Governesses' Benevolent Institution. Nevertheless, there were gaps in their provision, and these the Evangelicals discovered and did their best to fill.

The important and lasting aspect of this welfare work for working men and women was the focusing of attention upon the duty of the employer to provide such services himself. Except for some highly enlightened employers in the food-producing, sugar and confectionery trades, few felt any responsibility towards the comfort, health and well-being of those who worked for them. The example of these Evangelical societies among such groups as the navvies, railwaymen, theatrical girls and barmaids awakened their conscience to this aspect of their duties, and many began themselves to provide such services. But this process was slow, and only really began to take place on any scale in the early years of the First World War, when, as a result of the recommendation of the Health of Munitions Workers' Committee, clubs for recreation and amusement, educational schemes, nursing and sick visiting and the provision of canteens became more usual in industrial undertakings.

Thus at a time when the State was beginning to exercise some control through factory legislation, when the workers were trying to improve their wages and conditions of work through trade union organisation, and the benevolent and provident societies were available for the more highly paid workers, Evangelical societies were making attempts to provide welfare services in occupations where they were particularly needed. Though what was done by the Evangelicals was relatively small, the value of their services was gradually recognised by the community at large, and they were eventually to become established as a necessary part of industrial organisation.

CHAPTER XVI

These Evangelical Charities

THE MOST striking feature of Evangelical charity in the Victorian era is its vast dimensions. There were societies of all sorts and descriptions to meet a widespread variety of needs. Some were large; others small. Some were run by a committee; others were entirely under the control of a particular individual. Some were nation-wide in scope; others were completely local. It would be difficult to point to a need which was not catered for in one way or another. Societies dealing with children and young people vied with those helping the sick and the aged. There were organisations to cope with the aberrant groups in society—the criminals, the prostitutes and the drunkards. There were others to make life more bearable for the handicapped. The sailor and soldier and some other working men and women came in for their share; and finally there were the general missions which regarded few things as outside their scope of action.

These organisations formed the major part of the great growth in voluntary charity which took place during the nineteenth century, reaching a peak in the 1860's and 1870's, and then gradually declining. By no means all of them were Evangelical charities. In certain areas the Unitarians played an important part with their domestic missions which were noteworthy in such towns as Liverpool where contact with the Boston Unitarians was close, but because of their small and scattered membership throughout the rest of Britain it is doubtful if they were very widely known. Nevertheless they exercised a great influence through the work of certain of their outstanding members, particularly Mary Carpenter and William Rathbone, in the fields of juvenile delinquency and nursing. The High Church made some contribution in the form of "slum parish" work and in rescue work, and the Roman

Catholics and Jews each developed their own denominational social work. Christian Socialism had probably the greatest influence, since not only did it predominate in certain fields such as the improving of housing and of environmental conditions, which was the lifework of Octavia Hill, in the settlement movement initiated by Canon and Mrs. Barnett, and in the early attempts at co-operation, but it also provided the leadership for the change in the structure of society which was advocated in the later years of the century. But despite the important contributions made by these other groups, the part played by the Evangelicals was markedly predominant.

This great growth in voluntary charitable organisations was made possible by the surplus income in the hands of an expanding industrial society which was available for investment, and by the growing demand on the part of middle-class women folk for employment outside their homes. Compassion for the needy and a sense of guilt at the vast discrepancies in income between the different social classes undoubtedly played a part. But the Evangelicals had the added impetus of their religious beliefs, sharpened from time to time by revivals.

Evangelicalism was essentially a personal religion which placed the Gospel at the centre of its teaching, and made evangelism the primary purpose of every organisation. The individual soul was of inestimable value, and whatever else was attempted was of secondary importance. Each person, whatever his need, had to be won for Christ, and this involved a personal approach and a personal interest which superseded everything else. In addition the door-to-door visiting of the poorer areas, prior to the revival meetings, revealed the appalling conditions of poverty and distress, and so offered a challenge to existing Christians and a wide and ready range of service to the newly converted. This association of revival with social work was experimental in England until the mid-nineteenth century. The varied activities of the Clapham Sect, though they were Evangelical in origin, bore only an indirect connection with the eighteenth century revival, and the revival among sailors and soldiers of the first two decades of the nineteenth century led to spiritual work before it developed into social activities. But by the mid-century it had become an accepted fact of Evangelicalism that those who had experienced some spiritual renewal should straightway take part in the various efforts which were being made to help the less fortunate in the community. Some of the most important leaders in the social activities of the second half of the century and many of the social workers were converts of the mid-century revival. The visits of D. L. Moody to this country in 1873–5, 1881–4 and 1891 had a similar effect, and there are strong indications that he recommended certain forms of social work to his adherents, particularly that connected with young people.

Revivalism in America and Germany also had an effect upon social work in this country. The revivalism in the Protestant churches in America in the early decades of the century first associated social work with spiritual experience and so made this a feature of revivalist preaching in England in the second half of the century. It brought with it "Gospel temperance" which became closely linked with Evangelicalism and played an important part in changing the customary pattern of "drinking" in this country in the later decades. Similarly the methods of the Lutheran Inner Mission in Germany inspired some of the forms and ways of assistance which were used in such varied types of social work as nursing, the shelter of the homeless, the care of recalcitrant children, and the treatment of epileptics.

This personal approach, which the Evangelicals insisted upon, coloured the forms which their social work took, and had an important influence upon modern attitudes. It supplied the human touch that had been lacking in much of the earlier voluntary charity. When there was a need for residential treatment, the old type of institution tended to be replaced by the "home", and the greater freedom of a family relationship to supersede that of strict discipline. The orphan asylum gave way to the children's home; the penitentiary became the rescue home; the almshouse was converted into the old people's home; and those in charge were "father" or "mother" or "brothers" and "sisters". A similar change is noticeable in the case of the institute, which had provided for the spare time of young people and working men since the early nineteenth century. Personal as well as cultural needs found a place, and the institute tried to produce the informal atmosphere of the worker's own home. In order to maintain this personal relationship in circumstances where direct contact was no longer possible, new methods were introduced. Societies began to issue their own periodicals which were sent to all who had come into contact with them, personal correspondence was encouraged between social workers and those whom they helped, and an even closer link existed when a Christian Association was formed to keep in touch with all members however scattered they might be. Furthermore, when actual contact could not be made, the "letter" or "flower" mission was used to give a sense of personal interest to the housebound and to those in hospital or in prison. Today their influence can be found in the use of kindly and considerate treatment where censure had previously prevailed; in regarding the family as the norm for institutional care and in most cases as the unit for case work; and in the provision of the after-care in most fields of social work, usually with the purpose of rehabilitation to the life of the community.

This personal relationship is also to be seen in the ways in which these social organisations were financed. They relied almost entirely upon the donations and subscriptions of those who were interested, and the more strict Evangelical societies depended upon "faith" for their material needs. The example of George Muller in the thirties made this a fairly common practice, and it had the advantage of reducing the extensive and costly advertisement which was carried on by most societies to attract funds, but it could on occasions be decidedly harmful to those whom the organisation sought to help.

The Christian Missions and the Ragged Schools were the focal points for much of this social work. Their workers discovered the needs of the neighbourhood by careful and systematic visiting, they helped to provide the essentials of life through their thrift and provident societies, they undertook teaching in the care of the home and of children, and they offered rudimentary educational and recreational facilities to most age groups and sometimes also some special services such as home nursing and medical attention. In fact, through these varied activities they provided a fairly comprehensive system of welfare services for the ordinary needs of the poor. The less usual needs were met by the large number of specialised societies. In London and some of the more heavily populated provincial centres, voluntary organisations of these types were able to build their own premises, to employ numbers of paid workers and to develop their own particular techniques. But in the smaller cities similar organisations existed on a much less pretentious scale, and usually with far closer connections between them. It was often the city mission which organised most of the social services which were available.

Contemporary critics of this pattern of Evangelical charity pointed to the great amount of overlapping caused by the lack of unifying agencies; the waste of charitable funds since the "frivolous" public were moved by pity, fear or sheer carelessness to give whenever asked and with little enquiry as to need or as to the way in which the money would be used; the inefficiency of many societies; the pauperising effect of the large coal and bread clubs and the soup kitchens; and of holding such things as "thieves' suppers" and "prostitutes' meetings" which were regarded as highly emotional in character and likely to do little permanent good.

There is little doubt that many instances of these kinds of abuse were to be found, and the underlying purpose in the formation of the Charity Organisation Society in 1869 was to deal with them. It did so by trying to co-ordinate all the voluntary charities within an area, by drawing attention to the undesirable ones, by educating the public in the giving of money, by making enquiries into particular aspects of need, and by instituting certain techniques of case work and suggesting that social workers should be trained in their use.

The set-up of Evangelical charities, however, was not, in fact, as haphazard as it appeared. Some time before the formation of the Charity Organisation Society attempts had been made by the Ragged School Union and the Reformatory and Refuge Union to co-ordinate their particular forms of work, to direct applicants to suitable sources of help and to discourage inefficient and undesirable organisations. Different societies were linked together by common committee members, and prominent Evangelicals, like Lord Shaftesbury, Samuel Morley and George Williams, would have some part in the control of perhaps twenty or thirty organisations of very diverse types, and give to them a similar outlook and a consistent line of policy. There were the regular area meetings for Evangelical social workers which were held monthly or quarterly to discuss their cases and decide upon future forms and methods of work. In London they were held at the Mildmay Institution, the Home of Industry and the Clapham Conference Hall, and in the provincial towns they were frequently called by the city missions. The training of social workers was undertaken on an elaborate scale by Mrs. Pennefather and her methods were copied by other groups of deaconesses and social workers some time before the Charity Organisation Society emphasised this requirement. Moreover, the recommendations of the special committees of the Society often followed the lines of action already adopted by existing Evangelical societies. Thus, while the Charity Organisation Society performed much valuable work in relation to voluntary charity in the later decades of the century, in nearly every case its methods were already in use by existing Evangelical organisations, and what the Society frequently did was to clarify and make more widespread the practices of the more enlightened Evangelical bodies.

The other main line of criticism was that the Evangelicals were usurping the duties of the authorities, particularly in respect of providing food and shelter for the destitute and homes for children who would otherwise qualify for the pauper schools. The Evangelical organisations did, admittedly, undertake duties for which the Poor Law was responsible. But when they did so it was because the Poor Law was inadequately equipped to deal with all those who might justifiably appeal for its services, because its methods took no account of the need to treat these persons as human beings, and because in many areas out-relief was extremely meagre.

Whatever criticism is warranted, and some undoubtedly is, it must not be forgotten that the Evangelicals left hardly a need untouched. Christopher Dawson's views on the humanitarian movement of the period can be applied equally well to the work of the Evangelicals:

> It is easy to criticise this movement for its incompleteness and its inconsistencies; but if we look back to the England of 1837 ... we shall be astonished not at what was left undone, but by what was achieved.[1]

[1] Christopher Dawson, "The Humanitarians" in *Ideas and Beliefs of the Victorians*, 1949, p. 252.

Their missions were to be found in every poor quarter of the towns helping to meet the everyday needs of the people. They performed practically all the social services in the nineteenth century for certain groups such as the handicapped and young people. They filled important temporary gaps in the existing organisation of education with their ragged schools, and in the medical services with their medical missions. They cared for the prostitute and the prisoner and, by their insistence on temperance and their provision of coffee houses and cafés, made it possible for the working man to get his refreshments and meals at places other than the public house.

Where morality was concerned they were extraordinarily active, and this is to be expected in view of their determined religious beliefs. They were to the forefront in the demands for the repeal of the Contagious Diseases Acts, in the passing of the Criminal Law Amendment Act, in international legislation with regard to the "white slave trade", and in the protection of deep-sea fishermen from the excesses of the "bum-boats". They flung themselves wholeheartedly into each of these reforms, using methods, inherited from the Clapham Sect, which were based on urgent religious appeals to arouse the conscience of the community, prayer meetings and public gatherings to raise enthusiasm, with lectures, pamphlets, newspaper articles and the bill-board to gain publicity. These became the typical Evangelical methods of campaigning and were very similar to those of the Evangelical revivalists. This probably accounted for their acceptance by large sections of the community and so for their subsequent success.

Otherwise, in the legislative field, they did not often interfere with the right of the individual to pursue any profitable line of action on his own. They left this to the Benthamites and their followers, who were already making much headway along these lines. Thus, although the Evangelicals made strong efforts to reduce intemperance, few advocated the passing of the liquor licensing laws; they took little interest in the Education Acts either for normal children or for the handicapped; and only the more progressive of them encouraged the introduction of State insurance. Lord Shaftesbury was the exception, and his main motive was to protect the weak. He therefore pressed for legislation for the protection of women and children in the factories and mines, for the better treatment of the insane, and for the care of cruelly treated children.

The Evangelicals did, however, play an important part in drawing attention to social problems. While the more learned members of society were informed about these problems by the investigations of the London and Manchester statistical societies, and professional people and the more emancipated middle-class women read the blue books and the reports of the National Association for Promoting Social Science, the Evangelical publications found their way into almost every ordinary middle-class household. This was made possible through the popular and widely read books by persons such as Catharine Marsh, through the extensively circulated reports of the numerous societies, and through the addresses at such gatherings as the Mildmay conferences and the May Meetings. Not only were people made aware of the conditions of the poor and needy and what the Evangelicals were doing to help, but they were spurred on to do something themselves. Some became Evangelical social workers, others developed their own methods and lines of action, and it was by no means unusual to find that the social reformer of the early twentieth century had come from an Evangelical background or environment. This widespread circulation of information about social conditions by Evangelical workers and writers has been much overlooked, and should be classed with the more careful and detailed surveys of investigators, such as Charles Booth, as a contributory factor in leading to social reform.

Furthermore, the Evangelicals were largely instrumental in the evolution of many of the principles and concrete forms of social work which are followed today. Much of the present-day youth work closely follows Evangelical lines; they suggested many of the modern improvements in the practice of nursing; the N.S.P.C.C. still deals with the cruelly treated and neglected child; the welfare work for soldiers and sailors largely follows Evangelical methods; and the modern non-licensed restaurant and café for those of moderate means owes its origin to them. Similarly it was certain groups of Evangelicals who first recognised social work as a distinctive professional occupation, rather than a voluntary part-time one, offering training and payment to workers and making provision for their recuperation from sickness and for their old age. The mission visitor and the mission nurse performed many of the tasks which now fall to the school care committee representative and the health visitor. The probation officer can trace his direct descent from the police court missionary, and the modern moral welfare worker owes much of her techniques and methods to her Evangelical predecessors.

The Evangelicals have often been accused of a failure to follow up their widespread social work with a definite social policy. It is said that they fully accepted the prevailing class structure as the only permanent and right one, and based their methods of social work upon it. This is to some extent justified, and their motives were probably similar to those underlying their comparative lack of interest in social legislation. But this criticism is by no means universally true. A change in attitude among the Evangelicals appears in the "forward" movement of the churches in the 1880's by those who began to apply the conception of "salvation" to society as well as to the individual. This idea, much of which had been derived from the Christian Socialists, found support among the more advanced of the Nonconformist leaders, and it expressed itself in many of the new social activities and attitudes of the churches. It led to the formation of social unions whose members showed concern for the state of society, and were often in favour of a modification of the class structure. This was particularly apparent in the Christian Labour movement, whose members followed an Evangelical form of faith and who derived from the Gospels the example of socialism which they attempted to introduce into social and political life. Many of the early labour leaders were connected with the movement, using the Browning Settlement as their headquarters and the Brotherhood meetings as their mouthpiece. Here the campaign for old age pensions was strongly pursued at the end of the century, the demand was widely expressed for social security schemes to replace some of the social work then being done by voluntary charity, and the present combination of State action with the help of voluntary societies was urgently recommended. Nevertheless, these progressives, though they were highly vocal, represented only a small proportion of the Evangelicals and frequently had no support from the rest.

The twentieth century has brought great changes. The rise in the standard of life and the general improvement in employment has reduced the degree of material distress, and brought about a far greater equality in the size of income. The welfare state has gradually come into its own and now covers most of the ordinary needs of life, and the State and voluntary charity have reached a *modus vivendi* whereby the one is supplemented by the other. But there is still the need for personal service. The welfare state has necessarily to perform much of its work in a general and often impersonal manner and people need advice in ways of securing and using State aid. They want sympathy in the various perplexities of life which, with the lessening of anxiety over its necessities, have changed in kind rather than in magnitude. Though the nature of voluntary charity has altered from being something which the rich did for the poor, to that of an obligation on the part of all members of the community to help one another, the less privileged still need education in social living.

Here, the influence of the nineteenth century Evangelicals continues. The recognition by present-day social workers that human relationships are of primary importance and should be fostered at whatever cost owes much to the approach of these Evangelicals, who valued the demands of the spirit as highly as those of the body. This Evangelical attitude of personal interest and concern still plays an important part in the work of many of the existing voluntary societies and can be seen in the continued use of many of the methods of voluntary action which were suggested by the Evangelicals in the Victorian era. Though charitable effort has changed to social service and attention is now focused on the community rather than the individual, the concept of personal service, which was the basic principle of these nineteenth century Evangelical organisations is still fundamental to modern social work.

Lord Shaftesbury was right when he maintained in 1884 that "most of the great philanthropic movements of the century have sprung from the Evangelicals".[1] The Evangelicals, in their massive

[1] Edwin Hodder, *Life of Lord Shaftesbury*, 1886, vol. ii, p. 3

amount of philanthropy, emphasised old needs, pointed to new ones and dealt, according to their lights, with an enormous amount of destitution, distress and degradation among the poorer groups in the community. They set the precedent for many of the techniques which are followed today and their spirit of personal service still prevails. Criticism of their work was plentiful and often justified, but this does not detract from the fact that the Evangelicals supplied help at a time when it was greatly needed and not available to any significant extent from other sources.

Therefore, among the many hands which laid the foundations of the social services of the twentieth century the initiative and work of the Evangelicals must be given their full credit. Many authorities, in assessing the factors which helped to build the modern social services, point to the influence of Charles Booth's massive surveys, to the demands of socialism both Christian and secular, to the effects of a widened franchise, to the efforts of the women's movement, and to the pressures to maintain competitive efficiency in industry. But a factor of equal, if not greater, importance than these, was the work of the Evangelical voluntary organisations, which dealt in a practical manner with many of the numerous and varied social problems of the Victorian era and which set the pattern for much of the social welfare work of the present time.

Select Bibliography

CHAPTER I

Peter Quennell, ed., *Mayhew's Characters*, Spring Books, 1952.
Peter Quennell, ed., *Mayhew's London*, Spring Books, 1952.
Peter Quennell, ed., *London's Underworld*, Spring Books, 1952.
Thomas Beames, *The Rookeries of London*, Bosworth, 1850.
James Greenwood, *The Seven Curses of London*, Stanley Rivers, 1869.
George Sims, *How the Poor Live*, Chatto and Windus, 1889.
H. Taine, *Notes on England*, Strahan, 1872.
Sampson Low, *Charities of London*, S. Low, 1862.

CHAPTER II

William James, *Varieties of Religious Experience*, Longmans Green, 1903; Mentor paperbacks in U.S.
Robert Braithwaite, *Rev. W. Pennefather*, John Shaw, 1878.
Edwin Hodder, *Lord Shaftesbury*, Hodder & Stoughton, 1886.
Edwin Hodder, *Samuel Morley*, Hodder & Stoughton, 1887.
Mrs. Edwin Trotter, *Lord Radstock: an Interpretation and a Record*, Hodder & Stoughton, 1915.
J. Rendel Harris, *Life of Francis William Crossley*, Nisbet, 1899.
E. W. Jealous, *The Beaten Track: The Open Air Mission*, 1953.
John Wood, *The Story of the Evangelisation Society*, The Evangelisation Society, 1908.
S. G. Green, *The Story of the Religious Tract Society*, R.T.S. 1899.
G. E. Morgan, *R. C. Morgan: his Life and Times*, Morgan & Scott, 1909.

CHAPTER III

Ellen Barlee, *Our Homeless Poor*, Nisbet, 1860.
A. T. Alexander, *Fifty Years' Story of the Bedford Institute*, Bedford Institute Association, 1915.

John Campbell, *Memoirs of David Nasmith*, John Snow, 1844.

Robert Lee, *Ten Fruitful Years: a History of the Manchester City Mission*, Pickering & Inglis, 1937.

J. M. Weylland, *Round the Tower: or the Story of the London City Mission*, Partridge, 1875.

Elsbeth Platt, *The Story of the Ranyard Mission*, Hodder & Stoughton, 1937.

L.N.R. (Mrs. Ranyard), *The Missing Link*, Nisbet, 1860.

L.N.R. (Mrs. Ranyard), *God's Message in Low London*, Nisbet, 1871.

A.V.L., *Ministering Women and the London Poor*, Nisbet, 1870.

H. J. Cooke, *The Story of the First Deaconess Institution*, Elliot Stock, 1893.

Mrs. Bayly, *Ragged Homes and How to Mend Them*, Nisbet, 1859.

G. H. Pike, *Golden Lane*, James Clarke, 1876.

G. H. Pike, *Pity for the Perishing*, James Clarke, 1884.

Robert Sandall, *A History of the Salvation Army*, Nelson, 1947.

Edgar Rowan, *Wilson Carlile*, Longmans, Green, 1926.

CHAPTER IV

George McCree: his Life and Work, by his Elder Son, James Clarke, 1892.

R. G. Burnett, *These My Brethren: a History of the East End Mission*, Epworth Press, 1946.

Dorothy Price Hughes, *Hugh Price Hughes*, Hodder & Stoughton, 1904.

Marguerite Williams, *John Wilson of Woolwich*, Marshall, Morgan & Scott, 1937.

W. Y. Fullerton, *F. B. Meyer*, Marshall, Morgan & Scott, 1929.

J. C. Carlile, *C. H. Spurgeon*, R.T.S., 1934.

J. C. Carlile, *My Life's Little Day*, Blackie, 1935.

J. Scott Lidgett, *My Guided Life*, Epworth Press, 1936.

W. A. Hammond, *Eighteen Years in the Central City Swarm*, Browning Settlement, 1912.

Lewis Paton, *John Brown Paton: a Biography*, Hodder & Stoughton, 1914.

J. W. Tuffley, *Grain from Galilee: a History of the Brotherhood Movement*, Headley Bros., 1935.

CHAPTER V

C. J. Montague, *Sixty Years in Waifdom: a History of the Ragged School Movement*, John Murray, 1904.

Henry Hawker, *Recollections of John Pounds*, Williams & Norgate, 1889.

David Williamson, *Sir John Kirk*, Hodder & Stoughton, 1922.

Edwin Hodder, *John MacGregor*, Hodder & Stoughton, 1894.

J. D. Hilton, *Marie Hilton: her Life and Work*, Isbister, 1897.

Rosa Waugh, *Life of Benjamin Waugh*, T. Fisher Unwin, 1913.

CHAPTER VI

Barnardo & Marchant, *Memoirs of Dr. Barnardo*, Hodder & Stoughton, 1907.

A. Gammie, *A Romance of Faith: a History of Quarrier's Homes*, Pickering & Inglis, 1952.

William Bradfield, *Life of Thomas Bowman Stephenson*, Kelly, 1913.

W. Elfe Tayler, *Ashley Down*, J. F. Shaw, 1861.

V. I. Cuthbert, *Where Dreams Come True*, Shaftesbury Homes, 1937.

William Edmondson, *Making Rough Places Plain: a History of the Manchester & Salford Homes*, Sheratt & Hughes, 1921.

The First Fifty Years, a Chronicle of the Waifs & Strays Society, S.P.C.K. 1922.

W. Y. Fullerton, *J. W. C. Fegan*, Marshall, Morgan & Scott, n.d.

Marguerite Williams, *Charlotte Sharman*, R.T.S., 1932.

Phoebe Giniver, *A Retrospect: Kingsdown Orphanage*, 1912.

The Story of the Orphan Homes, Leominster, Partridge, 1880.

Ernest H. Jeffs, *Motherless: the Story of R. T. Smith and the First Home for Motherless Children*, Marshall, Morgan & Scott, n.d.

I. S. Robson, *The Story of the Little Boys*, Farningham Homes, 1910.

A. E. Hughes, *Lift up a Standard*, Irish Church Missions, 1948.

Lilian M. Birt, *The Children's Home-Finder*, Nisbet, 1913.

Clara M. Lowe, *God's Answer: the Home of Industry*, Nisbet, 1882.

CHAPTER VII

W. McG. Eagar, *Making Men*, University of London Press, 1953.

Hodder Williams, *Life of George Williams*, Hodder & Stoughton, 1906.

These Hundred Years, 1844–1944: the Story of the Y.M.C.A., Y.M.C.A., 1944.

Donald Fraser, *Mary Jane Kinnaird*, Nisbet, 1890.

Emily Kinnaird, *Reminiscences*, John Murray, 1925.

Lucy M. Moor, *Girls of Yesterday and Today*, Partridge, 1910.

F. P. Gibbon, *William A. Smith of the Boys' Brigade*, Collins, 1943.

Cuthbert & Lennox, *Henry Drummond*, Andrew Melrose, 1904.

Mary Heath, *Friendship's Highway*, Girls' Friendly Society, 1926.
Potter & Woodward, *Mary Sumner: her Life and Work*, Warren, 1921.
Ethel M. Hogg (Wood), *Quintin Hogg: a biography*, Constable, 1904.
Ethel M. Wood, *Robert Mitchell*, Muller, 1934.

CHAPTER VIII

Henry Carter, *English Temperance Movement*, Epworth Press, 1933.
William Gourlay, *National Temperance*, Richard J. James, 1906.
Autobiography of John Gough, Sampson Low, 1870.
J. M. J. Fletcher, *Mrs. Wightman of Shrewsbury*, Longmans, 1906.
Mrs. Charles Wightman, *Haste to the Rescue*, Nisbet, 1859.
Canon Ellison, *Twenty-Five Years of the C.E.T.S.*, C. of E. Temperance Society, 1887.
Ray Strachey, *Frances Willard: her Life and Work*, T. Fisher Unwin, 1912.
Robert Taylor, *The Hope of the Race*, Hope Press, 1946.
Arthur Reed Kimball, *The Blue Ribbon*, B. F. Stevens, 1894.
Marguerite Williams, *John Pearce*, R.T.S., 1929.
Mrs. Eliza Thompson, *Hillsboro' Crusade: Sketches & Family Records*, Cincinnati, 1896.

CHAPTER IX

W. J. Taylor, *The Story of the Homes*, the London Female Preventive & Reformatory Institution, 1907.
E. W. Thorne, *Twenty-Five Years' Labour among the Friendless & Fallen*, Shaw, 1886.
J. Butler, *An Autobiography*, Arrowsmith, n.d.
Madge Unsworth, *Maiden Tribute*, Salvationist Publicity & Supplies, 1949.
A Thread of Gold: the Story of Fifty Years' Work with the Church Army, Church Army, 1937.
R. M. Barrett, *Ellice Hopkins: a Memoir*, Wells Gardner, 1907.
Mary H. Steer, *The Bridge of Hope Mission*, Gillett Bros., 1928.
W. A. Coote, *A Romance of Philanthropy*, National Vigilance Association, 1916.
W. A. Coote, *A Vision and its Fulfilment*, National Vigilance Association, 1910.

CHAPTER X

W. L. Clay, *The Prison Chaplain*, Macmillan, 1861.
William Tallack, *Howard Letters and Memorials*, Methuen, 1905.
F. W. Robinson, *Female Life in Prison*, 2 vols., Spencer Blackett, 1862.

M. A. Lloyd, *Susanna Meredith*, Hodder & Stoughton, 1903.

Mrs. Meredith, *The Story of a Mission*, Partridge, 1886.

M. Lloyd-Pritchard, *Sarah Martin*, Howard League, 1950.

J. W. McDermid, *The Life of Thomas Wright of Manchester*, John Heywood, 1876.

Fifty Years: a Record of Child Saving and Reformatory Work, Reformatory & Refuge Union, 1906.

H. H. Ayscough, *When Mercy Seasons Justice*, C. of E. Temperance Society, 1925.

Inasmuch, the Story of the Police Court Mission, Williams & Norgate, 1926.

CHAPTER XI

Mary G. Thomas, *Edward Rushton*, National Institute for the Blind, 1949.

Mary G. Thomas, *The National Institute for the Blind*, N.I.B., 1954.

Frances Martin, *Elizabeth Gilbert and her Work for the Blind*, Cassell, 1891.

John Rutherford, *William Moon and his Work for the Blind*, Hodder & Stoughton, 1898.

Kenneth Hodgson, *The Deaf and their Problems*, Watts, 1953.

CHAPTER XII

H. Tuke, *The History of the Insane in the British Isles*, Kegan Paul, 1882.

Memoirs of the Life and Labours of Andrew Reed, by his Two Sons, Strahan, 1863.

Julie Sutter, *A Colony of Mercy, or Social Christianity at Work*, Hodder & Stoughton, 1893.

Agnes Hunt, *Reminiscences*, Wilding, 1935.

The Heritage Craft Schools and Hospital, Chailey, Heritage Craft Schools, 1948.

John A. Groom, *The Romance of John Groom's Crippleage*, John Groom's Crippleage, 1948.

CHAPTER XIII

Evans & Howard, *The Romance of the British Voluntary Hospital Movement*, Hutchinson, 1930.

E.A.W., *William Fairlie Clarke*, William Hunt, 1885.

Patricia Davies, *Fifty Years of Midwifery: the Story of Annie McCall*, Health for all Publishing Company, 1950.

Charlotte Mason, *God Answers Prayer: the Home for Christian Workers*, Marshal, Morgan & Scott, 1909.

L. French, *The Royal Hospital and Home for Incurables, Putney*, Home for Incurables, 1936.

Charlotte Winkworth, *Life of Pastor Fliedner*, Longmans Green, 1867.

Eleanor Rathbone, *William Rathbone: a Memoir*, Macmillan, 1908.

L.N.R. (Mrs. Ranyard), *Nurses for the Needy*, Nisbet, 1875.

Memorials of Agnes Jones, by her Sister, Strahan, 1871.

J. L. Hazelton, *Inasmuch, a History of the Aged Pilgrims' Friend Society*, Farncombe, 1922.

CHAPTER XIV

E. W. Mathews, *The King's Brotherhood: the Memoirs of W. H. Angas*, Partridge, 1911.

Hill of the Ratcliffe Highway, Cambridge University Press, 1932.

Mary L. Walrond, *Launching out into the Deep, an account of the Missions to Seamen*, S.P.C.K., 1904.

J. Radcliffe, *Recollections of Reginald Radcliffe*, Morgan & Scott, 1896.

Agnes Weston, *My Life among the Bluejackets*, Nisbet, 1911.

E. J. Mather, *Nor'ard of the Dogger, the Mission to Deep-Sea Fishermen*, Nisbet, 1888.

Aldershot, a Record of Mrs. Daniell's Work among Soldiers, by her Daughter, Hodder & Stoughton, 1879.

S. Robinson, *The Soldier's Friend*, T. Fisher Unwin 1913.

Elise Sandes, *Enlisted, or My Story*, Partridge, 1915.

Porter & Matheson, *Elise Sandes & Theodora Schofield*, Marshall, Morgan & Scott, 1934.

CHAPTER XV

L. E. O'Rorke, *Life and Friendships of Catharine Marsh*, Longmans, 1918.

Catharine Marsh, *English Hearts and English Hands*, Nisbet, 1857.

Catharine Marsh, *A Tale of Old Beckenham*, Nisbet, 1876.

D. W. Barrett, *Life and Work among the Navvies*, Wells, Gardner & Darton, 1880.

J. M. Tritton, *A Beloved Lady: The Recollections of the Life and Work of Catharine Gurney*, International Christian Police Association, 1933.

C. B. Firth, *Constance Louisa Maynard: Mistress of Westfield College*, Allen & Unwin, 1949.

Index